MIND OVER MACHINE

The Power of
Human Intuition and Expertise
in the Era of the Computer

Hubert L. Dreyfus

Stuart E. Dreyfus

with Tom Athanasiou

THE FREE PRESS
A Division of Macmillan, Inc.
NEW YORK

The Free Press
A Division of Macmillan, Inc.
866 Third Avenue, New York, N.Y. 10022

Collier Macmillan Canada, Inc.

Printed in the United States of America

printing number
1 2 3 4 5 6 7 8 9 10

We acknowledge the authors and publishers of the following works for material quoted in this volume:

Marvin Minsky, *Semantic Information Processing*, MIT Press, 1968, pp. 3–4, 13, 18, 25–27. Copyright © 1968 by Marvin Minsky. Reprinted with permission (on pp. 68–71).

E. Feigenbaum & P. McCorduck, *The Fifth Generation*, © 1983, Addison–Wesley, Reading, Massachusetts, pp. 18, 38, 55, 56, 64, 76–77, 79–80, 82, 84–85, 229, 236. Reprinted with permission (on pp. 103–7, 118–19).

From *Mindstorms: Children, Computers, and Powerful Ideas* by Seymour Papert, pp. 27–29, 36–37, 96–98, 113, 152, 153. Copyright © 1980 by Basic Books, Inc. Reprinted by permission of the publishers (on pp. 133, 146–147, 148, 155).

Library of Congress Cataloging-in-Publication Data

Dreyfus, Hubert L.
    Mind over machine.

    Includes index.
    1. Artificial intelligence. 2. Computers. 3. Expert systems (Computer science) I. Dreyfus, Stuart E.
II. Athanasiou, Tom. III. Title.
Q335.D73 1986   006.3   85–20421
ISBN 0–02–908060–6

*To our Mother
and the memory
of our Father*

CONTENTS

PREFACE

WISHFUL THINKING has probably always complicated our relations with technology, but it is safe to assert that before the computer, and before the bomb, the complications weren't quite as dangerous as they are today. Nor was the wishful thinking as fantastic. Consider a typical military wish list:

> As a result of a series of advances in artificial intelligence, computer science, and microelectronics, we stand at the threshold of a new generation of computing technology having unprecedented capabilities. . . . For example, instead of fielding simple guided missiles or remotely piloted vehicles, we might launch completely autonomous land, sea, and air vehicles capable of complex, far-ranging reconnaissance and attack missions.[1]

Military managers, like their civilian brethren, have long dreamed of autonomous machines, freed of their reliance on fallible, contentious humanity, able finally to go it alone. Now the speed of computerized warfare has added new urgency to the pursuit of machine intelligence. After all, nuclear attack times are down to seven or eight minutes, and computers, more alert, faster, more constant than we human beings, seem the obvious solution. Thus, faith in the perfectibility of computer intelligence has become a means of avoiding the truth of our circumstances. With it comes a temptation to avoid confronting the perils of our existence by handing over our fate to electronic machines.

That dream may become a reality in the Strategic Defense Initiative ("Star Wars"). Describing the system, *Time* writes in its March 11, 1985, issue:

> Humans would make the key strategic decisions in advance, determining under what conditions the missile defense would start firing, and devise a computer system that could translate those decisions into a program. In the end the defensive response would be out of human hands: it would be activated by computer before U.S. commanders even knew that a battle had begun.

Today, after twenty years of support for artificial intelligence (AI) research, the military is moving to call in its chips. But does the military hold the cards to realize its hopes? It does not. The human mind has the upper hand over any machine. The "series of advances" upon which hopes for "autonomous computer systems" depend have been greatly exaggerated, with serious negative consequences.

At present, large-scale efforts are under way to develop artificial intelligence systems capable of conversing fluidly in natural language, of providing expert medical advice, of exhibiting common sense, of functioning autonomously in critical military situations. Debates about the political, moral, ethical, and social consequences of such systems are each year more prominent than the last, yet they still take place within a haze of misinformation about the genuine potential of machine intelligence. Marvin Minsky, for example, recently said:

> Today our robots are like boys. They do only the simple things they're programmed to. But clearly *they're about to cross the edgeless line past which they'll do the things we are programmed to.* . . . What will happen when we face new options in our work and home, where more intelligent machines can better do the things we like to do? What kind of minds and personalities should we dispense to them? What kind of rights and privileges should we withhold from them? Are we ready to face such questions?[2]

Even Joseph Weizenbaum, whose *cri de coeur* is still the best-known attack on the computerization of human affairs, as-

sumes the eventual success of the artificial intelligence enterprise: "It is technically feasible to build a computer system that
will interview patients applying for help at a psychiatric out-
patient clinic and will produce their psychological profiles
complete with charts, graphs, and natural-language commentary."[3]

Our goal here is not to take up the rationality or irrationality
of the arms race or the social problems posed by automation.
Those are concerns for society as a whole, and we claim no
special expertise in evaluating them. Our intention is more modest but more basic. Despite what you may have read in magazines and newspapers, regardless of what your congressman was
told when he voted on the Strategic Computing Plan,
twenty-five years of artificial intelligence research has lived up
to very few of its promises and has failed to yield any evidence
that it ever will. The time has come to ask what has gone wrong
and what we can reasonably expect from computer intelligence.
How closely can computers processing facts and making inferences approach human intelligence? How can we profitably use
the intelligence that can be given to them? What are the risks
of enthusiastic and ambitious attempts to redefine our intelligence in their terms, of delegating to computers key decision-
making powers, of adapting ourselves to the educational and
business practices attuned to mechanized reason?

In short, we want to put the debate about the computer in
perspective by clearing the air of false optimism and unrealistic
expectations. The debate about what computers should do is
properly about social values and institutional forms. But before
we can profitably discuss what computers *should* do we have
to be clear about what they *can* do. Our bottom line is that
computers as reasoning machines can't match human intuition
and expertise, so in determining what computers should do we
have to contrast their capacities with the more generous gifts
possessed by the human mind.

Too often, computer enthusiasm leads to a simplistic view
of human skill and expertise. To maintain the momentum of
automation, to carry its thrust from the production line and
office to the board room and classroom, computer boosters lean
on theories that emphasize those aspects of expertise that most
lend themselves to computerization. To the "knowledge engineers," skill and expertise are equivalent to the "rules of thumb"

that human experts articulate when asked how they solve problems.

We contend that those rules, though they lead to a view of expertise that supports optimism for the future of machine intelligence, do fundamental violence to the real nature of human intelligence and expertise. To safeguard both, we shall propose a nonmechanistic model of human skill, one that we claim:

- Explains the failure of existing AI systems to capture expert human judgment
- Predicts that failure will continue until intelligence ceases to be understood as abstract reason and computers cease to be used as reasoning machines
- Warns against attempts at too zealous computerization in fields such as education and management, which, while not AI proper, fall prey to similar misconceptions

We are at the same time in no way Luddites.[4] It seems obvious to us that there are tasks for which computers are appropriate and even indispensable. Computers are more deliberate, more precise, and less prone to exhaustion and error than the most caring and conscientious human being. Examples of computers as useful tools are numerous and easy to come by:

- As word processors, computers are changing our methods and styles of writing—making composition more responsive to our desires. To write this book we used the UNIX operating system, two VAX computers, and phone lines connecting our offices and our homes.
- Computer assisted design (CAD) is transforming engineering, making design more efficient and more flexible. At General Motors 42 percent of drafting is currently done on a screen, and in the next decade that figure will approach 100 percent. Designers will be able to summon up cross-sectional views from any perspective within solid objects, and from an object's dimensions and properties to estimate its strength and simulate its reaction to various kinds of stress.
- As telecommunications devices, computers are transforming our notions of collaboration and are beginning to change the ways we communicate written information. Excerpts of our book were sent to friends around the country on the ARPANET, which brought their criticisms to our screens the very same day. Such

exchanges would be common if personal computers could communicate easily, but so far computer manufacturers have offered their machines with operating systems that are either proprietary or shared by only a few manufacturers. Now, however, TOPS, a local area networking system developed by Centram West, makes possible a "simultaneous translation" between different machines so that all data and other computer resources can be fully shared.

• As aids for the handicapped, computers offer incredible new possibilities. Already they've radically increased the abilities of seriously disabled children to function in normal school environments, by allowing, for example, students to work on microcomputers equipped with special input devices. Reading machines for the blind are already available, as are machines that help the deaf learn to speak, and artificial vision systems, which translate a TV signal into tactile images on the user's back, are in development.

Tools enlarge our capacities and provide us with a range of abilities we could not otherwise claim. But computers are more than tools. When programmed to do so, they can automatically store, modify, and access vast files of data, and do so more quickly and more accurately than we ourselves. Here computers act not as tools but as automatic data-processing devices: keeping records, shuffling funds, maintaining inventories, optimizing railroad traffic, and coordinating airline reservations. Moreover, when problems can be translated into mathematical representations in objectively defined ways that require no subjective assessments, computers can take over functions previously seen as the work of management. That has happened, for example, in oil refineries, where computers decide how much crude oil of various grades to blend to produce a desired mix of final outputs.

But we shall focus neither on computers as tools nor on computers as automatic data processors. Our concern is the misguided effort to enlarge the capacities of data-processing systems to the point where more sophisticated skills, skills involving not only calculation but judgment as well, can be captured within electronic circuits. It is in this effort to create artificial intelligence that the nature, problems, and limits of mechanized reason are most clearly evident.

Computers are certainly more precise and more predictable than we, but precision and predictability are not what human intelligence is about. Human beings have other strengths, and here we do not mean just the shifting moods and subtle empathy usually ceded to humanity by even the most hard-line technologists. Human emotional life remains unique, to be sure, but what is more important is our ability to recognize, to synthesize, to intuit. There are good reasons to believe that those abilities as well are rooted in processes altogether different from the calculative reason of computer programs, and we shall explain, as best we can, what those processes are.

By so doing, we want to raise two warning flags: one against placing excessive faith in the possibility of mechanizing human skill and expertise, and the second against the increasing tendency, noted by Sherry Turkle in her book *The Second Self,* to regard ourselves as abstract reasoning machines. The truth is that human intelligence can never be replaced with machine intelligence simply because we are not ourselves "thinking machines" in the sense in which that term is commonly understood. Each of us has, and uses every day, a power of intuitive intelligence that enables us to understand, to speak, and to cope skillfully with our everyday environment. We must learn what this power is, how it works, where it fits into our lives, and how it can be preserved and developed.

We are not proposing to exalt the intuitive at the expense of the analytic abilities so highly developed in our Western culture. Zen Buddhism, Jungian mysticism, and other attempts to bypass or quiet the analytic mind have their place, but our book is not a defense of them. The hoary old split between the mystical and the analytic will not do in the computer age, for neither pole of that often misleading dualism names the ordinary, nonmystical intuition that we believe is the core of human intelligence and skill. Further, we shall show that analysis and intuition work together in the human mind. Although intuition is the final fruit of skill acquisition, analytic thinking is necessary for beginners learning a new skill. It is also useful at the highest levels of expertise, where it can sharpen and clarify intuitive insights.

The recognition that human expertise resists capture in formal rules has real consequences for our conception of the proper role of computers in the making of expert decisions. At the University of California Medical Center in San Francisco researchers have developed a system we think is on the right track. Rather than trying to embody the expertise of human doctors in an automated system, Dr. Marsden Blois and his co-workers have developed RECONSIDER, a "diagnostic prompting system," which addresses the real-world problem that "the most frequent diagnostic mistake is oversight." RECONSIDER is a simple system, far less sexy than well publicized expert systems like MYCIN or INTERNIST. It is a straightforward interactive encyclopedia designed to help the doctor determine the patient's disease. The doctor merely types in the symptoms, and the system presents a comprehensive list of associated diseases. Plausible diagnoses are ranked in order of their probability, and adding more symptoms reorders the list. The doctor uses RECONSIDER to avoid jumping to conclusions and to remind himself of other possibilities. But in the end, it remains the task of the doctor to make the diagnosis.

As used in AI, computers are analytic engines. They can apply rules and make logical inferences at great speed and with unerring accuracy. To exactly the extent that rules and inferences have a crucial place in everyday human affairs, the computer has a place in improving and implementing logical thought. Since the extent is limited, so also is the place of the analytic engine. By recognizing limits we shall find a greater clarity—about what we are and where we are going—than we could ever discern within the entrepreneurial haze of AI rhetoric. And we shall find as well that our intuitive expertise, irreducible to rules, casts the weight on the side of the human mind as we try to establish a new balance between ourselves and our ever more powerful, yet perhaps perpetually limited, machines.

ACKNOWLEDGMENTS

MANY PEOPLE contributed their expertise to this undertaking. Tom Athanasiou contributed most. Carefully reading and rereading our manuscript, he spotted arguments in need of further evidence and relentlessly tracked down the relevant details. Rather than trust published reports, in most cases he conducted extensive and searching interviews with those involved. Excerpts appear throughout the book. His journalistic expertise also enabled him to greatly improve our preface and to detect occasional weak or unclear passages and to revise them. Finally, Tom's sense of the broader political context forced us to face the distinction between our primary concern with what computers can and cannot do, and the social issues that must be addressed once the limits of what is possible are clearly drawn.

Denise Denniston, too, carefully read the entire manuscript, and her suggestions greatly improved the exposition and overall organization of the book. Various experts gave us detailed critiques of the chapters on their respective fields. Our thanks in particular to John Haugeland, Ned Block, Sandra Cook, Judah Schwartz, Nat Goldhaber, Eli Shlifer, and John Hancock. Much appreciated advice came from Ron Wolff, Terry Winograd, John

Balfe, Ron Shamir, James Unger, Robert Reinstedt, M. E. Maron, and the participants in our 1984 NEH Summer Seminar on "The Place of Computers in our Culture." The book would never have reached its present form without the enthusiasm, dedication, knowledge, and scrupulous attention to detail of our editor, Grant Ujifusa. Finally, our gratitude to Geneviève Dreyfus and Renée Dreyfus for providing a context of common sense and good judgment.

We are grateful to the Life Sciences Directorate of the Air Force Office of Scientific Research, the Berkeley Cognitive Science Program supported by the Alfred P. Sloan Foundation and the U.C. Berkeley Operations Research Center for financial support and the use of their facilities.

PROLOGUE

"THE HEART HAS ITS REASONS THAT REASON DOES NOT KNOW"

IN THE EARLY SIXTIES, when I* began to teach philosophy at M.I.T., I had never seen a real-world digital computer, though I had read about robots in science fiction. I was in for a surprise. When I tried to explain to my students the speculations of various philosophers from Plato to Immanuel Kant to Bertrand Russell about how perception, understanding, and meaning may operate, my students told me that such philosophy was now passé thanks to the development of the digital computer. Across the street, the students assured me, the robot project under the direction of Marvin Minsky was making real progress on a genuine research program aimed at programming a machine to perceive, understand, and even coordinate perception and understanding with movement. Philosophers, it seemed, had been wasting their time for two thousand years and had finally been replaced by serious researchers.

Such news was confusing and unsettling. On the one hand, I was no traditional philosopher. I knew that philosophers from

---

* This prologue, like the rest of this book, was written jointly by Hubert and Stuart Dreyfus. For stylistic reasons, however, we have chosen to present it from Hubert's point of view.

the time of Socrates and Plato had been trying to find the definitions and logical relations underlying perception and understanding without notable success, and yet went on insisting that such rules must nonetheless exist in the mind. I knew that Thomas Hobbes had said around 1600 that reasoning is really reckoning with parcels—what my students at M.I.T. had begun to call calculating with bits.

I had come to think of the whole tradition I was teaching as a see-saw battle between rationalist philosophers and philosophers who tried to do justice to common sense. It started with Plato, who named what his teacher, Socrates, was doing "philosophy"—the love of wisdom—and followed Socrates in thinking of wisdom as whatever could be spelled out in explicit principles or definitions. Socrates had not been able to find any definitions of his favorite concerns, such as piety, justice, and knowledge, that would stand up to sustained argument, so he concluded he knew nothing. Plato, however, loved mathematics and thought that if one put aside cooks, craftsmen, poets, and all the others acting on mere skill and intuition, it would be possible to find a whole system of theoretical, objective principles, which, like the truths of geometry, could be defended in rational argument and used to explain nature and justify actions. It was this claim that nurtured the main line of our Western philosophical tradition. After all, when one has to make important decisions in which lives may be at stake, one does not want to act on hunches or hearsay but on principles that can be laid out and justified to oneself and one's peers.

Yet each time a great philosopher came along with the claim that he had found the basic principles underlying all intelligible order, some other thinker would call the whole enterprise into question. Plato's famous protégé, Aristotle, while accepting a great deal of Plato's argument, tried to stay close to everyday experience and so had important doubts. He pointed out that underlying all explicit knowledge of the sort Plato championed there had to be a kind of judgment that enabled experienced practitioners in any domain to apply their principles to particular cases. So, Aristotle said, if you have an ethical problem, do not ask a philosopher what to do; ask a wise old man.

After Aristotle and Plato the breach widened. Galileo, an heir of Plato's rationalism, showed that Plato was at least half right, that the idea of finding abstract objective laws relating elements worked for nature. Descartes generalized that success and claimed that one could analyze *any* problem into its basic, isolatable elements, and explain the complex in terms of rule-like combinations of such primitives. Basic principles could be deduced by asking how a perfectly rational and good God would organize the world, and how he would want man to act. All knowledge and action could then be deduced from those first principles.

Descartes's grand scheme, in which man played God, gave rise to Pascal, who was himself a great mathematician and even built a calculator, but who was untainted by the tradition. He argued, opposing Descartes, that in matters of perception, every-day knowledge, and action, finite human beings had no access to basic elements and rational first principles. Instead one had to assume the risk of basing one's theories and actions on the ambiguous background of custom and experience. In deciding what to do, Pascal said, one had no choice but to trust one's emotions and intuitions. As he put it, "The heart has its reasons that reason does not know."

Of course, that assertion did not end the debate. The next round pitted Leibniz, who is considered the greatest of the seventeenth-century rationalists, against the great empiricist David Hume. Leibniz, a mathematician who is credited with inventing binary numbers, took Plato's and Descartes's project one step further and claimed that even those skills Plato had rejected as merely a kind of knack or "knowing how" could be salvaged as "knowing that." As he put it:

> [T]he most important observations and turns of skill in all sorts of trades and professions are as yet unwritten. This fact is proved by experience when, passing from theory to practice, we desire to accomplish something. *Of course, we can also write up this practice, since it is at bottom just another theory more complex and particular* . . . .[1]

David Hume, a historian, again came to the defense of concrete common sense. He held that knowledge was not grounded in principles and theories. Rather, knowledge was based on habits formed by successful coping. In ethics he held that we cannot justify our actions but have to trust our natural moral feelings. But even Hume said experience could be analyzed into basic elements.

Kant, probably the greatest philosopher of them all, thought that both Hume and Leibniz were partly right. Hume was right in criticizing Descartes, Leibniz, and all metaphysicians who claimed the ability to read God's mind. But the rationalists were on the right track. One could nonetheless find basic principles that applied to our world by understanding the rational human mind. And Kant had a new idea as to how the mind worked. He held that all concepts were really rules. For example, the concept for dog is something like the rule: If it has four legs, barks, and wags its tail, then it's a dog. After Kant the rule-following view of the mind was worked out in greater and greater detail. Finally Edmund Husserl, who can be regarded as the father of the information-processing model of the mind, argued that concepts were hierarchies of rules, rules which contained other rules under them. For example, the rule for recognizing dogs contained a subrule for recognizing tails. Husserl also saw that such rules would have to tell us not about any particular dog, or dogs in general, but about the typical dog. All the basic ideas used by Minsky and his students of artificial intelligence were in place.[2]

I saw the history of philosophy in those terms because the contemporary thinkers I preferred and whose books I taught in my courses—Martin Heidegger, Maurice Merleau-Ponty, and Ludwig Wittgenstein—like Pascal, set themselves against both sides of our philosophical tradition. These thinkers tried simply to describe everyday experience. They came to the conclusion that perception could not be explained by the application of rules to basic features. Human understanding was a skill akin to knowing how to find one's way about in the world, rather than knowing a lot of facts and rules for relating them. Our basic understanding was thus a *knowing how* rather than a *knowing that.*

For these thinkers, philosophy was finished all right, since its attempt to treat intelligence as rational or at least analytic had never worked. No philosopher had ever been able to propose a single rule or analysis for which another philosopher had not succeeded in finding a counter-example. Thus I was prepared and pleased to hear the news from the robot laboratory that philosophy was finished—replaced by a concrete research program.

But if my favorite thinkers (who might be called antiphilosophers) were right, the new computer approach should not work either, based as it was on using programs or rules to impart "knowledge" to machines. So I confidently continued to teach Merleau-Ponty's claim that perception and understanding are based in our capacity for picking up not rules, but flexible styles of behavior. For example, someone who knows how to drive a car with a shift on the steering column can easily transfer the skill to a shift on the floor, even though the rule describing the sequence of movements required would be very different. Explaining Heidegger, I continued to assert that we are able to understand what a chair or a hammer is only because it fits into a whole set of cultural practices in which we grow up and with which we gradually become familiar. As I taught I wondered more and more how computers, which have no bodies, no childhood, and no cultural practices but are disembodied, fully formed, nonsocial, purely analytic engines, could be intelligent at all. Clearly, if the word I was getting from the robot laboratory was right, then the antiphilosophers I was teaching were wrong. I realized that if I was going to go on teaching those antiphilosophers to skeptical students, whom I now thought of as the heirs of Plato, Kant, and Husserl, I had better find out just how intelligent computers were and how intelligent they were likely to become.

I wrote all this to my brother, Stuart, who was at the RAND Corporation programming JOHNNIAC, an early prototype computer designed by John Von Neumann, and Stuart conveyed it to RAND's token philosopher, Bill Maron. The time must have been right for such an encounter, since Maron told Stuart that *his* brother too had just sent a letter to advise RAND that it should not invest time and money in the new field of computer intelligence before someone studied the work of Merleau-Ponty. Two months later I was at RAND, hired as a consultant to evaluate their pioneering work in what was then called Cognitive Simulation (CS). CS was the first phase of what I now recognize as the four phases that have come to make up the history of the attempt to make intelligent machines.

When I arrived at RAND in the summer of 1964, Allen Newell, Herbert Simon, and Cliff Shaw (henceforth referred to as NSS) had recently finished the important work that was to launch machine intelligence research on its roller coaster career. Before NSS the digital computer had proved a great boon in solving numerical problems too complicated and time-consuming for human mathematicians, and so it was generally considered merely a very powerful and useful number-crunching device. While it was recognized that a computer could manipulate symbols that represented entities other than numbers, Newell and Simon were among the first to use the symbols to stand for real-world objects such as words, pieces on a chess board, or features of a picture.

NSS got people to think out loud as they tried to solve logic problems or other puzzles. Analyzing the way students proceeded to solve such problems, Simon and Newell noted that their subjects tended to use rules or shortcuts that were not universally correct but that often helped, even if they sometimes failed. Such a rule of thumb might be, for example: Always try to substitute a shorter expression for a longer one. Simon and Newell decided to try to simulate that type of analytic problem-solving on the RAND computer. They coined the term "heuristic program" to distinguish the programs using such shortcuts from those that are guaranteed to work—so-called algorithmic programs, which follow a systematic method guaranteed to deliver a solution but sometimes become unwieldy when dealing with large practical problems.

The notion of a rule of practice provided a breakthrough for those looking for a way to program computers to exhibit problem-solving ability. With this method NSS succeeded in programming the computer to solve several puzzles. They then abstracted the general principles they were using and wrote a program for solving a whole range of such problems, which they called the General Problem Solver (GPS).

The mood at RAND was even more enthusiastic than at M.I.T., as Newell and Simon announced that they had solved many of the problems that had plagued philosophers from Plato to the present. Not just understanding but even learning and intuition were at last about to be understood:

> We have begun to learn how to use computers to solve problems, where we do not have systematic and efficient computational algorithms. And we now know, at least in a limited area, not only how to program computers to perform such problem-solving activities successfully; we know also how to program computers to *learn* to do these things.
>
> In short, we now have the elements of a theory of heuristic

(as contrasted with algorithmic) problem solving; and we can use this theory both to understand human heuristic processes and to simulate such processes with digital computers. Intuition, insight, and learning are no longer exclusive possessions of human beings: any large high-speed computer can be programmed to exhibit them also.[3]

Work on Cognitive Simulation at RAND was in its manic phase. NSS were producing papers as fast as they could get the computer to manipulate symbols, and it appeared that Newell and Simon were well on their way to fulfilling the prediction they had made in 1958 that "in a visible future . . . the range of problems [computers] can handle will be coextensive with the range to which the human mind has been applied."[4]

I began reading NSS's landmark papers with a mixture of excitement and fear. Perhaps Hobbes, Kant, and Husserl were right after all, and the human mind was an analytic engine. But then what about the seemingly plausible arguments of Merleau-Ponty, Heidegger, and Wittgenstein, which I had come to accept? As I read the RAND papers my excitement and fear turned to disappointment and relief. It seemed to me that NSS had done original and impressive work in solving some specific problems and proving machines could perform symbol manipulation, but their broader claim to have cast any general light on understanding, intuition, and learning was not supported by their actual research.

The idea current at RAND at that time—an idea that still sustains artificial intelligence research in times of adversity— was called the continuum hypothesis. As Patrick Winston, the head of the M.I.T. AI Laboratory, put it recently: "Just as the Wright brothers at Kitty Hawk in 1903 were on the right track to the 747's of today, so AI, with its attempt to formalize common-sense understanding, is on the way to fully intelligent machines." In a report I wrote for RAND I disagreed with that kind of optimism and concluded that, in spite of NSS's impressive work, an overall pattern had emerged: success with simple mechanical forms of information processing, then great expectations, and finally failure when confronted with more intuitive forms of intelligence. Simon's claims fell into place as just another example of the phenomenon which Y. Bar-Hillel had called the "fallacy of the successful first step." In a talk I gave at RAND, I compared AI to alchemy to make the point. Like the alchemists trying to turn lead into gold, I said, AI had fancy equipment, a few flashy demos, and desperately eager patrons, but they simply had not discovered the right approach to the problem.

When I finished my report and submitted it to RAND to be distributed, I got my first taste of the unscientific character of the field. Workers in artificial intelligence, unlike most scientists, almost never acknowledge their difficulties and are highly sensitive to criticism.[5] RAND usually published the conclusions of the consultants it hired, but because I was criticizing RAND's cognitive simulation research, Simon and Newell insisted that my paper was nonsense and that RAND should in no way appear to condone it. That led to a year-long struggle within RAND as to whether the paper should be published or suppressed.

Meanwhile, Stuart, a computer specialist, was working at RAND with the internationally famous mathematician Richard Bellman to develop a young discipline called operations research. Workers in that area were creating mathematical models and methods that they hoped would allow computers to determine the best possible (optimal) decisions for various problems faced by generals, industrial planners, and public policy-makers. Although he and Bellman believed decision problems could be represented and solved mathematically, Stuart supported me and insisted that the paper be published. Both he and Bellman had long suspected that the grandiose claims and predictions made by Simon and associates were not based on sound empirical research. Stuart knew from his own experience as a tournament chess player that human decision-making was an inscrutable business, a mysterious blending of careful analysis, intuition, and the wisdom and judgment distilled from experience. He was therefore suspicious of the claim that a digital computer could so easily be programmed to learn, let alone exhibit intuition and insight; he was indignant upon learning Simon's and Newell's prediction, published in 1958, that within ten years a computer would be world chess champion.

Stuart, Bellman, and their friends finally prevailed. After a year's delay, my paper "Alchemy and Artificial Intelligence" was released. The abstract of the paper reads:

Early success in programming digital computers to exhibit simple forms of intelligent behavior, coupled with the belief that intelligent activities differ only in their degree of complexity, have led to the conviction that the processing underlying any cognitive performance can be formulated in a program and thus simulated on a digital computer. Attempts to simulate cognitive processes on computers have, however, run into greater difficulties than anticipated.

An examination of these difficulties reveals that the attempt to analyze intelligent behavior in digital computer language systematically excludes three fundamental human forms of processing (fringe consciousness, essence/accident discrimination, and ambiguity tolerance). Significant developments in artificial intelligence must await computers of an entirely different sort, of which the only existing prototype is the little-understood human brain.[6]

The fears of those who tried to prevent the distribution of the paper were justified. It was the first detailed criticism of work in CS, and it sparked debate all over the world—at Novosibirsk in the USSR, in Japan, and among the top scientists at large companies such as Bell Telephone. But it was not seriously discussed at the principal AI centers such as M.I.T. and Carnegie–Mellon. Indeed, at M.I.T. the rejection was so total that students and professors working on the robot project dared not be seen having lunch with me without risking getting into trouble with their superiors. When Joseph Weizenbaum, the only professor who had any doubts, wanted to discuss his concerns with me, we had to meet at his home in the suburbs. I spent the next semester at the Harvard Computer Laboratory, which, not being committed to artificial intelligence, offered to make me a research associate in computer science so I could continue my investigation.

Stuart stayed at RAND working on formal models of optimal decision-making and running them on the JOHNNIAC computer, which he shared with Simon, with whom he was now barely on speaking terms.

During those days of the infancy of operations research and of the digital computer, the average man or woman at a cocktail party had not heard that machines could think, learn, and create as Simon and Newell had claimed or could be used to determine optimal decisions for real-world problems as Stuart believed. Hence in social situations Stuart found himself frequently called upon to explain what he was working on at the mysterious and supersecret RAND Corporation and how it was that computers could become decision-makers, not merely number crunchers. His favorite example became the problem of when to replace one's car. Supposing one planned to drive a car for the next thirty years or so, how often should an old one be replaced by a new? It's simple, he would say, given a digital computer. You estimate the costs of operating an aging car and the cost of buying a new one; throw in other factors such as the need for reliable performance, depreciation, and the pleasure derived from ownership; weigh all of these factors appropriately; and let the computer determine the most desirable sequence of decisions to replace. It's really all number crunching, after all, once you program the appropriate facts and tradeoffs between various factors.

One evening at a cocktail party, after this standard answer to the customary question, an unusual thing happened. Instead of thanking Stuart and moving on to something else more comprehensible, a listener innocently asked, "Oh, and is this the way you decide when to replace *your* car?" "Of course not" Stuart replied without hesitation. "That was only an example of how to use the formal procedure. Buying a new car is for me much too important to be left to a mathematical model. I mull it over for awhile, and buy a new car when it feels right."

The next morning Stuart began to reflect upon what had happened. How could he tell generals, businessmen, and policymakers that they should use a decision-making technique that he himself wouldn't use in his own personal life? Why did he trust his feelings rather than his formal car replacement model? Trying to answer the question led to this book. Hunches and intuitions, and even systematic illusions, are the very core of expert decision-making, so whether one seeks to use a digital computer to model the heuristic rules behind actual problem-solving, as Newell and Simon did, or whether one tries, like Stuart and Richard Bellman, to find optimal algorithms, the result fails to capture the insight and ability of the expert decision-maker. Once Stuart saw this, he saw that no matter how much more work was done in computer simulation and operations research, and no matter how sophisticated the rules and procedures became, such analytic abstractions would never allow the computer to attain expertise. As Stuart put it: "There's no continuum. Current claims and hopes for progress in models for making computers intelligent are like the belief that someone climbing a tree is making progress toward reaching the moon."

Thus Stuart was converted and now cautions people against making the same first-step fallacy in operations research that I observed in artificial intelligence. He points out that while operations research had early successes in modeling operational problems in the military and industry—how to search for a submarine or when to reorder inventory—that is no reason to believe that the same mathematical modeling techniques can tell experienced generals what military strategies are optimal, business executives whether to diversify their companies, or public policy-makers how to allocate their budgets. Problems involving deep understanding built up on the basis of vast experience will not yield—as do simple, well-defined problems that exist in isolation from much of human experience—to formal mathematical or computer analysis.

Stuart's observations confirmed my own, so I returned to M.I.T. in the fall of 1964 convinced that the robot project had much to learn from Heidegger, Merleau-Ponty, and Wittgenstein. If philosophy in the tradition of Socrates and Plato was indeed defunct, so were its computer-oriented heirs.

Twenty years have passed since I first challenged the optimism of the artificial intelligence community. During that time, research in machine intelligence has taught us much about ourselves, more by its failures than by its successes. But suddenly, and without open debate, we have turned from the millions-for-basic-research phase of the past twenty years to a crash development program that will ultimately cost billions. AI spokesmen themselves have the bulk of the responsibility. It is they who, sometimes naively and sometimes cynically, proclaimed the "successes" of AI and then created a bogus Japanese–U.S. "AI gap" that, in the tradition of the phony "missile gap" and "bomber gap," justified the massive R&D effort of Strategic Computing.

The Department of Defense's *Strategic Computing Plan* of October 1983[7] seeks immediate funding of more than $500 million, the first two years of which have already been approved, and states that "within the past few years, a series of important advances have occurred across a wide range of areas." It lists, among those "advances," expert systems with common sense and artificial intelligence systems with natural language understanding. The report cites no specific recent "advances" in AI, and you will discover as you read on that no such advances have occurred. The "common sense" and "natural language understanding" problems, both alleged by the Department of Defense's Advanced Research Projects Agency (DARPA) to have been solved, are closely intertwined, unsolved, and, given AI's current approach, probably unsolvable. Likewise, computers are no more able today to deal intelligently with "uncertain data" than they were a few years ago, when radar reflections from a rising moon were interpreted by the computerized ballistic missile warning system as an enemy attack. In its evaluation of the Strategic Computing Program, the Office of Technology Assessment cautions:

> Unlike the Manhattan Project or the Manned Moon Landing Mission, which were principally engineering problems, the success of the DARPA program requires basic scientific breakthroughs, neither the timing nor nature of which can be predicted.[8]

Even if the Department of Defense invests billions in AI, there is almost no likelihood that this state of affairs will change.

Let us hope that, after having wasted hundreds of millions on their artificially intelligent decision-making systems, military managers will still be wise enough to see their obvious shortcomings and refrain from deploying them. Still we should note the risk: Once vast sums of money have been spent, the temptation will be great to justify the expenditure by installing questionable AI-based technologies in a variety of critical contexts—from data-reduction to battle management. And, to justify its expenditures to the general public, the military may feel compelled to encourage the adoption of similar technologies in the civilian sector: Automated air traffic control systems and the overzealous adoption of computerized teaching machines are both very real possibilities.

Unless illusions concerning AI are dispelled we are risking a future in which either computers make crucial military decisions and spinoffs from military development flood unplanned into civilian life or hundreds of millions of dollars are wasted pursuing false hopes. Knowledgeable practitioners of artificial intelligence have already learned from bitter experience that the success of initiatives like Strategic Computing are highly unlikely. We hope that military decision-makers, or the politicians who fund them, will see the light and save the taxpayer money by terminating the effort until basic research results justify the expenditure. In the meantime, we believe it appropriate that more people understand the real nature of artificial intelligence technology. No unprecedented and potentially dangerous reliance on automated systems should be adopted without the widespread and informed involvement of the people to be affected.

At this point the reader may reasonably ask: But if symbol-manipulating computers cannot attain the skill level of an expert human being, and if the "Japanese challenge in Fifth Generation Systems" is essentially a money grab on the part of ambitious AI entrepreneurs, why don't we or at least the military technologists already know it? The answer is that the spokesmen for the artificial intelligence community have a great deal at stake in making it appear that their pure science of artificial intelligence and its engineering offspring, expert systems, are solid, established, and noncontroversial. They will do whatever is required to preserve that image.

When a Silicon Valley PBS affiliate television station, KCSM in San Mateo, wanted to do a program on AI and expert systems to be shown nationally, Stanford's AI expert, John McCarthy, was happy to take part, as was a representative of IntelliCorp, an expert systems company that wished to air a promotional demonstration film. I was asked to be on the show as a discussant to provide a balanced perspective. After much negotiating, an evening was finally agreed upon for taping. That evening the producer and technicians were standing by at the studio, and I was already in San Mateo when word came at the last minute that McCarthy would not show up and that IntelliCorp had withdrawn its demo because Dreyfus was to be on the program. The third participant, expert systems expert Michael Genesereth, also backed out.

All of us standing by were stunned. I had already been interviewed about AI on NOVA and on the CBS television network news and had recently appeared on a panel with Marvin Minsky, Seymour Papert, John Searle, and McCarthy himself at a meeting sponsored by the New York Academy of Sciences. Why not on KCSM? The reason seemed to be that no one could prevent NOVA or Dan Rather from interviewing me, and the discussion in New York reached an audience of only five hundred. But when it came to a half-hour discussion aired nationally, the experts wanted to give the impression that they represented a

successful science with marketable products and so didn't want
to have to face any potentially embarrassing questions.

The shock tactic worked. The executive producer and show
anchor man, Stewart Cheifet, rescheduled the taping with
McCarthy and the demo from IntelliCorp and decided that the
planned discussion with me had better be dropped. In the interest of fairness, I was asked to submit my questions to him, to
be used at his discretion. I suggested he ask the following questions:

1. What are the unsolved problems in AI?
2. Has there been any progress toward solving them?
3. Why should we expect they will be solved?
4. Do expert systems ever do as well as the experts whose
   rules they run?
5. If not, why not?
6. What makes you think experts follow unconscious rules,
   anyway?

When I watched the program I saw that just as time was
running out, my questions were, indeed, asked, although in a
somewhat revised form. To the question, "How smart can machines become?" John McCarthy answered that he saw no limits
short of human intelligence, and that even that might be surpassed by faster machines. Nils Nilsson of SRI, who had replaced
Genesereth, admitted that it was "proving a little difficult to
represent commonsense knowledge." The reason, he said, was
that "very few people are willing to pay for putting commonsense knowledge into a computer." There was no hint of the
fact that a decade of research on commonsense knowledge at
the main AI centers of the world had produced no progress.

To the next question, "Has AI turned out to be harder to
produce than you thought?" McCarthy took issue with Nilsson's
claim earlier in the program that one could at present put into
expert systems the knowledge of a world class expert. McCarthy
pointed out, quite sensibly, that one could do so only if the
knowledge could be captured in if–then rules. Other knowledge
used in a vaguer way, he said, is harder to program. No one
asked just what that other knowledge was or whether it could
be put into a computer at all. Time was up.

The viewers were left with the impression that AI is a solid,
ongoing science, which, like physics, is hard at work solving

its quite manageable current problems, while expert systems are its equally successful engineering offspring. Thus the public's chance to hear both sides was lost again, and the myth of steady progress in AI and the usefulness and reliability of expert systems was maintained. The real story remained to be told, and we propose to tell it here.

To deal with the questions I put to the TV panel, we first need to understand human skills and what goes into becoming a human expert. We must also see how computers as logic machines actually work and to what extent human skill can be simulated by using them. That is an empirical question and can be answered only by looking into the successes and failures of artificial intelligence and expert systems. Then we will be in a position to apply our understanding of the limits of logic machines to two professions especially concerned with the role of computers in their work—education and management. Finally we can begin to bring the history of Western philosophy up to date, restoring the proper balance between calculative reason and intuition.

CHAPTER 1

FIVE STEPS FROM NOVICE TO EXPERT

Mathematical formalizers wish to treat matters of intuition mathematically, and make themselves ridiculous. . . .
The mind . . . does it tacitly, naturally, and without technical rules.

Pascal
Pensées (1670)

YOU PROBABLY KNOW how to ride a bicycle. Does that mean you can formulate specific rules that would successfully teach someone else how to do it? How would you explain the difference between the feeling of falling over and the perfectly normal sense of being slightly off balance when turning? And do you really know, until it happens, just what you would do in response to a certain unbalanced feeling? No, you don't. You can ride a bicycle because you possess something called "know-how," which you acquired from practice and sometimes painful experience. The fact that you can't put what you have learned into words means that know-how is not accessible to you in the form of facts and rules. If it were, we would say that you "know that" certain rules produce proficient bicycle riding.

The issue, of course, is not confined to riding a bike. All of us know how to do innumerable things that, like bike riding, cannot be reduced to "knowing that." You know how to carry on a conversation, and how to do so appropriately in a wide variety of contexts with your family, your friends, in the office, at a party, and with a stranger. Not only do you know what sorts of things to say in various social settings, but how far to stand from your conversational partner and what tone of voice to use. You almost certainly know how to walk. Yet the mechanics of walking on two legs is so complex that the best engineers cannot even come close to reproducing it in artificial devices. If you are a carpenter, you know how to use tools in a way that escapes verbalization. A blind person knows how to use his cane, not as an object that transmits messages through impacts, each requiring interpretation, but in the same way you know how to use your arm to grope about in a dark room. You know how to get along with people, do your job, lead your life.

Maybe you take your know-how so much for granted that you don't appreciate the extent to which it pervades your activities except in situations in which it has deserted you. Have you ever been driving effortlessly along a city street in a stick-shift car and suddenly found yourself consciously thinking about the gear you are in and whether it's appropriate? Chances are the sudden reflection upon what you were doing and the rules for doing it was accompanied by a severe degradation of performance; perhaps you shifted at the wrong time or into the wrong gear. Here you fell victim to "knowing that" as it interrupted and replaced your "knowing how."

Practice is required for maintaining know-how. It can be lost through inactivity. When we were engaged in Air Force–sponsored research into flying skill, Captain Drew Poston, an expert pilot who had been promoted to instructor and then became an evaluator who tested the competence of trainees, described an embarrassing experience. As an evaluator, his only opportunity to fly the four jet KC-135s at which he had once been expert was during the return flight after completing an evaluation. He was approaching Castle AFB on one such flight when an engine failed. That is technically an emergency, but the experienced and practiced pilot will respond effortlessly to compensate for the pull to one side. Being out of practice, Captain Poston thought about what to do and then overcompensated. He then consciously corrected himself, and the plane shuddered back and forth as he landed. Consciously using rules, he had regressed to flying like a beginner.

Here is an experiment that will perhaps bring home to you the difference between "knowing how" and "knowing that." A version of it was first performed in England about ten years ago.[1] Imagine that you have been asked to perform two tasks.

In the first, you are presented with a stack of cards. One side of each card has either the letter A or the letter D. The opposite side of each card has either the number 4 or the number 7. The cards are now stacked with either side up, at random, and shuffled, so that thumbing through the deck you would see some A's, some D's, some 4s and some 7s. Your task is to determine whether or not the cards of this deck satisfy the rule "If the letter side of a card is an A, then the number side must be a 4." To make that determination, you are to imagine that you are going through the deck, looking at the turned-up side of each card, one at a time, and turning over whichever cards you must, but only those cards, in order to verify or contradict the rule that every A must be accompanied by a 4.

Think about the task for a moment. Would you turn over only those cards with A's showing? Or those showing A's and 4s? Or showing A's and 7s? Or perhaps those showing A's, 4s, and 7s? Or did you choose some other combination? Write down your choice and proceed to task two. And don't feel discouraged. Task one is difficult, and most of the English college students upon whom the experiment was first performed failed to give the correct answer.

As task two, you are to imagine that you are the cashier at a supermarket and have the checks received that day stacked before you; some face up and some face down. Your supermarket has a rule. The checkout people are to accept checks for more than $50 only if approved on the back by the manager. Imagine that you are to go through the checks, one at a time, and turn over only those checks necessary to establish if the approval rule has been followed.

Again, think about the task for a moment. Would you turn over only checks bigger than $50? Or those, plus checks with their face down bearing the manager's approval? Or those for over $50 and those with no approval on the back? Or perhaps checks exceeding $50, plus all checks with their faces down? Or some other combination?

As before, jot down your answer. If you are typical of most subjects of this experiment, you did not find task two nearly as difficult as task one. You probably correctly answered two by turning over checks for more than $50 and those with no approval on their backs. You were more likely to miss on task one, for which the correct solution is to turn over A's and 7s only.

Why this pair of experiments? Because the two tasks are essentially identical. If you designate "over $50" as A, "not over $50" as D, "approved on back" as 4 and "unapproved" as 7, task two becomes task one. But while they are abstractly identical, the statement of task two draws, for many, on "knowing how," whereas task one is perceived as a logical puzzle requiring the application of logical rules, that is, requiring the reduction to "knowing that." All of you who did task two easily and correctly and had trouble with task one have learned from this experience that "knowing how" is quite distinct from "knowing that" and in no way requires using conscious abstract rules.

Moreover, the fact that a reduction to rules of logic exists for the specific problem we have just posed does not mean that such a reduction is even possible for unstructured and poorly defined problems found in the real world. Our cashier could choose to use logic rather than know-how to deal with check approval, but he also knows how to tell if a customer's face matches that on an ID, and no one knows a set of rules or procedures that can produce this ability.

Five Stages of Skill Acquisition

The know-how of cashiers, drivers, carpenters, teachers, managers, chess masters, and all mature, skillful individuals is not innate, like a bird's skill at building a nest. We have to learn. Small children, and sometimes adults, learn through trial and error, often guided by imitation of those more proficient. Children learn to walk and adults learn bicycle riding in this manner. More commonly, however, adults begin to acquire new skills by means of either written or verbal instruction. It is this process that concerns us here.

As human beings acquire a skill through instruction and experience, they do not appear to leap suddenly from rule-guided "knowing that" to experience-based know-how. A careful study of the skill-acquisition process shows that a person usually passes through at least five stages of qualitatively different perceptions of his task and/or mode of decision-making as his skill improves. Understanding the dynamic process of human skill acquisition provides the framework for our investigation of machine intelligence. Once we adequately appreciate the full development of human skilled behavior, we can ask how far along this path the digital computer can reasonably be expected to progress.

We're painfully aware of the fact that we shall continually be referring to "he" as the subject in what follows. Let us make it clear that women become experts based on their concrete experiences as readily as men. Some fields may be dominated by male or female experts, but we all share expertise equally in most everyday activities such as conducting conversations, recognizing faces, and walking through traffic.

As we examine in detail how a novice, if he possesses innate ability and has the opportunity to acquire sufficient experience, gradually becomes an expert, we shall focus upon the most common kind of problem area, sometimes called "unstructured." Such areas contain a potentially unlimited number of possibly relevant facts and features, and the ways those elements interrelate and determine other events is unclear. Management, nursing, economic forecasting, teaching, and all social interactions fall into that very large class. Examples of "structured areas" of decision-making, on the other hand, are mathematical manipulations, puzzles, and, in the real world, delivery truck routing and petroleum blending. Here the goal and what information is relevant are clear, the effects of decisions are known, and verifiable solutions can be reasoned out. A high level of skill in any *unstructured* problem area seems to require considerable concrete experience with real situations, and any individual will have had more experience with some types of situations than with others. Consequently an individual will be at the same time expert with respect to certain types of problems in his area of skill, but less skilled with respect to others. A businessman, for example, may show expertise at marketing while at the same time being only competent as a financial planner, and a mere novice when it comes to negotiating a merger.

We studied the skill-acquisition process of airplane pilots, chess players, automobile drivers, and adult learners of a second language and observed a common pattern in all cases, which we call the *five stages of skill acquisition.* You need not merely accept our word but should check to see if the process by which you yourself acquired various skills reveals a similar pattern. After we developed our five-stage description, a group of research nurses who had amassed considerable data about the acquisition of nursing skill found that our model fitted their data very well. The results of that study may be found in the book *From Novice to Expert* by Professor Patricia Benner.[2]

Not all people achieve an expert level in their skills. Some areas of skill—chess, for example—have the characteristic that only a very small fraction of beginners can ever master the domain. That, of course, is one of the great attractions of the game. Other areas, such as automobile driving, are so designed that almost all novices can eventually reach the level we call expert, although some will always be more skilled than others. Being an expert, or being at any particular stage of our skill acquisition model, does not necessarily mean performing as well as everyone else exhibiting the same type of thought process. We refer to "stages" because (1) each individual, when confronting a particular type of situation in his or her skill domain, will usually approach it first in the manner of the novice, then of the advanced beginner, and so on through the five stages, and (2) the most talented individuals employing the kind of thinking that characterizes a certain stage will perform more skillfully than the most talented individuals at an earlier stage in our model.

The five stages we shall lay out are called novice, advanced beginner, competent, proficient, and expert.

Stage 1: Novice

During the first stage of the acquisition of a new skill through instruction, the novice learns to recognize various objective facts and features relevant to the skill and acquires rules for determining actions based upon those facts and features. Elements of the situation to be treated as relevant are so clearly and objectively defined for the novice that they can be recognized without reference to the overall situation in which they occur. We call such elements "context-free," and the rules that are to be applied to these facts regardless of what else is happening "context-free rules." The manipulation of unambiguously defined context-free elements by precise rules is called "information processing." If you recognize a letter E because it has certain horizontal and vertical lines in a certain relationship, you have done so by information processing. If you recognize it because it matches what you have seen before and learned is an E, you have used holistic template matching, not information processing.

Here are some examples of context-free features and rules as they are sometimes presented to beginners in a variety of skill areas. The beginning automobile driver learning to operate a stick-shift car is told at what speed (a context-free feature) to shift gears and, at any given speed, at what distance (another such feature) to follow a car preceding him. These rules ignore context. They do not refer to traffic density or anticipated stops. Similarly, the beginning chess player is given a formula for assigning point values to pieces independent of their position and the rule "always exchange your pieces for the opponent's if the total value of pieces captured exceeds that of pieces lost." The beginner is generally not taught that in certain situations the rule should be violated. The novice nurse is taught how to read blood pressure, measure bodily outputs, and compute fluid retention, and is given rules for determining what to do when those measurements reach certain values. A business school student of marketing learns consumer behavior theories and cost-profit modeling and plugs into such models context-free features like market share, sample survey results, demographic data, and production costs.

The beginning student wants to do a good job, but lacking any coherent sense of the overall task he judges his performance mainly by how well he follows learned rules. After he acquires more than just a few rules, the exercise of his skill requires so much concentration that his capacity to talk or listen to advice is severely limited. Like the training wheels on a child's first bicycle, these first rules allow the accumulation of experience, but soon they must be put aside to proceed.

Stage 2: Advanced Beginner

Performance improves to a marginally acceptable level only after the novice has considerable experience in coping with real situations. While that encourages the learner to consider more context-free facts and to use more sophisticated rules, it also teaches him a more important lesson involving an enlarged conception of the world of the skill. Through practical experience in concrete situations with meaningful elements, which neither an instructor nor the learner can define in terms of objectively recognizable context-free features, the advanced beginner starts to recognize those elements when they are present. How? Thanks to a perceived similarity with prior examples. We call the new elements "situational" to distinguish them from context-free elements. Rules for behavior may now refer to both the new situational and the context-free components.

Take a few real-world examples. A dog owner learns through experience to recognize his pet's distinctive bark, but he cannot list any particular facts about that bark which would allow *you* to recognize it. If the dog's bark were displayed on an oscilloscope as a sound wave, facts about that wave could be used to identify it. But those are not the sort of facts to which the owner has any conscious access. Similarly, nobody combines facts or features to identify the smell of coffee.

The advanced beginner automobile driver uses situational engine sounds as well as context-free speed in his gear-shifting rules. He also learns to distinguish between the behavior of the distracted or drunken driver and that of the impatient but alert one. With experience, the chess beginner learns to recognize and avoid overextended positions. Similarly, after much experience he can spot such situational aspects of positions as a weakened king's side or a strong pawn structure despite the lack of precise and universally valid definitional rules. The student nurse learns from experience how to distinguish the breathing sounds that indicate pulmonary edema from those suggesting pneumonia. Rules of treatment can now refer to the presence or absence of such sounds. The advanced beginner marketing decision-maker learns not by rules but by experience how to assess his company's competence in the manufacture of a new product, which becomes a factor in his decision-making. In all those cases, experience seems immeasurably more important than any form of verbal description.

Stage 3: Competence

With more experience, the number of recognizable context-free and situational elements present in a real-world circumstance eventually becomes overwhelming. A sense of what is important is missing, as is beautifully illustrated in an expert nurse's description of her advanced-beginner students:

> I give instructions to the new graduate, very detailed and explicit instructions: When you come in and first see the baby, you take

the baby's vital signs and make the physical examination, and you
check the I.V. sites, and the ventilator and make sure that it works,
and you check the monitors and alarms. When I would say this
to them, they would do exactly what I told them to do, no matter
what else was going on . . . They couldn't choose which one was
the most important . . . They couldn't do for one baby the things
that were most important and then go to the other baby and do
the things that were the most important, and leave the things that
weren't as important until later on.[3]

The expert goes on to note:

If I said, you have to do these eight things . . . they did those
things, and they didn't care if their other kid was screaming its
head off. When they did realize, they would be like a mule between
two piles of hay.[4]

To cope with such problems, people learn, or are taught, to
adopt a hierarchical procedure of decision-making. By first
choosing a plan to organize the situation, and by then examining
only the small set of factors that are most important given the
chosen plan, a person can both simplify and improve his performance.

In general, a competent performer with a goal in mind sees
a situation as a set of facts. The importance of the facts may
depend on the presence of other facts. He has learned that when
a situation has a particular constellation of those elements a certain conclusion should be drawn, decision made, or expectation
investigated.

A competent driver, for example, is no longer merely following rules designed to enable him to operate his vehicle safely
and courteously but drives with a goal in mind. If he wishes
to get from point A to point B very quickly, he chooses his
route with attention to distance and traffic, ignores scenic beauty,
and as he drives selects his maneuvers with little concern for
passenger comfort or courtesy. He follows other cars more
closely than normally, enters traffic more daringly, and even
violates the law. A competent chess player[5] may decide, after
studying his position and weighing alternatives, that he can attack his opponent's king. He would then ignore certain weaknesses in his own position and the personal losses created by
his attack, while removal of pieces defending the enemy king
becomes his overriding objective.

One of us, Stuart, knows all too well what it is to think like a competent chess player, as he is stuck at that level. He recalls:

> I was always good at mathematics and took up chess as an outlet for that analytic talent. At college, where I captained the chess team, my players were mostly mathematicians and mostly, like me, at the competent level. At this point, a few of my teammates who were not mathematicians began to play fast chess at the rate of five or ten minutes a game, and also eagerly to play over the great games of the grandmasters. I resisted. Fast chess was no fun for me, because it didn't give me time to *figure out* what to do. I found grandmaster games inscrutable, and since the record of the game seldom if ever gave rules and principles explaining the moves, I felt there was nothing I could learn from the games. Some of my teammates who through fast chess and game studying acquired a great deal of concrete experience have gone on to become masters.
>
> As I look around at my mathematical academic colleagues, most of whom play chess and none of whom have gotten beyond my own competent level, I see how our view of chess as a strictly analytic game has cut us off from absorbing concrete chess experience. While students of mathematics and related topics predominate in the population of young people enthusiastic about chess, you are as likely to find a truck driver as a mathematician among the world's best players. You are more likely to find an amateur psychologist or a journalist. In a way I am glad that my analytic approach to chess stymied my progress, because this helped me to see that there is more to skill than reasoning.

We once asked the chess champion of The Netherlands, Jan Donner, why women had never risen to the highest levels in chess. Donner's puzzling reply was that women in chess lack intuition. Twenty years later we finally understood. Young women who are attracted to chess are, like future mathematicians, seduced by its analytic challenge. Accordingly, the self-selected group of women fails to make the leap to intuitive play that characterizes expertise. If less analytically inclined women took up chess in sufficient numbers, one might well soon find women among the strongest players. Interestingly, a fifteen-year-old Hungarian woman, Susan Polgar, has suddenly risen to the International Master level of chess. She has played since she was four, by which age she could hardly have learned to see herself as analytically talented. In fact, in a recent *New York Times* interview she boasted: "I play chess by instinct."

The competent nurse will no longer automatically go from patient to patient in a prescribed order but will assess the urgency of their needs and plan work accordingly. With each patient, such a nurse will develop a plan of treatment, deciding that if certain signs are present a certain number of days after surgery, say, the time has come to talk with a patient about his wound and its care outside the hospital. When discussing the matter, various medical aspects of the patient's condition will be ignored, and psychological aspects will become important. The competent manager of marketing will decide first whether there is need for a change in the *status quo,* then the scale of any planned undertaking, and finally the actual sequence of events. During each decision in the hierarchy he will pay attention to only a few of the immense number of factors impinging on the overall project.

Choosing a plan is no simple matter for the competent individual. There is no objective procedure like the novice's context-free feature recognition. And while the advanced beginner can get along without recognizing and using a particular situational element until a sufficient number of examples renders identification easy and sure, to perform at the competent level *requires* choosing an organizing plan. Furthermore, the choice crucially affects behavior in a way that one particular situational element rarely does.

That combination of nonobjectivity and necessity introduces an important new type of relationship between the performer and his environment. Recall that the novice and advanced beginner recognize learned components and then apply learned rules and procedures. As a consequence, they feel little responsibility for the outcome of their acts. Assuming that they have made no mistakes, an unfortunate outcome is viewed as the result of inadequately specified elements or rules. The competent performer, on the other hand, after wrestling with the question of the choice of a plan, feels responsible for, and thus emotionally involved in, the product of his choice. While he both understands and decides in a *detached* manner, he finds himself intensely *involved* in what occurs thereafter. An outcome that is clearly successful is deeply satisfying and leaves a vivid memory of the plan chosen and of the situation as seen from the perspective of the plan. Disasters, likewise, are not easily forgotten.

When cognitive scientists, psychologists, and others who think about thinking speak of "problem-solving" they have in mind the thought processes that characterize competence. Herbert Simon is typical of such information-processing psychologists, for his concern is to understand how we choose plans, goals, and strategies, and how situations represented as sets of facts and figures can be transformed by rule-like procedures into new sets that conform with our goals. Those psychologists have produced convincing evidence that we act as problem-solvers when confronted by puzzles or by unfamiliar situations. However, they typically go on to generalize their results too far, accepting as essentially true, without supporting this claim by any arguments or empirical evidence, that *all* intelligent behavior is of the problem-solving form. They thus uncritically accept the information processing assumption that intelligence consists in drawing conclusions using features and rules. Simon has written that the entire cognitive research enterprise "rests implicitly on the physical symbol system hypothesis: possession of the basic resources of a physical symbol system is both the necessary and sufficient condition for intelligent behavior."[6] We agree that problem-solving is "sufficient" to produce certain intelligent behaviors; that has been well documented. But there is not a shred of evidence that it is "necessary," that we cannot be intelligent without solving problems. Clearly we are not *conscious* of solving problems, that is, of selecting goals and combining elements by rule to reach them, during much of our life's activity. When we ride a bicycle, recognize a face in a crowd, exhibit common sense, use natural language, or cope skillfully with the great bulk of everyday situations, are we acting on the basis of rules? If not, are those activities therefore somehow not intelligent? And what of the processes by which we recognize problems that ought to be solved, are they too reducible to operations on sets of elements? Perhaps they are, but there is certainly no empirical evidence for assuming that they are.

The two highest levels of skill, levels we shall now describe in detail, are characterized by a rapid, fluid, involved kind of behavior that bears no apparent similarity to the slow, detached reasoning of the problem-solving process.

Stage 4: Proficiency

Up to this point the learner of a new skill, to the extent that he has made decisions at all rather than merely following rules, has made conscious choices of both goals and decisions after reflecting upon various alternatives. This Hamlet model of decision-making—the detached, deliberative, and sometimes agonizing selection among alternatives—is the only one recognized in much of the academic literature on the psychology of choice. While that type of carefully thought-out behavior certainly sometimes occurs, frequently for learners of new skills and occasionally for even the most skillful, an unbiased examination of our everyday behavior shows it to be the exception rather than the rule.

Usually the proficient performer will be deeply involved in his task and will be experiencing it from some specific perspective because of recent events. Because of the performer's perspective, certain features of the situation will stand out as salient and others will recede into the background and be ignored. As events modify the salient features, plans, expectations, and even the relative salience of features will gradually change. No detached choice or deliberation occurs. It just happens, apparently because the proficient performer has experienced similar situations in the past and memories of them trigger plans similar to those that worked in the past and anticipations of events similar to those that occurred.

Recall that an advanced beginner recognizes situational elements such as the smell of coffee after experiencing several examples. No evidence suggests that this is done by identifying components of that smell and combining those elements by a rule. Similarly, no evidence suggests that we recognize whole situations by applying rules relating salient elements. A boxer seems to recognize the moment to begin an attack, not by combining by rule various facts about his body's position and that of his opponent, but when the whole visual scene in front of him and sensations within him trigger the memory of earlier similar situations in which an attack was successful. We call the intuitive ability to use patterns without decomposing them into component features "holistic similarity recognition."

When we speak of intuition or know-how, we are referring to the understanding that effortlessly occurs upon seeing similarities with previous experiences. We shall use "intuition" and "know-how" as synonymous, although a dictionary would distinguish them, assigning "intuition" to purely cognitive activities and "know-how" to the fluid performance of a bodily skill.

Intuition must not be confused with irrational conformity, the reenactment of childhood trauma, and all the other unconscious and noninferential means by which human beings come to decisions. Those all resist explanation in terms of facts and inferences, but only intuition is the product of deep situational involvement and recognition of similarity. Nor is guessing what we mean by intuition. To guess is to reach a conclusion when one does not have sufficient knowledge or experience to do so. Some people believe there is a kind of enlightened guessing based on neither principles nor past experience. That kind of mystical attunement, if it exists at all, is not what we mean by intuition. *Intuition or know-how, as we understand it, is neither wild guessing nor supernatural inspiration, but the sort of ability we all use all the time as we go about our everyday tasks,* an ability that our tradition has acknowledged only in women, usually in interpersonal situations, and has adjudged inferior to masculine rationality.

The proficient performer, while intuitively organizing and understanding his task, will still find himself thinking analytically about what to do. Elements that present themselves as important, thanks to the performer's experience, will be assessed and combined by rule to produce decisions about how best to manipulate the environment. The spell of involvement in the world of the skill will thus be temporarily broken.

Here are a few examples of involved, intuitive understanding followed by detached decision-making. On the basis of prior experience, the proficient driver, approaching a curve on a rainy day, may intuitively realize that he is driving too fast. He then consciously decides whether to apply the brakes, remove his foot from the accelerator, or merely reduce pressure. The proficient chess player[7] can recognize a very large repertoire of types of positions. Grasping almost immediately, and without conscious effort, the sense of a position, he sets about calculating a move that best achieves his intuitive plan. He may, for example, know that he should attack, but he must deliberate about how best to do it. Recall that earlier we described how the competent nurse will figure out an organizing goal and gave as an example the nurse who decided it was time to discuss with the patient the surgical wound and how it would heal. The proficient nurse will *notice* one day, without any conscious decision-making, that the patient is psychologically ready to deal with his surgery and impending release. However, during the conversation, words will be carefully and consciously chosen. The proficient marketing manager will keep his finger on the pulse of the product market through reading and listening to everything from formal reports to gossip. One day he may decide, intuitively, that a problem or opportunity exists and that product repositioning should be considered. He will then initiate a study of the situation, quite possibly taking great pride in the sophistication of his scientific analysis while overlooking his much more impressive talent—that of recognizing, without conscious thought, the simple existence of the problem.

Stage 5: Expertise

An expert generally knows what to do based on mature and practiced understanding. When deeply involved in coping with his environment, he does not see problems in some detached way and work at solving them, nor does he worry about the future and devise plans. We usually don't make conscious deliberative decisions when we walk, talk, drive, or carry on most social activities. An expert's skill has become so much a part of him that he need be no more aware of it than he is of his own body.

The expert driver becomes one with his car, and he experiences himself simply as driving, rather than as driving a car, just as, at other times, he certainly experiences himself as walking and not, as a small child might, as consciously and deliberately propelling his body forward. Airplane pilots report that as beginners they felt that they were flying their planes but as experienced pilots they simply experience flying itself. Chess grandmasters,[8] engrossed in a game, can lose entirely the awareness that they are manipulating pieces on a board and see themselves rather as involved participants in a world of opportunities, threats, strengths, weaknesses, hopes, and fears. When playing rapidly, they sidestep dangers in the same automatic way that a teenager, himself an expert, might avoid missiles in a familiar video game, or as we avoid familiar obstacles when we dash to the phone. Similarly, the expert business manager, surgeon, nurse, lawyer, or teacher is totally engaged in skillful performance. *When things are proceeding normally, experts don't solve problems and don't make decisions; they do what normally works.*

Expert air traffic controllers don't experience themselves as seeing blips on a screen and deducing what must be going on in the sky. They "see" planes in the sky when they look at their screens, and they respond to what they see, not by rules but as experience has taught them. Presumably in time of attack military commanders would "see" a situation based on whatever data are available and would respond using common sense and experience. The frightening prospect with the "Star Wars" defense system, which requires that all contingencies be anticipated and rules for response be programmed into a computer, is that the expert's ability to use intuition will be forfeited and replaced by merely competent decision-making. In a crisis competence is not good enough.

The acquisition of medical diagnosis skill using x-ray film has recently been studied. After a few years of training, radiologists seem to form diagnostic hypotheses and draw conclusions from sets of relevant features as described in our third stage of skill acquisition, competence. But do experts perform in that way? Our skill acquisition model suggests that after enough experience with the films of patients with a particular condition the pattern of dark and light regions associated with that condition is stored in memory, and when a similar pattern is seen, the memory is triggered and the diagnosis comes to mind. There would be no decomposition of the patterns on the film into features, and no need for rules associating conditions with features. If you doubt that a dark and light pattern could look to the specialist like a collapsed lung lobe without need for detection of features and application of rules, imagine a patient with a glass chest. Even a novice doctor would see at a glance that a lung lobe was collapsed. Why should it be surprising that with enough experience an x-ray might look as familiar and informative to the expert as the actual chest looks to the novice doctor and that the expert should be able to "see" an abnormality through the x-ray as the novice doctor would see it through glass?

In the idealized picture of the skillfully coping expert that we have just presented it might seem that experts never think and are always right. Of course, in reality things are otherwise. While most expert performance is ongoing and nonreflective, when time permits and outcomes are crucial, an expert will deliberate before acting. But as we shall show shortly, this deliberation does not require calculative problem solving, but rather involves critically reflecting on one's intuitions. And even after critical reflection, experts' decisions don't always work out. An expert may, for example, in spite of great experience, be thrown a curve by events he could not have foreseen. Furthermore, where experts are pitted against other experts, only one can win.

If you have followed our description of how experience-based holistic recognition of similarity produces deep situational understanding, no new insight is needed to explain the mental processes of the expert. With enough experience in a variety of situations, all seen from the same perspective or with the same goal in mind but requiring different tactical decisions, the mind of the proficient performer seems to group together situations sharing not only the same goal or perspective but also the same decision, action, or tactic. At this point not only is a situation, when seen as similar to a prior one, understood, but the associated decision, action, or tactic simultaneously comes to mind.

An immense library of distinguishable situations is built up on the basis of experience. A chess master, it has been estimated, can recognize roughly 50,000 types of positions, and the same can probably be said of automobile driving. We doubtless store many more typical situations in our memories than words in our vocabularies. Consequently, such situations of reference bear no names and, in fact, seem to defy complete verbal description.

With expertise comes fluid performance. We seldom "choose our words" or "place our feet"—we simply talk and walk. The skilled outfielder doesn't take the time to figure out where a ball is going. Unlike the novice, he simply runs to the right spot. Taisen Deshimaru, a Japanese martial artist, remarks: "There is no choosing. It happens unconsciously, automatically, naturally. There can be no thought, because if there is thought, there is a time of thought and that means a flaw. . . . If you take the time to think 'I must use this or that technique,' you will be struck while you are thinking."[9] Tennis players "react" when expert, and, a surprising amount of the time, so do business managers and experienced doctors and nurses when deeply involved in their professional activities. The expert driver not only knows by feel and familiarity when an action such as slowing is required, but generally knows how to perform the act without evaluating and comparing alternatives. An expert American driver turning a corner would have to *decide* to keep to the left if he were driving in England, where he is no expert, but he does not have to decide to keep to the right in the United States.

The grandmaster chess player can recognize a large repertoire of types of position for which the desirable tactic or move immediately becomes obvious. Excellent chess players can play at the rate of five to ten seconds a move and even faster without serious degradation in performance. At that speed they must depend almost entirely on intuition and hardly at all on analysis and comparing alternatives.

We recently performed an experiment in which an International Master, Julio Kaplan, was required to add heard numbers at the rate of about one number per second while at the same time playing five-second-a-move chess against a slightly weaker, but master level, player. Even with his analytic mind completely jammed by adding numbers, Kaplan more than held his own against the master in a series of games. Deprived of the time necessary to see problems or construct plans, Kaplan still produced fluid and coordinated play.

Kaplan's performance seems somewhat less amazing when one realizes that a chess position is as meaningful, interesting, and important to a professional chess player as a face in a receiving line is to a professional politician. Bobby Fischer, perhaps history's greatest chess player, once said that for him "chess is life." Almost anyone can add numbers and simultaneously recognize and respond to faces, even though the face will never exactly match the same face seen previously, and politicians can recognize thousands of faces just as Julio Kaplan can recognize thousands of chess positions similar to ones previously encountered.

Herbert Simon has studied the chess master's almost instantaneous understanding of chess positions and accompanying compelling sense of the best move. He found that chess masters are familiar with thousands of patterns, which he calls chunks. Each chunk is a remembered description of a small group of pieces in a certain relationship to each other. He conjectures that a desirable move or chess idea is associated with each such chunk. Hence moves spring to mind as chunks are recognized without need for rule-like calculations.[10]

There are at least two problems with Simon's speculation. Because most chess positions are composed of several chunks, more than one move would come to mind and would need to be evaluated before the player gained a sense of which was best. Yet Julio Kaplan seems not to require such evaluation when he plays rapidly while simultaneously adding numbers. Hence Simon's conceptualization of chess in terms of chunk recognition, while providing a theory about why moves spring to mind, still seems to fall far short of the actual phenomenon of masterful play. Furthermore, for Simon chunks such as a standard castled king's formation are defined independently of the rest of the position. A configuration that didn't quite fit the description of a chunk, but in a real chess position played the same role as the chunk, would not count as such. But chess players can recognize the functional equivalence of configurations that don't fall under a single definition. For example, in some cases a configuration would count as a standard castled king's formation even if one pawn were advanced, but in other cases it would not. For these reasons it seems more plausible that expert chess players recognize and respond to whole positions, not component chunks.[11]

Expert nurses will sometimes sense that a patient lies in danger of an imminent relapse and urge remedial action upon a doctor. They cannot always provide convincing, rational explanations of their intuition, but very frequently they turn out to be correct. Pat Benner quotes an expert psychiatric nurse clinician, highly regarded for her judgment: "When I say to a doctor, 'the patient is psychotic,' I don't always know how to legitimize the statement. But I am never wrong. Because I know psychosis from inside out. And I feel that, and I know it, and I trust it."[12]

The nurse's desire to justify her intuition shows the pressure which often leads to rationalization, especially in our modern Western culture. There are, of course, two interrelated senses of the word "rationalization." Once a decision intuitively presents itself, rationalization in the first sense describes the attempt to find a valid *explanation* by identifying the elements of the situation and combining those elements by a decision rule to justify the chosen decision. That is the sort of rationalization the nurse who "knows psychosis from the inside out" is seeking when she gets "some in-service [people] in to talk to us about language." She realizes, however, that "all I am really trying to do is find words within the jargon to talk about something that I don't think is particularly describable."[13] If, indeed, elements and principles play no role in mature, practiced decision-making, rationalization in this sense amounts to the *invention of reasons*—rationalization in its second and generally derogatory sense.

SOMEONE AT A PARTICULAR STAGE of skill acquisition can always imitate the thought processes characteristic of a higher stage but will perform badly when lacking practice and concrete experience. For example, a beginner can, like a competent performer, set goals, but without experience he won't know how to set them sensibly. Similarly, anyone who has seen one situation in a skill domain and an accompanying action can then act intuitively like the expert by seeing all situations as similar to that one and always repeating the same action. Of course, he will perform quite badly. Our skill model represents a *progression* in the sense that a typical learner's *best* performance in a particular type of situation will initially stem from novice rule-following, then from the advanced beginner's use of aspects, and so on through the five stages. If the performer is talented, ultimately his best performance will result from the intuitive use of similarity and experience, and he will perform as an expert.

Now you have an overall view of our five stages of changed perception of the task environment and mode of behavior that accompanies skill acquisition. What should stand out is the progression *from* the analytic behavior of a detached subject, consciously decomposing his environment into recognizable elements, and following abstract rules, *to* involved skilled behavior based on an accumulation of concrete experiences and the unconscious recognition of new situations as similar to whole remembered ones. The evolution from the abstract toward the concrete reverses what one observes in small children dealing with intellectual tasks; they initially understand only concrete examples and gradually learn abstract reasoning. Perhaps it is because of the well-known pattern seen in children, and because rule-following plays an important, early role in the learning of new skills by adults, that adult understanding and skill are so often misunderstood as abstract and rule-guided.

Recall that we have been discussing how we acquire skills in unstructured problem areas, by which we mean areas in which the goal, what information is relevant, and the effects of our decisions are unclear. Interpretation, whether conscious, as in the case of the competent performer, or nonconscious and based upon perceived similarities, as for the more skilled, determines what is seen as important in a situation. That interpretive ability constitutes "judgment." Thus according to our description of skill acquisition the novice and advanced beginner exercise no judgment, the competent performer judges by means of conscious deliberation, and those who are proficient or expert make judgments based upon their prior concrete experiences in a manner that defies explanation.

The moral of the five-stage model is: there is more to intelligence than calculative rationality. Although irrational behavior—that is, behavior contrary to logic or reason—should generally be avoided, it does not follow that behaving rationally should be regarded as the ultimate goal. A vast area exists between irrational and rational that might be called *arational*. The word rational, deriving from the Latin word *ratio*, meaning to reckon or calculate, has come to be equivalent to calculative thought and so carries with it the connotation of "combining component parts to obtain a whole"; arational behavior, then, refers to action without conscious analytic decomposition and recombination. *Competent performance is rational; proficiency is transitional; experts act arationally.*

Deliberative Rationality

The conscious use of calculative rationality produces regression to the skill of the novice or, at best, the competent performer. To think rationally in that sense is to forsake know-how and is not usually desirable. If decisions are important and time is available, a more basic form of rationality than that of the beginner is useful. This kind of deliberative rationality does not seek to analyze the situation into context-free elements but seeks to test and improve whole intuitions.

Serious tournament chess involves deep deliberation, although, as we saw in the experiment where a player was deprived of the time to use it, quality of move choice depends surprisingly little on anything beyond pure intuitive response. You must be wondering: What does a masterful chess player think about when time permits, even when an intuitively obvious move has already come spontaneously to mind? Often he uses his time to follow out sequences of moves. Players at all levels of skill have been shown to be equally good at this. But strong intuitive players think about other things, too. What could be going through their heads? We raise the question not merely because chess is an intriguing mental activity, but because any decision-maker—all of us, when facing important social or financial decisions—encounters a problem very similar to the chess player's. We stay away from technical chess vocabulary, so you should find it easy to translate what we say into an account of your own deliberations when you are faced with decisions when planning a vacation, replacing an expensive appliance, bringing up your children, or managing a household.

Few if any situations in chess or life are seen as being of *exactly* the kind for which prior experience intuitively dictates what move or decision must be made. Usually certain aspects of the situation are slightly, yet disturbingly, different from what would make one completely comfortable with a decision based on what has happened before. The master chess player contemplates the differences, looking for a move that keeps all intuitively desirable options open while reducing his sense of uneasiness. Failing that, he tries to modify slightly the intuitively suggested move to account for the situation change.

A second focus of deliberation is the overall strategy being pursued. A master player never calculates the best strategy by a formula applied to decontextualized features of a position, as a merely competent player might, rather, he always *experiences* his position as raising issues prior experience causes him to see as important. Those issues gradually evolve as moves are made, however, so any organizing perspective, while an indispensable asset to intuitive understanding, holds as well the potential for disaster. Maintaining a perspective in the face of persistent and disquieting evidence is called tunnel vision. Tunnel vision is failing to recognize a potential new perspective that better explains recent past events and better dictates future actions.

While the novice and the advanced beginner are taught how to respond to present situations, context-free rules can, in principle, also be provided for what to expect next in each objectively defined situation. Those *reasoned-out expectations* can then enter into the competent performer's choice of a plan. Once the competent performer becomes involved in and remembers whole situations, he of course also remembers what happened next. That becomes the basis of the *intuitive expectations* of the proficient performer. While he knows not *why* certain situations often lead to certain others, when they do, expectations become associated with the remembered situations. The expected, should it occur, has a tendency to stand out as salient; even the nonappearance of the expected is noteworthy. The occurrence of the unexpected, however, may recede into the background of inconsequential features. Thus, while expectation seems to play an essential role in producing our ability to make sense out of a potentially infinitely complex environment, it also might produce tunnel vision, the inability to recognize and adapt to unexpected events.

Tunnel vision can sometimes be avoided by a type of detached deliberation. By focusing on aspects of a situation that seem relatively unimportant when seen from one perspective, it is possible for another perspective, perhaps that of one's opponent, to spring to mind. Should that happen, blunders caused by failing to anticipate an opponent's move can be avoided. To experience a change of perspective by looking at a nonsalient element until it becomes salient, consider the figure below. You probably see it as a three-dimensional cube with a certain face projecting out of the page toward you. Now concentrate your attention on the corner of the cube behind that particular face. Most likely, a face of the cube containing that corner suddenly becomes the face closest to you, and you see the cube from a new perspective, with the face that originally stood out receding into the background. If you saw the figure only as a pattern of rather unrelated lines on a flat page, you saw it as a beginner perceives his skill domain, before he attains competency and imposes a perspective. Most real situations aren't as fluid as the cube, be-

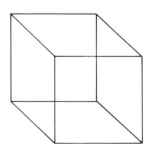

cause they frequently have only one interpretation consistent with past experiences.

We once heard an Israeli fighter pilot recount how deliberative rationality may have saved his life by rescuing him from tunnel vision. Having just vanquished an expert opponent, he found himself taking on another member of the squadron who seemed to be brilliantly eluding one masterful ploy after another. Things were looking bad until he stopped following his intuition and deliberated. Trying other ways of seeing his situation, he realized that all the surprising maneuvers of his opponent were really the predictable, rule-following behavior of a beginner. From then on, seeing the situation in terms of his experience with beginners, he easily won.

Another form of deliberation, considering the relevance and adequacy of past experiences that seem to underlie a current intuition, can also be useful. One can ask: Is what would normally appear to be the best move or strategy still the best in view of the time pressures of a particular game or one's current standing in a particular tournament? And even if past experience seems relevant, might there be a better move or decision than what experience brings to mind? A chess master sometimes senses opportunities beyond what he can immediately see in a position, presumably because much better results would be anticipated in several similar positions, which, while not enough like the present one to trigger an intuitive move, are still similar enough to produce a sense of opportunity. In this case he puts calculation in the service of intuition by examining sequences of moves which lead to other situations which he then evaluates intuitively.

One aspect of chess makes it a much more challenging subject of deliberative rationality than real everyday situations. Envisioned future positions are just as much real chess positions as the present one, and they are equally subject to deliberation. So a chess player can deliberate not only about his present position but about each possible position that he foresees. An imagined future in the everyday world is usually so incomplete as to make deliberations that compare it to actual past situations impossible.

Those sorts of issues would rarely, if ever, come to mind during the involved, fluid, expert performance of such everyday activities as driving a car, playing a sport, using a tool, or greeting a friend. Here, as in most things, we function exclusively as intuitive experts. But when time permits and much is at stake, detached deliberative rationality of the type described can enhance the performance of even the intuitive expert. We reiterate, however, that such deliberation tests and improves whole intuitions. No rules or principles are used to arrive at conclusions, and so it is not the sort of calculative rationality used by the beginner or competent performer as a surrogate for intuitive understanding.

Beyond Rationality

We have so far neglected to some extent those processes by which the human mind learns from experience. Involvement is essential for the holistic similarity recognition of proficient and expert performers. But if learning is to occur, some part of the mind must remain aloof and detached. A monitoring mind must decide when results justify reinforcement of chosen actions, when events indicate that expectations or decisions should be modified in future similar situations, or when what were seen as similar situations in the past should be differentiated in the future for purposes of expectation or decision. A portion of the mind is thus responsible for the fine tuning or disaggregation of current memories for more effective guidance of future behavior.

There are rare moments, however, when all monitoring ceases. We are referring to those brief periods of what is sometimes called "flow," when performance, accompanied by a feeling of euphoria, reaches its peak. Athletes describe the phenomenon as playing "out of your head." They are sometimes taught that the "inner game" of their sport is the mental struggle to achieve that state during competition. From our perspective "flow" is not a sixth stage of the mental activities that produce skilled behavior but rather the cessation of the monitoring activity that normally accompanies the higher levels.

Creativity is another phenomenon that we note but do not examine. What we have been describing—the fine-tuned response to events based upon the lessons of concrete experience—ignores the truly imaginative act for which there is no detectable historical precedent. Much of what passes for creativity is actually unconventional and unexpected interpretations of past events. Even Einstein, whose discovery of the elementary laws of physics is often held up as the paragon of creative genius, seems to have held a view rather like ours. He claimed neither that his insights followed from logic nor that they went beyond all experience, but rather: "To these elementary laws there leads no logical path, but only intuition, supported by being sympathetically in touch with experience."[14] If so-called creative geniuses do more than intuitively see new ways to use past experience, such radical breaks must be extremely rare.

Experiments and Expertise

To forsake rationality in favor of unrationalized know-how is to sail on uncharted seas, and there will always be those, especially in our Western culture, who challenge the wisdom of the venture. A number of academic psychologists have even gone so far as to create experiments purporting to show not only the occasional fallibility of the human expert, a fact that no one would deny, but consistent flaws in human decision making that might imply the general superiority of rational mathematical approaches to real-world problems. More cautious psychologists are just now beginning to recognize the overwhelming complexities attendant upon such research and to question experimental evidence that claims to show systematic human deficiencies and the superiority of rational models.

Let's summarize and discuss some experimental evidence:

Experiment 1

When assimilating new evidence, people sometimes do not take sufficient account of base rates—that is, the frequency with which certain events have occurred in the past. As a result they put too much weight on new evidence.

Consider the following hypothetical situation:[15] Two cab companies operate in a city, the Blue and the Green, the names coming from the color of their cabs. Of all taxis, 85 percent are Blue, and 15 percent are Green. One night a cab was involved in a hit-and-run accident. No information is available about how many cabs of each color were on duty that night or what cabs were in that part of the city at the time of the accident. A witness later identified the cab as Green. The court tested the witness's ability to distinguish between Blue and Green cabs at night under the same conditions as were present at the time of the accident and found that the witness was able to identify the color of a cab correctly 80 percent of the time and was wrong 20 percent of the time. What are the chances that the cab involved in the accident was Green, as claimed by the witness?

A mathematical calculation using what is called Bayes' Law shows that the correct answer is .41. That is, it is more likely than not that the witness was wrong. That is because the possible error in the witness's vision is compounded with the large likelihood (85 percent), assuming no witness, that the cab was Blue. Most individuals respond to this question with an answer at, or close to, the 80 percent figure, paying too little attention to the base-rate fact that most cabs in the city are Blue.

But does the poor performance of most subjects in the experiment really show that people deal poorly with new evidence in real-world situations? Note that the base-rate frequency can be defined only with respect to some specific group. In the experiment the appropriate group was all of the cabs operating in the city, since nothing more was known about events that particular night. Things are not so simple in the real world. The question of what group to use when determining the base rate is often open to judgment.

What more typically occurs in the real world of skilled activity is illustrated by a medical diagnostician's judgment about the likelihood of a patient's having a particular disease, given specific laboratory test results that indicate presence of the disease but have a certain known likelihood of being wrong. One would be wrong to equate the likelihood that the test is accurate with the probability that the patient has the disease, just as one would be wrong to accept the witness's 80 percent accuracy in identifying cabs as the likelihood the cab was Green. According to probability theory, the probability that the test results are correct should be used to adjust the prior likelihood of the patient's having the disease based on what is already known from other facts about him. But to what reference group should this individual be compared to obtain the prior likelihood? Everyone with the same symptoms for which prior tests had ruled out the same possible other diseases? Everyone of his sex? his age? his ethnic group? his country of origin or residence? his body type? his personality traits? If all conceivable characteristics are specified, the individual is unique, and there are no prior examples against which a comparison can be made. If too few are specified, the comparison group is inappropriate. In the real word, unlike the experiment, there are rarely objectively correct choices of what reference group to use. Expert doctors, guided by their experience-based know-how, wisely diagnose without specifically addressing the judgmental issue of relevant reference group. Only when facing unfamiliar situations in which the diagnostician feels that he is merely competent might it be sensible to think about appropriate reference groups and then use probability updating to combine base-rate data with additional tests. Here the computer can be immensely useful.

So the experiment really shows that people are not very good at performing a task that is rarely relevant in the real world. Naturally, if there is seldom any reason to do something like update base-rate probabilities using uncertain evidence, people will not master it.

Experiment 2

Human beings have been shown to be inferior to mathematical procedures for revising probability estimates when additional factual evidence is provided.

In a typical experiment[16] the subject is presented with two identical-looking bags filled with poker chips. He is told that one bag contains 70 red chips and 30 blue ones, while the other bag holds 30 red chips and 70 blue ones. The subject does not know which bag contains which. A coin is flipped in the presence of the subject to determine which bag is to be sampled, and a chip is drawn from that bag. The subject notes its color, the chip is returned to the bag, and the contents are thoroughly mixed. Another chip is drawn from the same bag, the subject again notes its color, and it is returned to the bag. Suppose that after ten draws the subject has seen six red chips and four blue chips. The subject is then asked what he now believes are the chances that the bag selected is the one with 70 red chips and

30 blue ones. Almost all subjects, realizing that the odds before the sampling were 50–50 and that now the odds appear to favor the predominately red bag, answer with odds adjusted in favor of that bag. But by how much should one adjust the odds, based on ten observations which split 6–4 in favor of red?

This problem has a precise mathematical answer that is indisputable under the hypotheses of the experiment. Most subjects are surprised to learn that the odds are now better than 5 to 1 that the bag being sampled is indeed the predominately red one. Almost all subjects adjust the odds much less from 50–50, putting much too little emphasis on the sample result and too much on the fact that each bag was equally likely to be the one chosen. Intuition does not perform well here. The term conservatism describes the unwillingness of a subject to accord new evidence the significance it in fact has.

But does the experiment tell us anything about experience-based real-world behavior? Note that explicit assumptions about the situation are needed in order to calculate any probability revisions at all. Usually problems to be modeled assume, among other things, that (1) the true situation is one of a certain known set of possibilities (one of two bags for example) and the odds are known before further evidence is introduced; (2) the true situation remains fixed rather than changing over time; (3) all possible pieces of evidence that might be observed can be enumerated; and (4) the probabilities of pieces of evidence being observed, given the true situation, are known and do not change as time passes. In short, the situation is assumed to be structured and stationary. The correct probability revision based on additional evidence is then defined as the revision that is mathematically correct, given the assumptions of the model. No matter what the particular assumptions made in order to compare human beings against models, those assumptions must be made explicit and held constant to be represented in the model. Because they are fixed and explicit, the situation will not mirror the uncertain, nonstationary, unstructured world in which we live. Probability revisions that might work extremely well in the real world are not necessarily accurate in the simple world assumed in the stated problem and the model. Consequently, all that life has taught us is simply misleading, and the calculations based on the model, unaffected by real life and reflecting in exact fashion the assumed environment, produce better performance than human competitors. Given the world assumed in the experiment, the human subjects are not experts, and the fact that they may well be experts in some skill involving real-world uncertainties actually prejudices their performance.

Experiment 3

Simple mathematical models have been shown to predict the quality of future academic performance of newly admitted graduate students better than the committee of professors making the decisions.

One study compares the actual performances of graduate students in the psychology department at the University of Oregon with the predictions of their performances made by the four-professor admissions committee.[17] Human accuracy was compared with various simple mathematical models that considered only three factors: a graduate record examination score, overall undergraduate grade point average, and a subjective assessment of the quality of the undergraduate school attended. The predictions made by the models were all better correlated with observed results than were the committee's predictions.

Should we conclude that experts are inferior to models when making decisions? We note, with some embarrassment, that the professors on such committees meet only once or twice a year, perform this duty as only one of a great many responsibilities, are generally too busy with their research and other activities to spend more than about ten minutes on each case or to follow up on the results of their decisions, and finally constitute a rotating committee. Thus, while the individuals who make up admission committees may have unusual talents, they have no particular expertise in predicting academic performance and no special involvement in their committee task. Several of the shortcomings were indeed acknowledged in the report on the research performed at the University of Oregon. Others we know from experience. We have an example here of experts in one domain performing and being evaluated in another. It would be interesting to compare the predictive ability of models against those professionals responsible on a full-time basis for the admission decisions at elite undergraduate colleges. Our guess is that full-timers would fare better.

But the established superiority of computerized mathematical models to less-than-expert human beings shows us one proper place for computers in our society. When expertise is nonexistent, too expensive, or locally unavailable, computers can be programmed to produce better decision-making than inexperienced or less-than-involved human beings.

Experiment 4

People make inconsistent decisions.[18] Faced with a hypothetical choice between (A) being awarded $10 million and (B) participating in a lottery where there are 10 chances out of 100 of receiving $50 million, 89 chances out of 100 of receiving $10 million, and 1 chance in 100 of receiving nothing, most subjects prefer A, the sure $10 million. Those same subjects are then presented with the following hypothetical choice: Would you prefer to participate in (C) a lottery where you have 11 chances out of 100 of receiving $10 million and 89 chances out of 100 of receiving nothing or, instead, (D) a lottery where you have 1 chance out of 10 of receiving $50 million and 9 chances out of 10 of receiving nothing? Here, most subjects prefer choice D. Do you, like most subjects, prefer A to B and D to C?

Why is this behavior inconsistent? After placing 89 balls representing the $10 million prize in an urn out of which a ball determining the payoff is to be drawn, the choice between A and B is equivalent to the choice between (1) adding 11 more balls also representing the $10 million prize to the urn or, instead, (2) adding 10 balls representing a $50 million prize and one representing zero payoff. Similarly, after placing 89 balls representing zero payoff in an urn out of which a ball determining the payoff is to be drawn, the choice between C and D is again equivalent to the choice between (1) and (2). So interpreted, in the first case most subjects want the last 11 balls to represent the $10 million prize, while in the second case, given the same alternatives for the last 11 balls, most subjects prefer that 10 balls represent the $50 million prize and one ball represent the zero payoff. Assuming that the choice concerning the last 11 balls should not depend on the first 89 balls placed in the urn, that is inconsistent behavior. The conclusion to be drawn is that computational models that avoid such inconsistent behavior are superior to people who exhibit it.

To argue that people are inconsistent in experiment 4, the choice between payoffs was reduced to one between two alternatives for the last 11 balls to be placed in an urn by arguing that the choice shouldn't depend on the other 89 balls already in the urn. But this eliminates from any possible relevance all holistic considerations that might depend on the first 89 balls as well as the last 11. One such holistic consideration thus automatically omitted is the act of gambling itself, since what does or does not constitute a gamble, and the extent of the gamble, depend on the nature of all 100 balls in the urn and not on only the last 11. If the subjects have feelings about the act of gambling itself or expectations of feeling guilty, should excessive greed lead to blown opportunities, and should those feelings enter into their decision-making, their behavior may well be beyond reproach. Perhaps choice A is preferred to B because it guarantees a fortune while avoiding the unpleasantness of gambling and the risk of perpetual self-recrimination should the 1 in 100 chance of zero payoff occur. Choice D may be preferred to C because, in this case, the subject *must* gamble and suffer the accompanying pain and possible guilt, and feels that lottery D is superior to lottery C if the pain, common to both, is factored out. The subjects then behave consistently with respect to their criterion, and the experiment constitutes no evidence for the fallibility of intuitive human decision-making.

ONE CAN PRODUCE a long list of individual thought patterns that are functional in the real world of expertise but, in contrived experiments, lead to bizarre behavior. For example, in experiments involving unchanging environments, *recent* events are treated by subjects with too much emphasis. Yet in the real world, where the environment clearly changes, that behavior may well be functional.

When discussing competent decision-making, stage three of our five-stage model, we explained how a plan causes certain elements in a situation to stand out and thus makes comprehensible what would otherwise be an overwhelmingly complex situation. This powerful cognitive strategy, without which we would be doomed to beginner understanding and skill, has its risks. The same situation, seen from two different perspectives, can look different and dictate different decisions. Ingenious recent research by Amos Tversky has brought the phenomenon to the fore. He shows that various wordings of the same question can affect perspective and hence decision. If the decision is a choice between two alternatives, the rewording can produce a reversal in choice.

Here is a striking example. Imagine that, should nothing be done, a certain flu will kill about 600 people this year, and you must choose between two treatment options. Option one will save about 200 people. Option two will save all of the people with probability one-third and no people with probability two-thirds. Which option do you prefer? Answer the question and then read on. Now imagine the same impending flu epidemic and that you again have a choice between two options. Option one will result in about 400 deaths. Option two gives a one-third probability that none will die and a two-thirds chance that about 600 will die. Which option do you prefer?

The shift of perspective from doing something good, saving lives, to one of doing something bad, letting people die, changes most subjects' preference between what are *really identical choices.* Most subjects will not gamble if a sure gain is attainable without risk but will gamble to avoid an otherwise sure loss.

These findings can be interpreted as showing a human weakness: If there is a best choice, the wording of a problem should not change it. Certainly computer models, which lack perspective, will not suffer from the deficiency. We prefer to regard the experimental results as interesting elucidations of the price human beings may have to pay for understanding organized by perspective, not as evidence that the unorganized understanding of the beginner is preferable. And, of course, one must realize that the skeletal definition of the hypothetical situation (in our example, the one-sentence description of the impending epidemic) hardly grounds the subject in reality. Thus whatever perspective occurs to the subject is tentative at best and more easily dislodged than one's perspective of the real world. Accordingly, despite any problems raised by the existence of perspective, the indisputable fact remains that human skill level increases when tasks are approached from a point of view.

IN SUM, subjects do many strange things in experiments. That, however, does not demonstrate inappropriate real-world behavior by experts.[19] While we make no claims that experts have been experimentally proved to outperform mathematical models when confronted by real-world unstructured problems, we strongly deny that the available evidence proves the superiority of rational calculation.

If experiments are to have any direct bearing on the substitution of computer power for human expertise, they must pit truly experienced and talented experts against computers or mathematical models within the context of the unstructured tasks that are required of the experts in the normal exercise of their skill, and for which there are clear measures of success.[20] Most arenas of skill involve uncertainty, and human learning is more difficult when the resulting feedback is contaminated by random events. So, out of fairness to the model, uncertainty should be present in the problem. Fields of man–machine combat that satisfy such conditions are not easy to find. The problem given must be repeatable, because in any environment containing uncertainties a good decision can sometimes lead to a bad result owing to some improbable chance event. Accordingly, most business management situations must be ruled out. Furthermore, the area of comparison should not have an objective or scientific basis that would allow substituting objective knowledge and brute-force calculation for human understanding. Chess and card games become, for this reason, unsuitable subjects for the ultimate confrontation, although it is interesting to see just how well the computer can do, given the edge. Chess and games like bridge and poker are so complex that not even the computer can rely completely on brute-force enumeration of all possibilities. So it is by no means obvious that man eventually will lose the upper hand here. We shall see later how chess-playing computers, performing immense amounts of enumeration but relying also on evaluative rules, compare with skilled human players.

What skills are left? Not many, unfortunately. Weather forecasting seems an appropriate skill for studying human deficiencies and, in fact, has already been investigated extensively. Significantly, biases found in decontextualized laboratory experiments or in inappropriately chosen real-world tasks did not appear in those real-world tests.[21] Perhaps, subject to a breakthrough in biochemical understanding, diagnosing mental disease based on a full range of personal interviews and tests might make for a fruitful arena. Another might be the prediction of performance on a job, should the job be sufficiently important that a staff of professional interviewers has acquired, through experience and feedback, expertise at prediction. A valid comparison might be forthcoming in stock market security analysis, but the experts would have to be professional analysts and not brokers. Questions appropriate to the subject's everyday activities would have to be asked, and the comparison extended over enough time to make sure that market behavior during the experiment was typical. Some of those tasks have already been the subject of comparisons between mind and machine, but in flawed ways that our suggestions have attempted to circumvent. In general, experimental results thus far reported do not support the confidence by aficionados of artificial intelligence or computer modeling.

TABLE 1–1 summarizes what we said earlier about the five stages in the human skill acquisition process. We shall refer to the table later as we describe and discuss the attempts of computer scientists to create intelligent machines. The distinction between the detached, rule-following beginner and the involved, intuitive expert is crucial. The advanced beginner's recognition of situational elements based on experience rather than rules and the competent performer's use of plans and a point of view are also important. Soon you will discover which of the human capabilities shown have been successfully simulated using digital computers, which are currently the subject of research efforts

TABLE 1–1. Five Stages of Skill Acquisition

Skill Level	Components	Perspective	Decision	Commitment
1. Novice	Context-free	None	Analytical	Detached
2. Advanced beginner	Context-free and situational	None	Analytical	Detached
3. Competent	Context-free and situational	Chosen	Analytical	Detached understanding and deciding. Involved in outcome
4. Proficient	Context-free and situational	Experienced	Analytical	Involved understanding. Detached deciding
5. Expert	Context-free and situational	Experienced	Intuitive	Involved

holding some promise of success, and which clearly lie beyond the reasonable expectations of an artificial intelligence based on information processing. Then we can draw conclusions about the possible role of reasoning machines in our future.

CHAPTER 2

LOGIC MACHINES AND THEIR LIMITS

IT IS HARD to think about thinking machines. For one thing, computers become more powerful and cheaper at a dizzying rate. For another, some well-meaning and well-informed people tell us that computers are assuredly so literal and inflexible that they can never be made intelligent, while others in equally authoritative fashion announce that computers are already experts in some areas and will soon be programmed to contain all the world's expertise. Can machines really think? To have an informed opinion on this important question, one has to have a firsthand grasp of the nature of human skill and expertise and an understanding of the way computers are programmed to perform tasks that ordinarily require intelligence.

Our five-stage skill model, we hope, has helped you to recall what it is like to be an expert. Now we turn to the computer. To begin with, we must find out what kind of machine a computer is, what principles have governed its operations throughout its rapidly changing history, what would be required to program it to behave intelligently, and what has been accomplished so far. Only then will we be able to form a reliable perspective from which to consider the proper place of thinking machines in our lives.

Digital computers are basically highly complicated structures of simple switches, which are either on or off. The theory of such machines preceded their actual development. Philosophers like Descartes, Pascal, and Leibniz and mathematicians like Boole and Babbage sensed the potential power of combining many simple elements in rule-like ways. So by 1950, when high-speed digital computers were just beginning to be built, logicians such as Alan Turing were already accustomed to thinking of computers as devices for manipulating symbols according to exact rules. The symbols themselves didn't mean anything. So the operations that combined the symbols according to the rules of logic were meaningless too. They are just formal rules for transforming formal squiggles.

Computers are general symbol manipulators, so they can simulate any process which can be described exactly. When digital computers were actually constructed they were first used for scientific calculation. But, as noted, by the end of the 1950s researchers like Allen Newell and Herbert Simon began to take seriously the idea that computers were general symbol manipulators. They saw that one could use symbols to represent elementary facts about the world and use rules to represent relationships between them. Computers could then follow such rules or programs to deduce how those facts affect each other and what happens when the facts change. In this way computers came to be used to simulate logical thinking. *We shall call computers used in this way "logic machines" or "inference engines."*

Newell and Simon believed that computers so programmed could not only prove theorems in logic but could, in principle, solve problems, recognize patterns, understand stories, and, indeed, do anything that an intelligent person could do. All provided—and the importance of this proviso has yet to be fully appreciated—that the symbols in the computer were used to represent context-independent, objective features of the real world and that the relationships between those objective features obeyed strict rules so that they could be represented in computer programs. That means the features could not be dependent on interpretation, like a car is going "too fast," but had to be specified in a way free of interpretation, like going "20 miles an hour." The rules too had to be utterly precise, like "shift to second at 20 miles an hour," not commonsense rules like, "under normal conditions, shift to second at about 20 miles an hour."

The precision essential to a computer's way of manipulating symbols constitutes both a great advantage and a severe limitation. Since what the symbols in a computer represent must be absolutely precise, and the programmer must be absolutely clear as to what he lets each symbol mean, the attempt to write a computer program inevitably exposes hand-waving, fuzzy thinking, and implicit appeals to what everyone takes for granted. Submitting to this rigor is an immensely valuable discipline.

The analytic power of the computer used as a logic machine also has its limitations, however. They show up when we consider the way such computers deal with images and with the recognition of similarity or analogy. Electronic machines can store an image as a set of dots and can rotate it so that a human designer can use the computer to see the same object from any desired perspective, but in order to know what the image depicts computers have to recognize what objects are in the picture. It has turned out to be very difficult to program computers to analyze scenes and recognize the objects in them. Scene-analysis programs require a great deal of computation and work only in special cases when just a few objects are involved whose shapes the computer has been programmed to recognize in advance.

But that is just the beginning of the problem. The computer, if used to simulate logical thinking, can only make inferences from lists of facts. It's as if, in order to read a newspaper, you had to spell out each word, find its meaning in the dictionary, and diagram every sentence, labeling all the parts of speech. Brains don't seem to decompose either language or images this way, but logic machines have no choice. Being unable to make inferences from images, they must decompose them into the objects they contain and into descriptions of those objects in terms of their features before drawing any conclusions. In converting a picture into a description, however, much information is lost. For instance, given a photo one can see immediately just which objects are between, behind, and in front of which others. All those relationships must be listed in the computer's description, or else the information must be recalculated each time it is needed.

One could argue that logic machines' inability to see images doesn't matter since images play no role in thinking. But the research psychologist Roger Shepard has shown that people actually use images, not descriptions, in some situations. When asked to compare two figures, such as those in Figure 2–1, to see if they are the same, the time subjects take to decide is directly proportional to how much one figure must be rotated in order to be superimposed on the other. Moreover, subjects report they mentally rotate one of the figures to see if it matches the other.

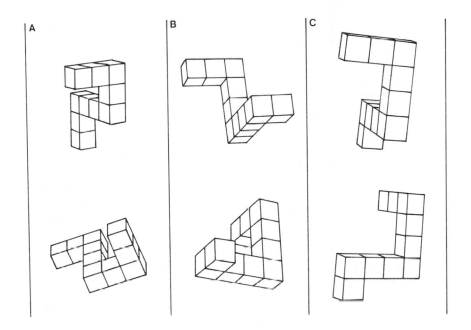

Some drawings similar to those used in Shepard and Metzler's 1971 experiments on mental rotation. The ones shown in (A) are identical, as a clockwise turning of this [page] by 90 degrees will readily prove. Those in (B) are also identical, and again the relative angle between the two is 90 degrees. Here, however, it is a rotation in depth that will make the first coincide with the second. Finally, those in (C) are not at all identical, for no rotation will bring them into congruence. The time taken to decide whether a pair is the same was found to vary linearly with the angle through which one figure must be rotated to be brought into correspondence with the other. This suggested to the investigators that a stepwise mental rotation was in fact being performed by the subjects of their experiments.

FIGURE 2–1 Mental Rotation Exercise. (From David Marr and H. Keith Nishihara, "Visual Information Processing: Artificial Intelligence and the Sensorium of Sight," *Technology Review,* 81, No. 1 [October 1978]. Reprinted with permission from *Technology Review,* copyright 1978. Drawings based on R. N. Shepard and J. Metzler, "Mental Rotation of Three Dimension Objects," *Science,* 171 [February 19, 1971]: 701–703. Copyright 1971 by the AAAS.)

Of course, computers can also rotate images and check to see if one image can be superimposed on another. Shepard's experiments were neither for nor against computer simulations. They were designed to demonstrate that people actually do form and use images.

The question immediately arose for cognitive scientists: Why would the time it takes to compare two descriptions be a function of the difference in orientation between the two images? And gradually most researchers have become convinced that human beings form images and compare them by means of holistic processes quite different from the logical operations computers perform.[1] Some AI workers hope for help from parallel processors, machines that can do many things at once and hence can make millions of inferences per second, but if human image processing operates on holistic representations that are not descriptions and relates such representations in other than rule-like ways, the appeal to parallel processing misses the point. The point is that human beings seem to be able to form and compare images in a way that cannot be captured by any number of procedures that operate on descriptions.

Human beings not only compare objects with images but also use images to predict how events in the world will turn out. Computers too can use their logical powers to make predictions, but they proceed in an utterly different way. If a person is told that there is a large box with a small box resting on it and is then asked what will happen if the large box is moved, he can imagine the box moving and read off what happens. If one adds that the small box is tied to the door, he can add that to his picture of things and again imagine the result.[2] A computer, however, must be given a list of facts about boxes, such as their size, weight, and frictional coefficients, and facts about strings such as their elasticity and strength, as well as how each is affected by various kinds of movements. Given enough precise information about boxes and strings, the computer can deduce whether the small box will move with the large one in various conditions. People too reason things out in the explicit, step-by-step way computers do if they must think about relationships they have never seen and so cannot imagine. However, when dealing with familiar situations people proceed in a way which does not seem to involve listing facts and rules and drawing logical conclusions at all.

That people can think by using images while logic machines can only make inferences from descriptions is only one of the important differences that must concern us. Another human skill that logic machines cannot simulate is the ability to recognize the similarity between whole images. Recognizing two patterns as similar, which seems to be a direct process for human beings, is very complicated for a logic machine. Each pattern must be defined in terms of objective features. Only then can the computer determine whether by some objective criterion the set of preselected features defining one pattern match the features defining the other pattern. Take, for example, face recognition. A person not only can form an image of a face, he can see one face as similar to another. Sometimes the similarity will depend on specific features, such as both faces having bright blue eyes and beards. A computer, if it has been programmed to abstract such features from a picture of a face, could recognize that sort of similarity. But in addition human beings can recognize similarity of what might be called aspects of faces. Aspects are not abstractable elements like blue and beard; rather, judgment or interpretation is required to recognize them. Two faces might appear to be alike because both have gentle, mocking, or puzzled expressions. Recognizing that does not involve finding certain features they share. Indeed, there is no reason to think that expressions have any elementary features. So there is no reason to assume a logic machine can capture the kind of similarities, such as those of expression, human beings are able to discern almost instantaneously.

Douglas Hofstadter, author of *Gödel, Escher, Bach,* makes this point graphically when he discusses letter A's in various type fonts. Computers, used as logic machines, he notes, must always decompose letters into a list of features such as "the width of its serifs, the heights of its crossbar, the lowest point on its left arm, the highest point along some extravagant curlicue, the amount of broadening of a pen, the average slope of the ascenders, and so forth and so on."[3] Hofstadter argues persuasively, however, that such a list of features cannot capture human judgments of similarity. He concludes:

[N]obody can possess the "secret recipe" from which all the (infinitely many) members of a category such a "A" can in theory be generated. In fact, my claim is that no such recipe exists.[4]

Similarity recognition is so difficult for logic machines that it is usually neglected, so there have been very few attempts to write similarity recognition programs. The most successful such program is generally acknowledged to be Thomas Evans's M.I.T. doctoral thesis, a program that performs analogical reasoning. In his 1966 *Scientific American* article Minsky says of Evans's program that it "displays qualities we usually think of as requiring 'intuition,' 'taste' or other subjective operations of the mind." He goes on to praise the success of Evans's analysis of the perceived similarity between simple figures into relations between identical elements:

> With his analysis of such operations and his clarification of their components in terms precise enough to express them symbolically and make them available for use by a machine, Evans laid a foundation for the further development of programs employing analogical reasoning.[5]

The promised development, however, did not take place. Evans's work on analogy or similarity is not even mentioned in a discussion of important contributions to AI published in the October 1982 issue of *Scientific American*. [6] The latest edition of *The Handbook of Artificial Intelligence* notes:

> Many key thought processes—like recognizing people's faces and reasoning by analogy—are still puzzles; they are performed so "unconsciously" by people that adequate computational mechanisms have not been postulated for them.[7]

How should we envisage such "unconscious computational mechanisms"? The information processing assumption is that they are just like our conscious mechanisms, based on rules and features, but unreachable by introspection and no doubt faster and more complicated. So information processing theorists think the unconscious mind of someone seeing a similarity between two objects must be detecting objective features and then checking in memory for a description of an object having many of the same features, and the brain must be doing the mechanical, computer-like processing that underlies those mental operations.

Mechanistic Systems Versus Holistic Systems

There is no evidence for the mechanical model, but it is taken for granted by AI theorists because it is the way people proceed when they are reflecting consciously and because AI theorists think any alternative must be mystical, that is, antiscientific. Of course, it would be mystical to say that the mind is some special sort of substance that does not even exist in space and so could not be explained in terms of anything material. That was Descartes's view, and it still lives on, but we consider this view implausible. Any modern thinker, we believe, must admit that whatever the mind does, it does it because of the processing capacities of the brain. So the question is not whether the mind is a machine but whether the *mind/brain* is a machine, that is, whether the mind/brain is an information processing mechanism. Before we jump to the conclusion that it is, it is important to realize that there are physical systems that can detect similarity without using any features and rules at all. So as not to become locked into the information processing prejudice for lack of imagination, it helps to consider how one such device works.

You have no doubt heard of holograms, but you may not realize how many mindlike properties they can be made to exhibit, or that neurons have actually been shown to behave in ways that fit the holographic model.[8] An ordinary hologram is made by taking a picture of an object using two beams of laser light, one reflected from the object to be pictured and the other shining directly onto the film. The result, unlike an ordinary picture, looks like a blur all over the negative. Technically it is an interference pattern, like the pattern of intersecting waves produced by throwing several pebbles into a pond. When a laser beam is projected through the blur the entire scene reappears, projected away from the plate, so that the viewer can see different aspects as he changes position (see Figure 2–2).

What first attracted neuropsychologists to the hologram was that it really is holistic. Any small piece of the blur has the whole scene in it. If you cut off a portion of the picture and shine a laser beam through what remains, the scene reappears, a bit more blurry but all there. For example, if you take a hologram of a table and cut off one corner and shine a laser beam through what remains, you do not get a scene with no corner on the table. The whole table is still there, but with less resolution. Certain areas of the visual cortex also have that property. When a piece is cut out, nothing specific is lost from a person's vision; instead everything seen is less distinct.[9] An even more mindlike property of holograms is that they can be used as an associative

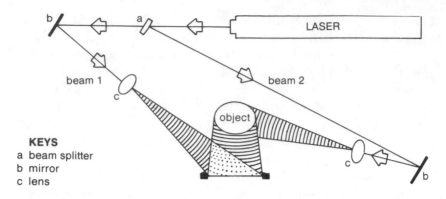

KEYS
a beam splitter
b mirror
c lens

After the laser's original beam is split (at point a), one part is deflected toward the film plate and the other is bounced off the object. When the beams reconverge, they form a light interference pattern that is recorded. The image is reconstructed when a second beam is reflected off the plate and diffused in the same pattern.

FIGURE 2–2 How a Hologram Works. (© Museum of Holography, 1976.)

memory. If one uses a single hologram to record two different scenes and then illuminates the hologram with laser light bounced off one of the scenes, an image of the other will appear.

For us, the most important property of holograms is the way they detect similarity. For example, one can make a hologram of this page and then make a hologram of one of the letters on the page, say the letter F. If one then superimposes the light beamed through the resulting two holograms, the astonishing result is a black field in which a bright spot appears at the location of each letter F on the page. Moreover, the brightness of the spot is proportional to the similarity between the particular letter F picked out and the letter F used as the model. Dimmer spots appear where there are imperfect or slightly rotated versions of the reference letter. Thus holograms can act as virtually instantaneous similarity recognizers.

What is crucial about this is that the process makes no use of features. According to the information processing assumption, a letter F would be recognized by noting that it has one vertical line and two horizontal lines that intersect but do not cross the vertical, or some other such set of objective features. But in a holographic similarity recognition device two whole wave fronts interact, and the bright spots indicate peaks of energy or resonance. In recognizing similarities that way, the question "similar with respect to what" does not arise.

The way a hologram can instantly pick out any occurrence of a specific letter on a page is reminiscent of the way a familiar face stands out when you look at a crowd even when you do not expect the acquaintance to be present. Generally you can't give rules using objectively identifiable features such as beard, glasses, or red hair for distinguishing that face from all other faces you can recognize. It is *possible* that such rules are used unconsciously, but that explanation, while conceivable, is certainly implausible. To implement a rule-governed procedure, your mind would have to examine each face in the crowd, detect its features, and compare them to lists of features describing each of your acquaintances. Some variation on the holistic model both is more plausible and fits experience better.

The human mind seems to have the remarkable ability to recognize whole scenes without decomposing them into features, an ability that far transcends current holographic techniques. The mind, unlike holography, can sometimes detect faces in crowds even with expressions unlike any previously seen on the face, and sometimes despite dramatic changes such as the growth of a beard, the acquisition of glasses, or the ravages of time. While holography provides an instructive example of the possibility of recognition without using the sort of features and rules demanded by the digital computer used as a logic machine, its limited capabilities highlight how little we know about the workings of the brain.

We take no stand on the question of whether the brain does or does not function holographically. We simply want to make clear that the information processing computer is not the only physical system that can exhibit mindlike properties and that other devices, such as holographic pattern recognizers, may be closer analogies to the way the mind actually works.

But haven't we avoided the mystical only to fall into the mechanical? What about our title *Mind over Machine?* How can we argue that the mind/brain is superior to any mechanistic system, that is, any machine, while admitting that the mind/brain is some kind of physical system, perhaps a holographic one? If you've been subtle enough to ask this question you'll have to be prepared for a rather subtle and complicated answer.

In order to explain how anything works, three levels must be taken into consideration: the particle level, the component level, and the functional level. Anything does what it does thanks to the physical particles it is made up of and the fact that they obey the laws of physics and chemistry. But precisely because all elements obey physical laws and so behave in the same way, the basic physical level cannot explain the functional properties of a machine. In order to explain devices, one has to see how the basic physical elements are organized into parts or components, each of which performs some special task. At this second level a car can be described as made up of components such as spark plugs, pistons, crank shaft, wheels, and so on. To describe a digital computer at this level, one would talk about switches, circuits, and—still on this level but more organized—central processors, memories, and input/output devices. A holographic pattern recognizer would be described in terms of laser, lenses, and mirrors.

At the third and most important level, the functional level, one can at last explain how a device does its work. Here, finally, we can address the question: Is the mind/brain a machine? Devices turn out to do their work in two fundamentally different ways, which require two fundamentally different kinds of explanation. A machine does its work by dividing up the job among different components each with its different function and putting them all together so as to produce a result. So a mechanistic explanation necessarily involves showing how the components's funtions are combined to add up to the functioning of the whole. Thus one can take spark plugs, pistons, valves, wheels, and the rest, none of which are self-moving, and connect those components in such a way that the whole mechanism is an automobile. A digital computer, programmed to manipulate symbols, is a much more abstract and refined mechanism. It is sometimes called a virtual machine. Its components are not physical parts but strings of bits functioning as symbols, whose different jobs consist in representing different features in the problem domain. Its symbols are put together so that a sequence of logical operations on them can produce something none of the components separately could produce, new information. Conventional AI researchers assume that the computer and the brain both function in this mechanistic way. If that view is correct, the mind/brain is indeed a machine.

But there are devices which do what they do in an entirely different way. A holographic pattern recognizer does its work without dividing up the job between different components. True, at the second level one can describe the lenses, lasers, and so on, and one can explain what job each one does, but something essential is left out. The actual recognition work is accomplished by the interference of two beams of light, with no separate functional components doing any work. In the case of holograms, the result must be explained directly in terms of the laws of physics, in this case the properties of optical interference patterns. To distinguish such a system from a mechanistic system we might call such a pattern recognizer a *holistic* system. There are many holistic systems around us: light bulbs, lenses, screws, and levers would be examples. One learns in school that screws and levers are simple machines, even though they have no parts, which shows that this important distinction is lost by our lack of vocabulary, so that we end up calling all physical systems machines. This makes it seem that, if one denies the mind/brain is a machine, one must be some sort of antiscientific mystic. Neither mystics nor mechanists, we hold that all available evidence is consistent with the view that on the functional level the mind/brain underlying expertise is a holistic system.

Minds over Logic Machines

Given their rigor, reliability, and indefatigability, computers used as logic machines do extremely well what human beings do only poorly. For centuries the military has tried, without success, to discipline recruits to respond to precise commands and to follow rules without appeal to interpretation or judgment. And since the work of Frederick Taylor, factory workers have been subjected to a similar discipline. But despite the "rationalization" of work and its decomposition into precisely specifiable motions, and despite countless hours spent following preordained steps in rigid order, human beings never attain the precision of rule-following machines. Human beings, however, exhibit a flexibility, judgment, and intuition that resist decomposition into specification and inference and have proved equally difficult to instill into logic machines. The question therefore is, given the best programming available now and in the foreseeable future, what level of skill can logic machines be expected to reach?

Clearly computers programmed to be logic machines are ideal beginners. The essence of any such computer is to follow precise rules for combining objective features. A driving rule like "shift to second when your speed reaches 20 mph" or a chess rule like "trade when the value of the captured piece is greater than the value of the piece lost" could be learned instantly by a computer and applied at the speed of light. Since its memory is perfect, a computer never needs practice. It can get all the rules right the first time. And since it can be programmed with hundreds of rules relating hundreds of features, a computer can become what might be thought of as an instant expert novice in any well-structured and well-understood domain.

Some brain-damaged human beings, like computers, deal with familiar domains in that completely logical manner. Patients suffering from a neurological disorder called "agnosia" exhibit a total dependence upon analysis and rational explanation. For them everything must be decomposed into features and relationships before it can be understood. For example, a victim of agnosia presented with a triangular object will first report that it has three angular corners connected by straight sides and only then will conclude that it is a triangle. Restricted to understanding of only this kind, the patient is unable to function adequately in the everyday world.

When the programmer tries to get the computer to pass to the advanced beginner level, he encounters his first serious obstacle. Remember, the advanced beginner must be able to recognize repeated, meaningful elements such as the motor sound when the car is straining to leave first gear or the way the chessboard looks when the king's side is weak. Recognizing such situational elements requires remembering typical examples as well as the ability to see the current pattern as similar to a remembered one.

A growing new field of psychology is devoted to studying the role of typical cases in intelligent behavior. Such cases are called prototypes and accumulating evidence indicates that they play crucial roles in all sorts of human thought—from logic to childhood learning.[10] "Prototypicality effects," as the measurement of the role of prototypes is now called, embarrass information processing modelers. Why? Because no evidence has been found that to recognize a current pattern as similar to a prototypical one, the human mind forms a description of each of the two patterns and checks for identical features, as would a logic machine. Rather, so far as the evidence goes, a human being has images of many typical cases, and the current pattern is seen as more or less like one of these. That is, the mind seems to function not like a logic machine but like a holistic image device. Even if, at some deep unconscious level, the brain does match typical cases by using some subtle features no one has ever dreamed of, that is no help to the programmer, whose only way of finding such features other than sheer luck has to be his own introspection and the observation and interrogation of experts. It follows that the digital computer, used as a logic machine, cannot reach the stage of advanced beginner.

Although logic machines cannot recognize the situational elements relied upon by advanced beginners, they can be programmed to organize their context-free facts in terms of goals, like a competent human being. The computer can be given a rule which tells it that if certain facts are present, the situation should be organized in terms of a certain goal. A medical diagnosis program, for example, could be given the strategic rule: If the white cell count is high, look for evidence of infection. Given that goal, only certain available facts become relevant. If an infection is suspected, then facts about the patient's blood sugar level can be ignored, while anything about microorganisms in the blood stream should be evaluated according to appropriate rules. We shall see that such techniques have actually been used to produce so-called expert systems, in which the computer's precision and speed compensate for its blindness to situational elements. Such systems perform about as well as competent human beings.

The move to the last two levels of skill pushes the limits of logic machines. Proficient performers and experts are not aware of looking for facts and inferring goals or actions; they are unaware of *choosing* any goals or actions whatever. And with the shift to involved, intuitive coping, performance is improved dramatically. Performers feel and their behavior confirms that they are able to handle situations in a new rapid and flexible way. They know that to make the leap to intuition requires a great deal of experience, but they are not aware of what goes on in their brain when they do it. People sometimes speak of quieting the analytic mind and letting the emotional, involved, holistic right brain do its work.

The information processing model, on the contrary, dictates that the improved performance results from more and better rules of the sort once consciously followed. We believe, however, that a move to the new level of performance coincides with a shift from the logical processing of atomic facts to the recognition without recourse to isolable elements, of the similarity between a current situation and a stored image-like representation of a previous situation it resembles. No introspective evidence for either position exists, since all agree that whatever happens happens unconsciously. Moreover, there are no experiments that point clearly either way. We hold that in the absence of evidence to the contrary, our model, which accounts for the striking shift to involvement, flexibility, and spontaneity experienced by the proficient and expert performer is to be preferred on common-sense empirical grounds to the information processing model.

But this is finally a question to be settled in the laboratory. A crucial test is to what extent those who accept the information processing model have been able to capture human intelligence and expertise in programs that use the computer as a logic machine. Accordingly, we now turn to an examination of actual work done in AI laboratories.

CHAPTER 3

ARTIFICIAL INTELLIGENCE: FROM HIGH HOPES TO SOBER REALITY

Machines will be capable, within twenty years, of doing any work that a man can do.

Herbert Simon
The Shape of Automation for Men and Management (1965)

There is a tendency in AI today towards flashy, splashy domains. . . . Yet there is no program that has common sense; no program that learns things that it has not been explicitly taught how to learn; no program that can recover gracefully from its own errors.

Douglas Hofstadter
"Artificial Intelligence: Subcognition as Computation" (1983)

THE IDEA THAT the digital computer is a general symbol manipulator, and so can be used for making inferences as well as for calculation, created an exciting new field called Cognitive Simulation (CS). The first five years of work in CS was spent getting people to verbalize their problem solving strategies, then programming the computer to follow a procedure as similar as possible to the steps the problem-solver had articulated. The enterprise was based on the hope that certain general techniques human problem-solvers seemed to employ, such as using operations that reduced the distance between themselves and the solution, could be abstracted and applied to all cases of problem-solving. But as our analysis of Newell, Shaw, and Simon's work done at RAND led us to suspect, crucial aspects of problem-solving, such as separating relevant from irrelevant operations, were left out of the problem-solving programs. Consequently NSS's program, called the General Problem Solver and based on the attempt to abstract the general rules underlying intelligence, worked in only a very limited set of cases.

High Hopes for Artificial Intelligence

With the failure of the first five-year plan at RAND and Carnegie–Mellon University (where Newell had joined Simon on the
faculty), interest shifted from Newell and Simon's Cognitive Simulation to what Marvin Minsky and Seymour Papert at M.I.T.
called Semantic Information Processing. Researchers at M.I.T.
abandoned the approach of Newell and Simon for two reasons.
First, the work was based on trying to get the computer to follow
the same steps that a human being seemed to follow to solve
problems. Second, NSS dealt only with games and puzzles, never
with the sort of problems that required knowledge of the real
world. The researchers at M.I.T. were not interested in using
computers, as Simon did, to implement a new kind of empirical
psychology but were willing to use any processing methods whatever, plus knowledge about the world, to enable the computer
to solve problems that seem to require real-world understanding
and intuition.

In the introduction to a collection of his students' Ph.D. theses
entitled *Semantic Information Processing,* Minsky describes the
heart of the M.I.T. approach:

> If we . . . ask . . . about the common-everyday structures—that
> which a person needs to have ordinary common sense—we will
> find first a collection of indispensable categories, each rather com-
> plex: geometrical and mechanical properties of things and of space;
> uses and properties of a few thousand objects; hundreds of "facts"
> about hundreds of people, thousands of facts about tens of people,
> tens of facts about thousands of people; hundreds of facts about
> hundreds of organizations. As one tries to classify all his knowledge,
> the categories grow rapidly at first, but after a while one encounters
> more and more difficulty. . . . I therefore feel that a machine will
> quite critically need to acquire the order of a hundred thousand
> elements of knowledge in order to behave with reasonable sensibil-
> ity in ordinary situations. A million, if properly organized, should
> be enough for a very great intelligence.[1]

Looking back from 1983, Jerry Fodor, also at M.I.T., quite
aptly describes those early knowledge structures in his recent
book, *Modularity of Mind:*

> [T]he attempted simulations proceeded by supplying machines with
> very large amounts of more or less disorganized, highly topic-spe-
> cific facts and heuristics. The result was an account of central pro-

cesses which failed to capture precisely what is most interesting about them: their wholism. . . . What emerged was a picture of the mind that looked rather embarrassingly like a Sears catalogue.[2]

Moreover, even if we had the facts, how would we access them? To establish that a fact exists in its data banks a computer must retrieve it. Worse, to establish that some fact is not in the data bank requires examining the entire list of what the computer knows to determine that the fact in question is missing. But, as pointed out by Richard Shaffer in the *Wall Street Journal*, the mind clearly doesn't work this way:

> Unlike computers, man's memory . . . is instantly aware of what it does—and does not—contain. [N]o list is needed. When were you born? You know the answer immediately. When was your mother born? You may not have a ready answer, but you know that you know the date and will remember it if you think long enough. . . . When was Thomas Jefferson born? If you don't know, you know that you don't know and that no amount of thinking will bring the date to mind.[3]

We offer here no explanation of that amazing human ability, but its existence dramatically shows the inadequacy of lists or other data structures now used in AI.

Putting commonsense knowledge into the computer and organizing it so that it could be used when relevant has been the constant preoccupation of workers at M.I.T., and the task gradually became recognized as the basic unsolved problem of AI. The problem emerged in three stages. At first the problem seemed difficult but manageable; after all, we human beings manage to understand the world and get around in it. Minsky proceeded with cautious optimism:

> As everyone knows, it is hard to find a knowledge-classifying system that works well for many different kinds of problems: it requires immense effort to build a plausible thesaurus that works even within one field. Furthermore, any particular retrieval structure is liable to entail commitments making it difficult to incorporate concepts that appear after the original structure is assembled. One is tempted to say: "It would be folly to base our intelligent machine upon some particular elaborate, thesaurus-like classification of knowledge, some *ad hoc* syntopicon. Surely that is no road to 'general intelligence.' ". . . But we had better be cautious about this caution itself, for it exposes us to a far more deadly temptation: to seek a fountain of pure intelligence. I see no reason to believe that intelli-

gence can exist apart from a highly organized body of knowledge, models, and processes.[4]

Minsky acknowledged, however, that "the programs described in *Semantic Information Processing* will work best when given exactly the necessary facts, and will bog down inexorably as the information files grow."[5] Was there any reason, then, to suppose that these programs were approaching the "superior heuristics for managing their knowledge structure" which Minsky believed human beings must have?

Certainly there was nothing in *Semantic Information Processing* to justify confidence. Minsky criticized NSS's early programs for their lack of generality: "Each program worked only on its restricted specialty, and there was no way to combine two different problem-solvers."[6] But his students' solutions were equally *ad hoc*. Minsky did not deny this, but added jauntily: "The programs described in this volume may still have this character, but they are no longer ignoring the problem. In fact, their chief concern is finding methods of solving it."[7] But there was no sign that any of the programs presented by Minsky had solved anything. None of them had discovered any *general* feature of the human ability to behave intelligently. All Minsky presented were clever special solutions, which worked because the real problems had been put aside.

Indeed, none of the programs in *Semantic Information Processing* showed any generality at all, and none of the procedures have been generalized as promised. Nor do the programs have any semantics, that is, any understanding of what their symbols mean. A program like Daniel Bobrow's story-problem understander, STUDENT, is so far from semantic understanding that, as Bobrow himself points out "the phrase 'the number of times I went to the movies' . . . will be interpreted incorrectly as the product of the two variables 'number of' and 'I went to the movies,' because 'times' is always considered to be an operator."[8] Nevertheless, Minsky was satisfied with the book: "[O]ne cannot help being astonished at how far [these programs] did get with their feeble semantic endowment."[9]

In retrospect, the game in the second stage seems to have been to get as far as one could with the *appearance* of meaning and flexibility before the real problems had to be faced, and then, when one failed to generalize one's "solution," to claim to have at least made a first step. In the words of Minsky:

> The fact that the present batch of programs still appear to have narrow ranges of applications does not indicate lack of progress toward generality. These programs are *steps toward* ways to handle knowledge.[10]

The *ad hoc* character of such work is even more striking in a program called ELIZA written by the M.I.T. Computer Science Professor Joseph Weizenbaum. Weizenbaum set out to show just how much apparent intelligence one could get a computer to exhibit without giving it "any semantic endowment at all," thereby reducing Minsky's method to absurdity. The result was a program that imitated a nondirective therapist by such simple tricks as turning statements into questions: "I'm feeling sad," into "Why are you feeling sad?" When the program couldn't find a stock response, it printed out statements like "Tell me about your father." The remarkable thing was that people were so easily fooled by such tricks. Weizenbaum was appalled when some of those interacting with the program divulged their deepest feelings and asked others to leave the room while they were using the program.

We were eager to see a demonstration of the notorious program, and because Weizenbaum was the only one in the M.I.T. AI laboratory who would speak to us after the publication of the RAND paper, we were delighted when he invited us to sit at the console and interact with ELIZA. We spoiled the fun however, unintentionally exposing how shallow the *ad hoc* trickery really was, by typing "I'm feeling happy" and then correcting ourselves by typing, "No, elated." At that point ELIZA came back with the remark: "Don't be so negative." Why? Because it had been programmed to respond with the rebuke whenever there was a "no" in the input.

It took about five years for the shallowness of Minsky's students' semantic information processing theses to become apparent. Meanwhile, at Peter Drucker's suggestion, the controversial RAND paper was expanded into a book, *What Computers Can't Do.* The book asserted that AI research had reached a dead end since it could not come up with any general way to represent everyday, embodied, commonsense understanding. But just as

What Computers Can't Do went to press in 1970, a new approach to representing commonsense knowledge was developed at M.I.T. If one could not deal systematically with everyday commonsense knowledge all at once, then why not develop methods for dealing systematically with knowledge in isolated subworlds and then build from that gradually?

Since by all accounts Terry Winograd's natural language understanding program, SHRDLU, best exemplifies that "major advance," we shall turn to it first. SHRDLU simulates on a TV screen a robot arm that can move a set of variously shaped blocks and allows a person to engage in a dialogue with the computer, asking questions, making statements, issuing commands, within this simple world of movable blocks. An integrated system, the program uses grammatical rules, semantics, and facts about blocks. It is thus, as Winograd cautiously claimed, "a computer program which 'understands' language in a limited domain, by including a model of the subject being talked about and a context of discourse. . . ."[11] Furthermore, the program explored the then new idea of representing knowledge in the form of procedures—rules for moving blocks, stacking blocks, and so on.

The dialogue thus made possible is strikingly natural. Here is a sample. (The sentences in capital letters are computer printout. The parentheses contain Winograd's comments):

1. pick up a big red block.

   OK.

   (The system answers "OK" when it carries out a command. In order to pick up the red block, it had to clear it off by finding a space for the green one and moving the green one away.)

2. grasp the pyramid.

   I DON'T UNDERSTAND WHICH PYRAMID YOU MEAN.

   (There are three pyramids in the scene, so the program does nothing.)

3. find a block which is taller than the one you are holding and put it into the box.

   (The system has to figure out what is meant by "one" and "it," as well as using deduction to decide which block it is holding.)

BY "IT," I ASSUME YOU MEAN THE BLOCK WHICH IS
TALLER THAN THE ONE I AM HOLDING.

(Printed out to keep us informed.)

OK.

(The hand has to set down the red block to pick up the taller blue
one.)

4. what does the box contain?

THE BLUE PYRAMID AND THE BLUE BLOCK.

5. what is the pyramid supported by?

(Earlier the system responded to "the pyramid" by saying "I don't
understand which pyramid you mean." Now, it assumes that we mean
the one just mentioned.)

THE BOX.

. . .

9. can the table pick up blocks?

NO.

(The semantic rules make this a nonsensical question, which therefore
must be false.)

10. can a pyramid be supported by a block?

YES.

(The deductive systems finds an actual example, so it knows this is
possible.)[12]

If being a major advance means being more general than
its predecessors, then SHRDLU is a major achievement. Winograd himself points out the superiority of his effort over earlier
language understanding programs:

A program may succeed by carefully choosing the problem it will
attack, so that some simple special-purpose solution will work.
ELIZA and STUDENT are examples of programs which give impressive performances owing to a severe and careful restriction
of the kind of understanding they try to achieve. If a model is to
be of broader significance, it must be designed to cover a large
range of the things we mean when we talk of understanding. The

principles should derive from an attempt to deal with the basic cognitive structures.[13]

At the time SHRDLU seemed to be such an attempt. Workers in AI were certainly not trying to deny that it was SHRDLU's restricted domain which made apparent understanding possible. But they thought Winograd's restrictions were not *ad hoc*. They even had a name for his method of restricting the domain of discourse. He was dealing with a micro-world. Indeed, what characterized the period of the early 1970s and makes SHRDLU seem an advance toward general intelligence is the very concept of a micro-world—a domain that can be analyzed in isolation. In a 1970 internal memo at M.I.T., Minsky and Papert frankly noted:

> Each model—or "micro-world" as we shall call it—is very schematic; it talks about a fairyland in which things are so simplified that almost every statement about them would be literally false if asserted about the real world.[14]

But they immediately added:

> Nevertheless, we feel that [the micro-worlds] are so important that we are assigning a large portion of our effort toward developing a collection of these micro-worlds and finding how to use the suggestive and predictive powers of the models without being overcome by their incompatibility with literal truth.[15]

Given the admittedly artificial and arbitrary character of microworlds, why did Papert and Minsky think the restricted domains provided a promising line of research?

They simply had faith that though each area of discourse seems to open out into the rest of human activity, endless ramification is only apparent and will soon converge on a self-contained set of facts and relations—what Minsky and Papert call a microtheory. For example, in discussing the micro-world of bargaining, Papert and Minsky consider what a child needs to know to understand the following fragment of conversation:

> JANET: "That isn't a very good ball you have. Give it to me and I'll give you my lollipop."[16]

They remark:

> [W]e conjecture that, eventually, the required micro-theories can be made reasonably compact and easily stated once we have found

an adequate set of structural primitives for them. When one begins to catalogue what one needs for just a little of Janet's story, it seems at first to be endless:

Time	Things	Words
Space	People	Thoughts

Talking: Explaining. Asking. Ordering. Persuading. Pretending.

Social relations: Giving. Buying. Bargaining. Begging. Asking. Presents. Stealing. . .

Playing: Real and Unreal, Pretending

Owning: Part of, Belong to, Master of, Captor of

Eating: How does one compare the values of food with the values of toys?

Liking: good, bad, useful, pretty, conformity

Intention: Want. Plan. Plot. Goal. Cause. Result. Prevent.

Emotions: Moods. Dispositions. Conventional expressions.

States: asleep. angry. at home.

Properties: grown-up. red-haired. called "Janet".

Story: Narrator. Plot. Principal actors.

People: Children. Bystanders.

Places: Houses. Outside.

Angry: State

Caused by: insult
deprivation

Results: not cooperative
lower threshold
aggression
loud voice
irrational
revenge

Etc.[17]

They conclude:

But [the list] is not endless. It is only large, and one needs a large set of concepts to organize it. After a while one will find it getting harder to add new concepts, and the new ones will begin to seem less indispensable.[18]

But why suppose that the seemingly endless reference to other human practices that Minsky and Papert only begin to spell out will converge to produce simple micro-worlds that can be studied in relative isolation? It looks like the approach represents a naive transfer to AI research of methods that have succeeded in the natural sciences. Winograd characteristically describes his work in terms borrowed from physical science:

> We are concerned with developing a formalism, or "representation," with which to describe . . . knowledge. We seek the "atoms" and "particles" of which it is built, and the "forces" that act on it.[19]

Indeed, physical theories about the universe can be built up by modeling relatively simple and isolated systems and then making the model gradually more complex and integrating it with models of other domains. So much is possible because all the phenomena are presumably the result of the lawlike relations of a set of basic elements, what Papert and Minsky call "structural primitives."

This idea doesn't work in AI. There workers confused two domains, which we shall distinguish as universe and world. A set of interrelated facts may constitute a *universe,* like the physical universe, but it does not constitute a *world.* The latter, like the world of business, the world of theater, or the world of the physicist, is an organized body of objects, purposes, skills, and practices on the basis of which human activities have meaning or make sense. Thus one can contrast the meaningless physical *universe* with the meaningful *world* of physics. Subworlds, like the world of physics, the business world, and the theater world, make sense only against a background of common human concerns. They are local elaborations of the one commonsense world we all share. That is, subworlds are not related like isolable physical systems to larger systems they *compose,* but are rather, local elaborations of a whole, which they *presuppose.* If micro-worlds *were* subworlds, they would not have to be extended and combined to reach the everyday world, because the everyday world would have already been presupposed in programming each subworld. Micro-worlds, however, are *not* worlds but isolated meaningless domains, and there is no way they can be combined and extended to arrive at the world of everyday life. By failing to ask what a world is, a third five-year period of stagnation in AI was mistaken for progress.[20]

By 1973, while gestures were still made toward generalization, it was becoming obvious that SHRDLU and all similar micro-world programs were in trouble. An M.I.T. AI Laboratory memo admits that "since the Winograd demonstration and thesis, several workers have been adding new elements, regulations, and features to that system. That work has not gone very far."[21] Such failures to generalize no doubt lie behind the sober evaluation two years later:

> Artificial Intelligence has done well in tightly constrained domains—Winograd, for example, astonished everyone with the expertise of his blocks-world natural language system. Extending this kind of ability to larger worlds has not proved straightforward, however. . . . The time has come to treat the problems involved as central issues.[22]

Winograd himself soon gave up the attempt to generalize the techniques used in SHRDLU. He acknowledged that micro-world programming techniques cannot be extended to the real world:

> The AI programs of the late sixties and early seventies are much too literal. They deal with meaning as if it were a structure to be built up of the bricks and mortar provided by the words. . . . This gives them a "brittle" character, able to deal well with tightly specified areas of meaning in an artificially formal conversation. They are correspondingly weak in dealing with natural utterances, full of bits and fragments, continual (unnoticed) metaphor, and reference to much less easily formalizable areas of knowledge.[23]

By the end of the 1970s, after trying to write a new knowledge representation language, KRL, to deal with the central role of typical cases and similarity in commonsense knowledge representation, Winograd "lost his faith" in AI altogether.

Commonsense Understanding

Sober evaluations such as Winograd's initiated the fourth and so far final phase of AI work. From roughly 1975 to the present AI has been wrestling unsuccessfully with what has come to be called the commonsense knowledge problem: how to store and access all the facts human beings seem to know. This problem has kept AI from even beginning to fulfill Simon's prediction made twenty years ago, that within twenty years computers would be able to do everything human beings can do.

Of course, the representation of knowledge was always a central problem for work in AI, but earlier periods—cognitive simulation, semantic tricks, and micro-worlds—were characterized by an attempt to avoid the problem of commonsense knowledge by seeing how much could be done with as little knowledge as possible. By the middle 1970s, however, the difficulties were being faced. As Roger Schank of Yale remarked: "Researchers are starting to understand that tours-de-force in programming are interesting but non-extendible . . . the AI people recognize that how people use and represent knowledge is the key issue in the field."[24]

Minsky predicted a generation ago, in 1967, that "within a generation the problem of creating 'artificial intelligence' will be substantially solved."[25] The most dramatic way to see how early high hopes for AI turned to sober evaluation is to contrast Minsky's recent remark to a reporter: "The AI problem is one of the hardest science has ever undertaken."[26]

A recent (October 1982) *Scientific American* article confirms that the commonsense knowledge problem has stymied AI for at least a decade. The article, in which with one exception[27] all the research reported was work done more than ten years ago, concludes:

> Probably the most telling criticism of current work in artificial intelligence is that it has not yet been successful in modeling what is called common sense. [S]ubstantially better models of human cognition must be developed before systems can be designed that will carry out even simplified versions of common-sense tasks.[28]

The decade-long impasse has recently given rise to a promising reaction. There is growing interest in the commonsense knowledge problem itself, which has made apparent two deep philosophical issues that AI has been refusing to face.

There are really two different problems lumped together under the commonsense knowledge problem. Each highlights an aspect of human understanding that the heuristically programmed computer seems unable to copy; that is, each problem appears insoluble using the current methods of AI. We shall call those two problems the problems of *commonsense under-standing* and of *changing relevance*. As noted, micro-world work avoided both problems instead of contributing to their solution, and so had to be abandoned as an approach to general intelligence. It then seemed for a time that new data structures called frames and scripts would come to the rescue, but we shall see why they too have resulted in little progress. Indeed, although early micro-world work is turning out to have practical applications that create the illusion of exciting new develop-ments, the two problems have brought conventional theoretical AI to a halt.

We can understand how the problem of commonsense under-standing arises when we reflect that the computer comes into our world even more alien than a Martian. It does not have a body, needs, or emotions, and it is not formed by a shared lan-guage and other social practices. If the machine is to interact intelligently with us, it has to be endowed with an understanding of the human form of life. What we understand simply by virtue of being human—that insults make us angry, that moving physi-cally forward is easier than moving backward, that we can pass by things by moving toward them and then away from them, and that time constantly passes and future events become past events—all this and much more has to be programmed into the computer as facts and rules. As AI workers put it, the com-puter must be given our belief system. This, of course, assumes that the understanding in our emotions, our bodies, and our social practices is made up of beliefs, so that the computer could be told all the facts we supposedly believe.

The supposition that everyday understanding is produced by *reasoning* from facts we *know* creates the first unsolved prob-lem: How can a computer be made to store and access the mass of beliefs about human beings and their world that it must have if it is to share our commonsense understanding? That is not just a problem of size and complexity, but a problem of what language to use to store the facts. Unless they can be stored in a totally explicit and context-free form, the computer cannot use them because the problem of commonsense understanding will reappear. In his recent *Scientific American* article on AI, Douglas Lenat reports the discovery of this difficulty:

> Ideally an entire encyclopedia would somehow be stored in com-puter-accessible form, not as a text but as a collection of thousands

of structured, multiply indexed units. Preliminary work toward this goal by a few investigators has revealed that it is even more elusive than it sounds: the understanding of encyclopedia articles itself requires a large body of common-sense knowledge not yet shared by computer software.[29]

But Lenat does not plumb the real depth of the problem here, for even if the facts were stored in a context-free form the computer still couldn't use them. To do that the computer requires rules enabling it to draw on *just those facts which are relevant in each particular context.* Determination of relevance will have to be based on further facts and rules, but the question will again arise as to which facts and rules are relevant for making each particular determination. One could always invoke further facts and rules to answer this question, but of course these must be only the relevant ones. And so it goes. It seems that AI workers will never be able to get started here unless they can settle the problem of relevance beforehand by cataloguing types of context and listing just those facts which are relevant in each.

To put the same problem in another way: The sort of rules human beings are able to articulate always contain *ceteris paribus* conditions, that is, the rules are applicable "everything else being equal." What "everything else" and "equal" mean in any specific situation, however, can never be fully spelled out since one can only give further rules with further *ceteris paribus* conditions. Moreover, there is not just one exception to each rule but several, and all the rules for dealing with the exceptions are also *ceteris paribus* rules. So we not only get a regress of rules for applying rules but an exponential explosion of them; the number of rules required multiplies at an ever increasing rate. For example, a general rule of chess is to trade material when ahead material. However, exceptions include the rule that it should not be applied if the opposing king is much more centrally located than yours, or when you are ahead but an opposing pawn is about to promote, or when you are attacking the enemy king, and so on. But there are in turn exceptions to each of those exceptions; for example, the pawn-about-to-promote rule can be ignored if the piece it is to become can be captured immediately. A computer programmer's failure to include one such exception-rule was exploited by the chess master David Levy in an important match, which we shall discuss later.

A related problem arises because in the real world any system of rules has to be incomplete. Consider the California vehicle code. In any encounter between an auto and a pedestrian, the code grants the right of way to the pedestrian, and so we might think the matter is settled. But, in fact, certain "judgment calls" remain for the driver, the pedestrian, and ultimately the judge. The pedestrian normally has the right of way, but he shouldn't jaywalk through heavy traffic, but if blind he *always* has the right of way, and so on. And if the "pedestrian" is a skateboarder, does he remain a pedestrian in the eyes of the law? When do other circumstances impinge? And which?

The law always strives for completeness but never achieves it. "Common law" helps, for it is based more on precedents than on code. But the sheer number of lawyers in business tells us that it is impossible to banish ambiguity and judgment by specifying a code of law so complete that all situations are specified and prejudged.

Ceteris paribus conditions and incompleteness are not merely annoyances showing analysis to be what Edmund Husserl, a philosophical precursor of AI, called an "infinite task." Rather those problems point to something taken for granted: namely, a shared, human background that alone makes possible all rule-like activity. To explain our actions and our rules, we must eventually fall back on our everyday practices and simply say "this is what one does" or "that's what it is to be a human being." Thus in the last analysis all intelligibility and all intelligent behavior must hark back to our sense of what we *are*, which is, necessarily, on pain of regress, something we can never explicitly *know*.

Some of what we are, like having a body with certain capacities, is innate, but even what is learned need not be learned as facts. Human beings, as we said earlier, learn how to act in the world by seeing the similarity of the present situation to some typical past experience. For beings who can acquire that kind of "know-how," which need not be represented as "knowing that," there is no commonsense knowledge problem. You can learn to swim by practicing the necessary patterns of responses, without having to represent your body and muscular movements in some data structure. Likewise what you "know" about the cultural practices that enables you to recognize specific situations and act appropriately within them has been gradually acquired through imitation, trial-and-error, and training. No one ever did or could, again on pain of regress, make explicit in terms of facts and rules what you have learned.

The commonsense knowledge problem, a result of trying to turn human *know-how* into computable *knowing that,* was the first way the problem of making a computer act in a human world without having human capacities manifested itself in AI. More recently a related problem has surfaced: the problem of dealing with change.

Changing Relevance

In general skilled human beings have in the areas of their expertise an understanding that enables them, as events unfold, to distinguish what is relevant from what is not. However, during the first three phases of AI research, from cognitive simulation up through work on micro-worlds, computers, like beginners, advanced beginners, and competent performers, were programmed to confront all facts as isolated from each other and goals as just further facts. Thus whenever a change occurred the whole set of facts that made up the computer's representation of the current state of affairs had to be recalculated to update what had changed and what remained the same. The attempt to capture human, temporal, situated, continuously changing know-how in a computer as static, de-situated, discrete, knowing that has become known as the frame problem. It has been defined as "the problem of finding a representational form permitting a changing, complex world to be efficiently and adequately represented."[30] More specifically, it is the problem of representing in some systematic way that as time passes and/or actions are performed, some but not all facts change and only a few of the changes are relevant to current action.

To understand the frame problem we need to review the various ways of updating the computer's knowledge of the changing situation that have been tried:

1. Early programs such as GPS explicitly specified all possible situations and the new situation that would result from each possible action. But for all but the simplest problems that approach is not workable, because there are too many possible situations and actions.

2. Purely deductive systems use rules of logic to deduce the

new state of affairs and the action to be taken. Rules which researchers called frame axioms were then required for updating each fact about the situation that changes and for each fact that remains unchanged. But as Lars-Erik Janlert points out: "Clearly, this way of modeling is not practical in a more complex problem world; the frame axioms will occupy all space and the deductions of non-changes all time."[31]

3. Next, programmers tried constraining the use of deductive logic by adding the nondeductive rule: Whatever is not deduced by means of a frame axiom to have changed is assumed to remain the same. But it was discovered that what changes because of an action often depends on many facts about the current state of affairs, so frame axioms had to be specified for many different states of affairs. Again, in complex situations there are just too many.

4. The most plausible proposal seems to have been made simultaneously in several quarters of the AI community as extending micro-worlds led to overwhelming lists of frame axioms. The idea was to group many similar situations into a single class. One could then specify for each class just those facts which were typically relevant and general purpose rules, valid for all situations encountered in the class, for how the facts were normally changed by an event. Minsky called such data structures "frames," and describes them as follows:

> A frame is a data-structure for representing a stereotyped situation, like being in a certain kind of living room, or going to a child's birthday party. . . . Much of the phenomenological power of the theory hinges on the inclusion of expectations and other kinds of presumptions.[32]

Roger Schank proposed similar structures, called scripts, in which the attempt to account for change is even more obvious:

> We define a script as a predetermined causal chain of conceptualizations that describe *the normal sequence of things* in a familiar situation. Thus there is a restaurant script, a birthday-party script, a football game script, a classroom script, and so on.[33]

Schank's illustration of the restaurant script spells out the normally relevant facts and their normal sequence in a restaurant situation:

Script: restaurant
Roles: customer; waitress; chef; cashier
Reason: to get food so as to go down in hunger and up in pleasure

Scene 1 entering

go into restaurant
find table
go to table
sit down

Scene 2 ordering

receive menu
look at it
decide on order
tell order to waitress

Scene 3 eating

receive food
eat food

Scene 4 exiting

ask for check
give tip to waitress
go to cashier
give money to cashier
go out of restaurant[34]

This representation of restaurant behavior is a sequence of simple situations each with its own small set of relevant facts, so here the problem of changing relevance does not arise. But the script cannot comfort AI researchers, for it has in effect simply avoided the problem of continuous, branching, real-world change by substituting a sequence of static micro-worlds. The restaurant script may work fairly well for understanding *simple stories* about restaurant dining, for which it was intended, but it leaves out the complex way restaurant dining changes through time. We do not simply enter, order, eat, and leave. After we enter, we might or might not wait to be seated, and then we might or might not study a menu, for example. Schank recognizes that his initial script is much too skeletal and discontinuous and now acknowledges that there are various tracks for various sorts of restaurants and that there are many subscripts that need to be added to fill out his account:

In order to schematically represent just one track of the restaurant script we have left out considerable detail and many possible options in each of the scenes. We have excluded entire scenes such as the *wait to be seated* scene. . . . certainly there is room for a *seeing someone you know* scene, for example, as well as a *meeting someone new* scene. Some of the sideline events at a restaurant also can be scripts in their own right. For example, a *paying by credit card* script is a fairly simple script that is called up in many places besides restaurants.[35]

That is the typical way researchers in AI proceed. One first introduces a manageable, computational account of a domain, then adds complications as they are needed to account for what people can do. But, of course, as one adds more and more subscripts, each with its preselected relevant features and its own subscripts, the complexity of the whole account rapidly increases. It is purely an act of faith on the part of AI researchers like Schank that such a model can capture human restaurant behavior before the formalism becomes hopelessly complicated. The simple version is easily manageable. But that is no evidence it is a successful first step toward human understanding.

Even if one shares Schank's faith that scripts can eventually capture the stereotypical side of restaurant behavior, with the proliferation of frames comes the question: How does one move from one frame to another? To keep to the restaurant example, suppose in the "seeing someone you know" frame the conversation with that person gives you new information. The friend might tell you that an old friend is in town for only one more hour, or that he just saw your small child running down the street unescorted, or that the sashimi just made him sick, or that a company in whose stock you hold a short position is about to become the object of a takeover, or that someone you are trying to avoid is eating in the next room, and so on. Each bit of news would set you off in a different direction. From the frame point of view the next frame would be either leaving as soon as possible, running out of the restaurant, ordering only cooked food, telephoning your broker, or asking for a table on the terrace. In order to give the computer the capacity to cope with this kind of change, the frame approach would have to include rules for how to select a next frame. It seems incredible, and indeed no one has even tried to provide such rules.

Even if the problems of frame proliferation and frame change could be solved, it is a huge leap to Schank's claim that "the restaurant script contains all the information necessary to understand the enormous variability of what can occur in a restaurant."[36] Schank doesn't even try to deal with the question of motivation. Yet to make sense of restaurant behavior one has to understand not only *what* people typically do in eating establishments but *why* they do it. Thus, even if he could manage to list all that was *possibly* relevant in typical restaurant dining, we would be left with no understanding of what at any point in time was *actually* relevant for the person involved.

Going to a restaurant is like most everyday situations. We face a continually branching web of possible situations, each of which is sized up in terms of some issue. Only then do the actually relevant facts show up as salient. For example, if you go out to eat in Berkeley, you have a choice between smoking and nonsmoking sections. What might become relevant here includes, among other factors, whether a table is free in the section one prefers and, if not, at what stage of their meals the current customers are. Moreover, which of those factors actually becomes important to you depends on how hungry you are, how rushed, how comfortable the waiting area is, and many other things. As time passes, all such factors continually change. One's concerns also change, and with them one's sense of which factors are relevant. After you move to a table, you consider the question of who sits where, which introduces new factors such as comfort, view, sex, and age—all of which have no fixed relevance but whose importance again depends on your perspective. And when you order, you do not summon up a fixed frame in which everything relevant has been determined once and for all. Some *possible* concerns are: What is fresh, how long it takes to prepare, how much it costs, what you ate earlier that day and expect to eat later that day, what dietary principles you follow and how strictly. This open-ended list sets out what *might* be important to you, but only your sense of things, gained perhaps by talking to the waiter, and your past experience of restaurant dining determine what is actually relevant as you decide what to eat.

To bring out the proper place and limits of the frame approach, one can contrast restaurant dining with a situation in which static, discrete scripts might work nicely. That situation would, of course, have to be completely defined by a discrete and limited set of features that would permit only a discrete and limited set of responses. Moreover, motivation would play no part, because at each stage in the script there would be a right thing to do. Thus no expertise would be required or acquired, there being no question of seeing the issue in the current situation or of passing from issue to issue as events unfold. Placing a phone call may well constitute such a situation. It is so simple that no strategy is needed, and there is one right way to do things. Thus the frame problem is finessed simply by using a frame that lists all possible events and the appropriate reaction to each. For example, a super-smart modem could store some sort of frame for typical phoning situations, including misdialing, busy, wrong number, changed number, unlisted number, malfunctioning phone, no answer, poor connection, crossed lines, cut off, answering machine, successful connection, and so on. With each could be paired an appropriate response or set of responses. Eventualities not relevant to making a phone call need not be considered at all. True, when placing a call the phone ceases to be free to outside calls; the dial tone cuts off and gets replaced by beeps; something happens in a computer at the central exchange, and so forth. But those do not affect making an ordinary phone call. Such possibilities might be listed in the frame of a robot programmed for phone repair, but they are not something a person has to check out each time he or she dials a call.

Being electronic devices, phones lend themselves to modular designs—that's what makes a phone repair robot, or at least a phone fault diagnosis program, a possibility. But a mechanical device even as simple as an automobile has a high number of interacting components, connected together in ways that produce complex and synergistic patterns of breakdown, with multiple and poorly delimited submodules each capable of occupying a continuum of states between proper and improper functioning. Accordingly, no set of frames can capture the knowledge necessary for expert diagnosis. Indeed, to the extent that any electronic device has such properties, it too will resist expert automated diagnosis.

The shifting relevance of aspects of ordinary changing situations would certainly be grounds for despair in AI and Cognitive Science, were it not for the fact that human beings get along fine in a changing world; and so these researchers assume human beings must somehow be able to update their formal representations. This gives comfort to AI researchers who think it shows the frame problem must be soluble. We, however, hold that it can more plausibly be read as showing that human, skillful know-how is not represented as a mass of facts organized in frames and scripts specifying in a stepwise sequence which facts must be taken account of as the state of affairs evolves. Rather, as we saw when describing proficient performers, memories of our past experience with situations similar to our present one and our ability to recognize this similarity seem sufficient to account for our ability to cope with change. The important point is that we human beings proceed from the past into the future with our past experience always going before us organizing the way the next events show up for us. So we do not need to deal with real-world situations by listing in advance all possibly relevant features plus rules for determining under what circumstances each feature may become actually relevant, and rules for when these rules are relevant, and so forth.

According to our account, the proficient performer sees directly what is relevant in his current situation because the current situation calls up a similar experience from the past, already "gestalted" in terms of issues. But this at first glance seems very mysterious. If the current state of affairs were not given in terms of issues until it is seen in terms of a past situation how would the brain detect the similarity of a current *meaningless* state of affairs encountered in the real world which has not yet been seen in terms of salience, to a stored *meaningful* situation already organized in terms of what is important?

If we stood outside the world and represented states of affairs as meaningless objects, situational similarity recognition would be mysterious, indeed. However, we are generally already in a meaningful situation. Except perhaps when awakening in the morning, we do not normally come upon situations in a void. Even when we first wake up, we somehow automatically view the situation as similar to a paradigmatic wake-up situation created by prior experiences and stored in memory, causing us to see certain aspects related to washing and dressing. From then on throughout the day we move gradually from situation to situation, always entering a new one from the perspective of the old.

When we are in a situation, certain aspects stand out as salient, and many others go unnoticed. When salient aspects change their character—for example, if a smiling expression changes to a smug one or an anticipated interest rate of 13 percent drops to 12 percent—the current situation may not be as similar to the current guiding paradigmatic situation as to some other paradigmatic situation, which has roughly the same salient aspects but matches better. That new situation then becomes guiding. As we have said, we believe this similarity recognition is accomplished in a holistic fashion not using feature detection. Certain aspects of the new paradigmatic situation that now guides behavior will have more or less salience than in the old one, and other aspects that were of no significance in the old guiding paradigm may now acquire some importance. Thus the relevance of aspects gradually evolves. No detached choice or deliberation is involved in the evolutionary process.

Sometimes the occurrence of an anticipated event rather than the changing of a salient aspect triggers a new understanding. Should any anticipated event actually occur, it will be seen as salient in the present situation. This modified present situation will then resemble a previously experienced situation which will determine appropriate new plans and anticipations. The way one sees one's new situation may differ only slightly from the way one was just seeing the previous situation or it may differ greatly depending on the nature of the event that triggered the change.

The frame problem—the problem of keeping track of all facts affected by all changes—shows the difficulty of substituting the computer's static, discontinuous, flat descriptions for the human capacity to transform past experience into a continuous view of changing relevance. Unless AI scientists can produce programs in which representations of past experiences encoded in terms of salience can directly affect the way current situations are organized, they will be stuck with some version of the frame problem and be unable to get their computers to cope with change.

In his *Scientific American* article Lenat points out, quite in line with the views presented here, that what computers lack is the ability to learn from experience and to apply what they know by recognizing the similarity of past experience to the present situation. This problem literally throws the computer scientist for a loop:

> On the one hand, computer programs will have to become a lot
> more knowledgeable before they will be able to reason effectively
> by analogy. On the other hand, to acquire knowledge in such bulk
> it would seem that computers must at least be able to "understand"
> analogy when it is presented to them. . . . The problem is thus
> of the chicken-and-egg sort.[37]

Lenat acknowledges that no one knows how to program a computer to take account of similarities, to *"reason"* by analogy as
he tendentiously puts it, and falls back on the usual "first step"
claim plus an empty gesture toward future research:

> A little introspection and an attentive ear are all it takes to realize
> that people draw on analogy constantly in explaining and under-
> standing concepts and in finding new ones. This source of power
> is only beginning to be exploited by intelligent software, but it
> will doubtless be the focus of future research.[38]

As long as the use of images and analogy remains a vague promise, heuristically programmed digital computers will not be able
to approach the way human beings cope with changing relevance.

The outlook for AI is grim indeed. As we saw earlier, computers, programmed as logic machines, cannot use images or any
picturelike representations without transforming them into descriptions. Likewise, logic machines cannot deal with similarity
except by analyzing it into a list of identical features. There is
no reason to hope that one can use the computer's capacities
for making logical inferences from unambiguous facts and for
matching exactly defined features with other exactly defined
features to produce the sort of comparison of whole images that
yields judgments of similarity.

AI Without Information Processing

The digital computer, when programmed to operate by taking
a problem apart into features and combining them step by step
according to inference rules, operates as a machine—a logic machine. However, the computer is so versatile it can also be used
to model a holistic system. Indeed, recently, as the problems
confronting the AI approach remained unsolved for more than
a decade, a new generation of researchers have actually begun

using computers to simulate such systems. It is too early to say whether the first steps in the direction of holistic similarity recognition will eventually lead to devices that can discern the similarity between whole real-world situations. We discuss the development here for the simple reason that it is the only alternative to the information processing approach that computer science has devised.

Recall our description of skill acquisition: The expert remembers a great number of concrete situations, can apparently without searching through all remembered situations recognize a new and somewhat different situation as similar to one of them, and has learned from experience to associate an action, decision, or plan as well as various expectations with each remembered situation. A computational device with these abilities would represent a monumental step toward a genuine artificial intelligence. Remarkably, such devices are the subject of active research. Indeed, distributed associative memory systems having the required holistic properties can actually be simulated on digital computers. When used to realize a distributed associative memory, computers are no longer functioning as symbol-manipulating systems in which the symbols represent features of the world and computations express relationships among the symbols as in conventional AI. Instead, the computer simulates a holistic system.[39]

There are at least two quite different approaches to the design of distributed associative memories. One, called holographic, is based on the mathematical description of holography. Here, an input "scene" and its associated output is converted to a very different representation by a mathematical transformation called a convolution. The convolution produces something akin to the interference pattern stored on a negative in optical holography in that no one element of the convolution corresponds to an element of the input or output, but the input-output pair is distributed throughout all of the elements of the convolution. This distributed representation is combined with distributed representations of all previously learned associated pairs already in memory so that all share the same computing elements. The resulting memory trace has several remarkable brainlike properties. If an input scene which is one member of an associated input-output pair is combined with the trace using a mathematical formula called a correlation, the other member of the associated pair is produced. This happens even if the input scene is only a significant part of the original whole scene, or is similar but not identical with the original scene. A scene can be anything that can be represented as a string of digits. At one extreme, the most common, the scene is a digitized representation of a picture with the digits representing the light intensity at various points. At the other extreme, if one chooses to see the world in terms of a typical AI description, it can be a representation of features that are present and absent in a situation. But even in the latter case, features are not stored as lists in distinct locations or processed according to recognizable rules.[40]

A second approach to the design of distributed associative memories is based on a neuron-net model of the brain. A digital computer imitates such a net by simulating simplified neurons and strengths of connections between them. Such systems function like a soap bubble—an entity composed of molecules each physically attached only to its immediate neighbors and sensitive only to local forces—which is nonetheless formed by the interaction of all the local forces so that the whole determines the behavior of the local elements. Given an input, activity spreads among the simulated neurons according to an arbitrary rule based on strengths of connections, and eventually produces an output. To achieve a memory of an association between an input and output pair, the strengths of connections are suitably modified. The modification is tricky since the adjusted strengths must not only result in the new input yielding the new output, but all previously learned inputs for which connection strengths have already been adjusted must still yield their correct outputs. The strengths of connections constitute the associative trace and allow the associations to be recreated rather than located somewhere and later retrieved as in conventional AI. As in the case of associative holographic memory, inputs and outputs can be anything from digitized pictures to representations of features present and absent. But individual neuronlike units and connections represent neither individual features nor associations.[41]

What if the brain were organized, at least in part, as a distributed associative memory? To be concrete, let us speculate about our ability to recognize a friend's face rapidly, even seen with a different expression or from a different angle than ever before—a task currently well beyond the capability of conventional AI. The neurons and connecting nerves in a certain area of the brain might store, in distributed form as a memory trace, associations between images of familiar faces and names. Many such associations might be stored for each friend's face—each with a different typical expression or seen from a different angle. When we see the face, the light-intensity pattern would interact with the memory trace, and if it approximated any of the images that created the trace, the associated name would come to mind as the output. All known faces would share the same memory trace, and one interaction of input and trace would produce the output. No features would be detected or lists searched.

This speculation seems less than fantastic if one considers an experiment performed in Finland using a fairly unsophisticated distributed associative memory employing mathematics based on storing and modifying strengths of connections. The faces of ten people were each photographed five times, once from each of five different angles. Each of the fifty photographs, represented by their light intensities at many specified points, was associated with a bar in a bar graph as output. The location of the bar was different for each person, so the five views of each person were all associated with the same bar, but each person was represented by a different bar. A distributed memory trace was formed, which stored all fifty face-name pairs. A picture was then taken of one of the original ten people from an angle different from that of the previous five photographs. Its intensity pattern was combined mathematically with the memory trace. The outcome was a bar graph with various heights of bars corresponding to how much the input resembled each of the ten people. The height of the bar corresponding to the person actually photographed was many times higher than the other nine bars. Thus the system correctly identified the person.[42]

Impressive as this achievement is, it nonetheless highlights two major problems that must be solved before distributed associative memories can be developed that have human intuitive capacities. The face that was successfully recognized had to be the same size and in the same orientation to the vertical as the reference figures. To approach human capacities some technique would have to be developed by means of which memories and new inputs could all be converted to a standard form. Techniques for normalization are already being developed in pattern recognition engineering.

The problem of normalization of visual images is trivial, how-ever, compared to the second problem. Can experts describe for storage in computers their memories of typical lived situa-tions so the computers can likewise be experts? Light and shad-ows on a face can easily be digitized, but how can we enter into a computer the pattern of saliences, expectations, and emo-tional colorings, such as hopes and fears, that characterize a remembered whole situation? It is just because no one has the slightest idea how such experiences could be stored in distrib-uted associative systems that cognitivists feel justified in adopt-ing the implausible view that what we remember are descrip-tions.

The neuron-net approach should not be confused with a con-nection-based procedure also using spreading activation now be-ing investigated by Jerome Feldman and others. This third approach, like the two approaches based on distributed associa-tive memories, dispenses with heuristic rules that manipulate symbols one after another. Like conventional AI, however, Feld-man's symbols always represent context-free features of the real world and, unlike the other two approaches, he uses rules speci-fying relationships between symbols.[43]

Feldman's approach is sometimes lumped together with the neuron-net model under the term "new connectionist" despite their fundamental differences, since both stress connections of elements. Given our account of expertise as based on holistic representations rather than features and rules, we see the con-nectionism of distributed associative memories as really new and promising, while Feldman's approach is at best an improved model of the analytic reasoning used by beginners. Not that analytic reasoning should be ignored: Any intelligent computer must both be able to respond to holistic similarities and to make inferences involving symbols, just as, if we are to believe some brain researchers, the holistic right brain and the logical left brain are both involved in human intelligence.

All three models share one important feature rarely found in the highly sequential reasoning procedures of conventional AI. The computations involved can be done in parallel; that is, many different things can be going on at once, as is apparently the case in the brain.

Like all those advocating parallel processing, Douglas Hof-stadter is critical of the conventional AI approach to intelligence.

His counterproposal is subtle and complex and so is our disagreement with him. But if you have made it through *Gödel, Escher, Bach,* you may want to struggle through the next few pages. Hofstadter shares with the new connectionists and with us the conviction that one cannot capture intelligent behavior and expertise using the sort of context-free facts and rules that beginners consciously employ when they reason. He therefore breaks with heuristic rules as well as with Feldman's relationships between context-free symbols. But he still supposes that the mind processes symbols—context-dependent ones. Hofstadter speculates that thinking is produced by what he cryptically calls "strange loops" and tangled hierarchies, with all symbols depending on and affecting other symbols. In his words, "symbols activate other symbols and all interact heterarchically."[44] While avoiding the introduction of context-free features, he still maintains that all thinking involves a level of symbol manipulation where "the triggering of some symbol by other symbols bears a relation to events in the real world . . . while a group of neurons triggering another neuron corresponds to no outer event. . . ."[45]

Hofstadter argues that the symbol manipulation level, while dependent on the neuron level, is necessary in order to mediate between the brain and the world. Playing devil's advocate, he considers the possibility—which we have been defending—that such mediation, which he calls "funneling," may not be necessary. "Perhaps an object being looked at is implicitly identified by its 'signature' in the visual cortex—the collected responses of simple, complex, and hypercomplex cells. Perhaps the brain does not need any further recognizer for a particular form."[46] He then rejects this view. His arguments, however, are not convincing.

Hofstadter notes certain post-impressionist paintings require several seconds of scrutiny before "suddenly a human figure will jump out at you"[47] and claims that this suggests time-consuming unconscious symbol manipulation. We think that this may well be true, but this contrived case does not show that normal everyday associative recognition likewise requires the manipulation of symbols. Indeed, ordinary everyday recognition is virtually instantaneous, which can be seen as supporting our contention that recognition can be the direct result of brain associations between what Hofstadter would call "signatures."

We normally enter everyday situations from a perspective based on recent events, so that certain aspects of the current situation stand out as significant. We believe that such understanding is produced directly by brain signatures without any mediating symbol level. As the situation changes, its significant aspects change and the new situation calls up the signature of a similar situation from the past which directly triggers an appropriate action. The simplest case is when everything is changing continuously, as when driving down a highway. In more difficult but still normal cases, as in entering a room, our expectations based on experience with previous rooms triggers a brain state causing significant aspects like people and furniture to stand out. And if we turn our attention to a figure, an association using only brain states roughly corresponding to light intensities from that figure, such as that used in the Finnish procedure for face recognition, allows us to see that it is, let's say, grandmother. While not virtually instantaneous, this multistep process carried on at the brain rather than symbol level takes but a moment. Realistic pictures in a museum take a bit longer to recognize because while we expect to see familiar objects like landscapes, animals, people and furnished rooms, our brain presumably needs to try several associations before it gets one integrating the whole scene. Only in extreme, contrived cases, such as puzzles and the sort of paintings described by Hofstadter, do our brains have to start from scratch like waking up in a strange place. Then, we speculate, a great many different sets of aspects of the situation must each be seen as salient before an appropriate association is triggered at the brain level. Or, if Hofstadter is right, as he may be in such contrived cases, we use this time to manipulate symbols to figure things out. In these difficult cases, merely noting that processing takes time does not tell us what is going on. We wonder, however, how Hofstadter would explain the virtually instantaneous everyday cases in terms of his time-consuming strange loops and tangled hierarchies.

According to Hofstadter, "[a]nother difficulty with a non-funneling theory is to explain how there can be different interpretations for a single signature"[48]; for example, an Escher picture or a line drawing of a cube. But if one believes, as we do, that the brain stores differently the same scene as seen from different perspectives, that is, with different aspects salient, this phenomenon is just what one would expect. In the normal course of events we enter a situation from a particular perspective and we therefore see it in the way that is consistent with our ongoing perspective. If we enter from another perspective things may look rather different. Should we come across the situation in isolation as in looking at a picture, then we would have to try focusing on various different sets of aspects as salient. Each might then call up a different associated memory and cause the situation to show up in a different way.

Even Minsky, one of the founders of conventional AI, no longer thinks human beings store past experience in "a language at all—that is, an ordered string of symbols." He now suggests that the brain performs "pattern-matching on the current state of the process."[49] In a recent paper that speculates on a much more distributed and networklike model of thought than now in vogue in AI, Minsky remarks:

> [W]hat if feelings and viewpoints are the simpler things? If such dispositions are the elements of which the others are composed, then we must deal with them directly. So we shall view memories as entities that predispose the mind to deal with new situations in old, remembered ways—specifically, as entities that reset the states of parts of the nervous system.[50]

According to Minsky, what is stored when some strategy works and new knowledge is acquired is not facts and heuristic rules but an efficiently organized library of special cases.

> [W]e spoke . . . of creating an entirely new K-node for each memorable event. But surely there are more gentle ways to "accumulate" new subordinates to already existing nodes. Suppose that a chimpanzee achieves the too-high banana by using different means at different times—first using a box, then a chair, later a table. One could remember these separately. But, if they were all "accumulated" to one single K-node, this would lead to creation of a more powerful "how to reach higher" node: when reactivated, it would *concurrently* activate P-agents for boxes, chairs, or tables, so that perception of *any* of them will be considered relevant to the "reach higher" goal. In this crude way, such an "accumulating" K-node will acquire the effect of a class abstraction . . . "something to stand on."[51]

Thus Minsky appears to have abandoned the cognitivist model of higher processes.

Other researchers have given up the information processing

model at the lowest level of interaction between people and the world. M.I.T.'s David Marr did excellent work on vision, working out algorithms that calculate boundaries, depth, texture, and the like without abstracting features of objects at all. The first stages of sensory processing, as simulated by Marr, do not use symbolic descriptions. Nonetheless, he remained true to the assumptions of AI in holding that the job of the senses is to produce "symbolic descriptions" for the higher processors. The fact remains Marr gave no arguments for this claim, and his important work is all at the presymbolic level.[52]

NEWELL AND SIMON'S initially attractive idea of using heuristic rules to manipulate symbols representing objective features of the real world has been in trouble for the past twenty years. If we put together the idea that the senses or peripheral processors are not using features and heuristic rules at the lowest level with the idea that the highest or most central processing in the brain matches patterns of whole situations rather than using features and heuristic rules, we can see that the information processing model is gradually being squeezed out by the AI researchers themselves.

Thanks to AI research, Plato's and Kant's speculation that the mind works according to rules has finally found its empirical test in the attempt to use logic machines to produce humanlike understanding. And, after two thousand years of refinement, the traditional view of mind has shown itself to be inadequate. Indeed, conventional AI as information processing looks like a perfect example of what Imre Lakatos would call a degenerating research program.[53] It began auspiciously enough with Newell and Simon's early work showing that computers could be programmed to simulate certain forms of human symbolic manipulations. And with the successes of the early 1970s it rapidly established itself as a flourishing research program. Then, rather suddenly, AI ran into unexpected difficulties from which it has yet to recover.

The trouble started, as we have seen, with the failure of attempts to program children's story understanding, and it soon became obvious that common sense was a serious and pervasive problem. Related problems were also noted, although not often seen as related. Cognitivists discovered the importance of images and prototypes in human understanding, and logic machines turned out to be very poor at dealing with images and with seeing the similarity of a given case to a prototypical one.[54] Learning also turned out to be much harder than anyone had expected.

As we see it, all these problems are versions of one basic problem. Current AI is based on the idea, prominent in philosophy since Descartes, that all understanding consists in forming and using appropriate representations. Given the nature of inference engines, AI's representations must be formal ones, and so commonsense understanding must be understood as some vast body of precise propositions, beliefs, rules, facts, and procedures. Thus formulated, the problem has so far resisted solution. We predict it will continue to do so.

What hides the impasse is the conviction that the commonsense knowledge problem must be solvable, since human beings have obviously solved it. But human beings may not normally use commonsense *knowledge* at all. What commonsense *understanding* amounts to might well be *everyday know-how*. If that is indeed the case, we can understand both the initial success and the eventual failure of AI. While its techniques will work to some extent in isolated domains, they will fail in such areas as natural-language understanding, speech recognition, story understanding, and learning, whose structure mirrors the structure of our everyday physical and social world.

Like alchemy and behaviorism in their time, AI projects an image of good health in spite of its difficulties. However, its feverish activity and strident claims, and the tendency of its practitioners to abandon theory and exploit current techniques, may well be signs of its crisis. There are symposia, proceedings, press releases, and start-up companies galore, and recently something the alchemists and behaviorists never achieved: lots of military money. But there are also signs of trouble. Recently, for example, Roger Schank lamented that "AI would have a fairly difficult time justifying itself as a scientific discipline."[55] Schank points out that researchers do not know what constitutes a Ph.D. topic or an acceptable paper in AI, because there is no agreement on what the issues are. He argues, like Lenat, that learning is the central issue, since one cannot claim any intelligence at all for programs that remain unaffected by their successes and failures. Yet general learning programs are not even on the AI horizon.

Even if the degeneration of theoretical AI makes it seem increasingly likely that the information processing model of the mind is a dead end, the AI community, like the alchemists, has developed techniques that are useful as practical tools. Already at the time of micro-world optimism, a split was forming in AI ranks that would lead some researchers out of the AI impasse. Newell and Simon's early collection of protocols from people actually solving problems, together with the relative success of AI in micro-worlds completely cut off from human life, provided Edward Feigenbaum with an opportunity for systems of a new sort. Those new systems would use the rules of thumb by which experts allegedly negotiate their areas of skill, plus large collections of facts about the real world; each would be designed to capture human expertise within a specific isolated domain.

The restricted theoretical interest of work in restricted domains is becoming apparent. At the same time hope for the practical use of symbol manipulation systems is turning from AI proper, with its commonsense knowledge problem produced by trying to represent our commonsense know-how, and with its frame problem produced by trying to represent temporal skills, to the promise of expert systems for domains cut off from common sense and from change. It is this turn to expert systems engineering that gives the field a new lease on life, for, with the decision to avoid the problems of commonsense understanding and temporal change that arrested AI, practical success seems within reach. Following the entrepreneurs, we shall now turn from the difficulties of AI and Cognitive Science to the booming field of knowledge engineering.

CHAPTER 4

EXPERT SYSTEMS VERSUS INTUITIVE EXPERTISE

Expert systems are computer programs performing at the level of human experts in various professional fields.

Edward Feigenbaum
The Fifth Generation (1983)

The words "expert system" are loaded with a great deal more implied intelligence than is warranted by their actual level of sophistication.

Roger Schank
The Cognitive Computer (1984)

ALMOST NO COLLEGE teaches it, but a new kind of engineering has burst on the American scene. Many people believe it may ultimately exert as profound an influence on the workplace as factory automation did decades ago.

It is called "knowledge engineering," and its task is to interview leading experts in science, medicine, business and other endeavors to find out how they make judgments that are the core of their expertise. The next step is to codify that knowledge so computers can make similar decisions by emulating human inferential reasoning.

The knowledge engineer does this by reducing the expert's wisdom to a series of interconnected generalized rules called the "knowledge base." A separate computer program called an "inferential engine" is then used to search the knowledge base and draw judgments when confronted with evidence from a particular case, much the way an expert applies past knowledge to a new problem.

While knowledge engineering is still a primitive art, it has already been used with some success in prospecting for minerals, diagnosing disease, analyzing chemicals, selecting antibiotics and configuring computers. These programs are called "expert systems."

While industry has used computer scoring systems analytically to advise executives making decisions, designers of the new systems hope eventually to duplicate judgments by human experts.

[M]any say the possibility of aggregating the knowledge and insights of several experts in the same field opens the prospect of computer-aided decisions based on more wisdom than any one person can contain.[1]

Such reports can be read in almost any newspaper these days. The above report made the front page of the usually trustworthy *New York Times.*

In *What Computers Can't Do,* written in 1969, the main objection to AI was the impossibility of using rules to select only those facts about the real world that were relevant in a given situation. The "Introduction" to the paperback edition of the book, published by Harper & Row in 1979, pointed out further that no one had the slightest idea how to represent the common-sense understanding possessed even by a four-year-old. Since those were our basic reservations, we noted that in areas more or less cut off from the rest of human life, such as games, microworlds, and highly technical domains, good work had been done, and we implied that there was no limit to what one could expect in such isolated areas. We thought that a checkers champion had already been programmed; we were impressed with the performance of SHRDLU in the blocks world; and we admired the ability of an expert system named DENDRAL. In spite of some doubts as to whether chess masters use rules and make inferences, we came out solidly on the side of knowledge engineering as opposed to theoretical AI and expressed (on page 27) what was for us an uncharacteristic optimism:

> As long as the domain in question can be treated as a game, i.e., as long as what is relevant is fixed, and the possibly relevant factors can be defined in terms of context-free primitives, then computers can do well. . . . And they will do progressively better relative to people as the amount of domain-specific knowledge required is increased.

Now we think we were wrong, and our doubts about whether chess masters use inference rules have developed into our five-stage model of skill acquisition, which suggests that it is highly unlikely that expert systems will ever be able to deliver expert performance. (Actually, we'd prefer to call them "competent systems," since we can find no evidence that they will ever surpass the third stage of our skill model.) Much of the current wave of optimism concerning expert systems has been generated by Edward Feigenbaum and Pamela McCorduck's book *The Fifth Generation*,[2] so we can best show the relevance of our account of skill acquisition to the hopes of expert system builders by taking a critical look at Feigenbaum's facts, arguments, and assumptions.

Expert Systems and Calculative Rationality

Expert systems have been the subject of recent cover stories in *Business Week* and *Newsweek* as well as the *New York Times* article with which we began this chapter.[3] The heightened interest in machine intelligence is attributable not to any new theoretical accomplishment but rather to a much publicized competition with Japan to build a new generation of computers with built-in expertise. That is the so-called fifth generation. (The first four generations were based, in turn, on vacuum tubes, transistors, integrated circuits, and LSI or "large-scale" integrated circuits.) According to *Newsweek* lead heading: "Japan and the United States are rushing to produce a new generation of machines that can very nearly think." Feigenbaum, professor of computer science at Stanford University and one of the original developers of expert systems, spells out the goal:

> In the kind of intelligent system envisioned by the designers of the Fifth Generation, speed and processing power will be increased dramatically; but more important, the machines will have reasoning power: they will automatically engineer vast amounts of knowledge to serve whatever purpose human beings propose, from medical diagnosis to product design, from management decisions to education.[4]

The knowledge engineers claim to have discovered that in areas cut off from everyday common sense and social intercourse, all a machine needs in order to behave like an expert are some general rules and lots of very specific knowledge. As Feigenbaum puts it:

> The first group of artificial intelligence researchers . . . was persuaded that certain great, underlying principles characterized all intelligent behavior. . . .
> In part, they were correct. [Such strategies] include searching

for a solution (and using "rules of good guessing" to cut down the
search space); generating and testing (does this work? no; try something else); reasoning backward from a desired goal; and the like.

These strategies are necessary, but not sufficient, for intelligent
behavior. The other ingredient is knowledge—specialized knowledge, and lots of it. . . . No matter how natively bright you are,
you cannot be a credible medical diagnostician without a great
deal of specific knowledge about diseases, their manifestations, and
the human body.[5]

That specialized knowledge is of two types:

The first type is the *facts* of the domain—the widely shared knowledge . . . that is written in textbooks and journals of the field. . . .
Equally important to the practice of the field is the second type
of knowledge called *heuristic knowledge,* which is the knowledge
of good practice and good judgment in a field. It is experiential
knowledge, the "art of good guessing" that a human expert acquires
over years of work.[6]

Using all three kinds of knowledge, Feigenbaum developed
a program called DENDRAL, an alleged expert in the isolated
domain of spectrograph analysis. From the data generated by
a mass spectrograph it can deduce the molecular structure of
a compound being analyzed. Another program, MYCIN, takes
the results of blood tests, such as the number of red cells and
white cells, sugar in the blood, and other measurements, and
comes up with a proposed diagnosis of which blood disease is
responsible for the patient's condition. It even gives an estimate
of the reliability of its own diagnosis. In their narrow areas, such
programs perform with impressive competence.

And isn't that success just what one would expect? If we
agree with Feigenbaum that "almost all the thinking that professionals do is done by reasoning,"[7] we can see that once computers
are used for reasoning and not just computation they should
be as good as or better than we are at following rules for deducing
conclusions from a host of facts. So we would expect that if
the rules an expert has acquired from years of experience could
be extracted and programmed, the resulting program would
exhibit expertise. Again Feigenbaum puts the point very clearly:

[T]he matters that set experts apart from beginners are symbolic,
inferential, and rooted in experiential knowledge. Human experts
have acquired their expertise not only from explicit knowledge

found in textbooks and lectures, but also from experience: by doing things again and again, failing, succeeding . . . getting a feel for a problem, learning when to go by the book and when to break the rules. They therefore build up a repertory of working rules of thumb, or "heuristics," that, combined with book knowledge, make them expert practitioners.[8]

Since each expert already has a repertory of rules in his mind, all the expert system builder need do is extract them and program them into a computer.

That view is not new. In fact, it goes back to the beginning of Western culture, when the first philosopher, Socrates, searched Athens for experts who could articulate their rules so he could test them. In one of his earliest dialogues, *The Euthyphro*, Plato tells us of an encounter between Socrates and Euthyphro, a religious prophet and so an accepted expert on pious behavior. Socrates asks Euthyphro to tell him how to recognize piety: "I want to know what is characteristic of piety . . . to use as a standard whereby to judge your actions and those of other men." But instead of revealing his piety-recognizing heuristic, Euthyphro does just what every expert does when cornered by a Socrates: He gives him examples from his field of expertise. Euthyphro cites situations in the past in which men and gods had done things everyone considered pious. Throughout the dialogue Socrates persists in interrogating Euthyphro about his rules, but although Euthyphro claims he knows how to tell pious acts from impious ones, he cannot state the rules that generate his judgments. Socrates encountered the same problem with craftsmen, poets, and even statesmen. None could articulate the principles on which he acted. Socrates concluded that no one knew anything—including Socrates, who at least knew his own ignorance.

That was an intolerable conclusion, so Plato, who admired Socrates and sympathized with his problem, developed an account of what caused the difficulty. Experts had once known the rules they use, Plato said, but then they had forgotten them. The role of the philosopher was to help people remember the principles on which they act.

In the Platonic view the rules are there functioning in the expert's mind whether he is conscious of them or not. How else could we account for the fact that he can perform the task? Knowledge engineers would now say that the rules the experts use have been put in a part of their mental computers, where they work automatically: "When we learned how to tie our shoes, we had to think very hard about the steps involved. . . . Now that we've tied many shoes over our lifetime, that knowledge is 'compiled,' to use the computing term for it; it no longer needs our conscious attention."[9]

Now, two thousand years later, thanks to Feigenbaum and his colleagues, we have a new name for what Socrates and Plato were doing—"we are able to be more precise . . . and with this increased precision has come a new term, *knowledge acquisition research.*"[10] But although philosophers and even the man in the street have become convinced that expertise consists in applying sophisticated heuristics to masses of facts, there are few available rules. As Feigenbaum explains, "an expert's knowledge is often ill-specified or incomplete because the expert himself doesn't always know exactly what it is he knows about his domain."[11] So the knowledge engineer has to help him recollect what he once knew:

> [An expert's] knowledge is currently acquired in a very painstaking way; individual computer scientists work with individual experts to explicate the expert's heuristics—to mine those jewels of knowledge out of their heads one by one . . . the problem of knowledge acquisition is the critical bottleneck in artificial intelligence.[12]

When Feigenbaum suggests to an expert the rules the expert seems to be using, he gets a Euthyphro-like response: "That's true, but if you see enough patients/rocks/chip designs/instruments readings, you see that it isn't true after all."[13] Feigenbaum comments with Socratic annoyance: "At this point, knowledge threatens to become ten thousand special cases."[14]

A History of Inflated Claims

There are also other hints of trouble. Ever since the inception of AI researchers have been trying to produce artificial experts by programming the computer to follow the rules used by masters in various domains. Yet, although computers are faster and more accurate than people in applying rules, master-level performance has remained out of reach. Arthur Samuel's work is typical. In 1947, when electronic computers were just being developed, Samuel, then at IBM, decided to write a checkers program. He did not try to make a machine play checkers by brute-force calculation of all chains of moves clear to the end. He calculated that if you tried to look to the end of the game with the fastest computer you could possibly build, subject to the speed of light, it would take 10 followed by twenty-one zeros centuries to make the first move. So he tried to elicit heuristic rules from checkers masters and program a computer to follow those rules. When the rules the experts came up with did not produce master play, Samuel became the first and almost the only AI researcher to make a learning program. He programmed a computer to vary the weights used in the rules, such as the tradeoff between center control and loss of a piece, and to retain the weights that worked best. After playing a great many games with itself, the program could beat Samuel, which shows that in some sense computers can do more than they are programmed to do.

The checkers program is not only the first and one of the best experts ever built, but it is also a perfect example of the way fact turns into fiction in AI. The checkers program once beat a state checkers champion. From then on AI literature has cited the checkers program as a noteworthy success. One often reads that it plays at such a high level that only the world champion can beat it. Feigenbaum, for example, reports that "by 1961 [Samuel's program] played championship checkers, and it learned and improved with each game."[15] Even the usually reliable *Handbook of Artificial Intelligence* states as a fact that "today's programs play championship-level checkers."[16] In fact, Samuel said in a recent interview at Stanford University, where he is a retired professor, the program did once defeat a state champion, but the champion "turned around and defeated the program in six mail games." According to Samuel, after thirty-five years of effort, "the program is quite capable of beating any amateur player and can give better players a good contest." It is clearly no champion. Samuel is still bringing in expert players for help, but he fears he "may be reaching the point of diminishing returns." That does not lead him to question the view that the masters the program cannot beat are using heuristic rules; rather, like Socrates and Feigenbaum, Samuel thinks the experts are poor at recollecting their compiled heuristics: "The experts do not know enough about the mental processes involved in playing the game."[17]

The same story is repeated in every area of expertise, even

in areas where unlike checkers expertise requires the storage of large numbers of facts, which should give an advantage to the computer. In each area where there are experts with years of experience the computer can do better than the beginner, and can even exhibit useful competence, but it cannot rival the very experts whose facts and supposed heuristics it is processing with incredible speed and unerring accuracy.

In the face of that impasse it was necessary, in spite of the authority and influence of Plato and two thousand years of philosophy, for us to take a fresh look at what a skill is and what the expert acquires when he attains expertise. As shown earlier, one has to abandon the traditional view that a beginner starts with specific cases and, as he becomes more proficient, abstracts and interiorizes more and more sophisticated rules. It turned out that skill acquisition moves in just the opposite direction— from abstract rules to particular cases. It seems that a beginner makes inferences using rules and facts just like a heuristically programmed computer, but with talent and a great deal of involved experience the beginner develops into an expert who intuitively sees what to do without applying rules. Of course, a description of skilled behavior can never be taken as conclusive evidence as to what is going on in the mind or in the brain. It is always possible that what is going on is some unconscious process using more and more sophisticated rules. But our description of skill acquisition counters the traditional prejudice that expertise necessarily involves inference.

Given our account of the five stages of skill acquisition, we can understand why the knowledge engineers from Socrates to Samuel to Feigenbaum have had such trouble getting the expert to articulate the rules he is using. The expert is simply not following any rules! He is doing just what Feigenbaum feared he might be doing: recognizing thousands of special cases. That in turn explains why expert systems are never as good as experts. If one asks the experts for rules one will, in effect, force the expert to regress to the level of a beginner and state the rules he still remembers but no longer uses. If one programs them on a computer, one can use the speed and accuracy of the computer and its ability to store and access millions of facts to outdo a human beginner using the same rules. But no amount of rules and facts can capture the knowledge an expert has when he has stored his experience of the actual outcomes of tens of thousands of situations.

The knowledge engineer might still say that in spite of appearances the mind and brain *must* be reasoning—making millions of rapid and accurate inferences like a computer. After all, the brain is not "wonder tissue," and how else could it work? But as we have seen, there *are* other models for what might be going on in the hardware. When asked in an interview whether holograms would allow a person to make decisions spontaneously in very complex environments, Karl Pribram, a Stanford neuropsychologist, replied: "Decisions fall out as the holographic correlations are performed. One doesn't have to think things through . . . a step at a time. One takes the whole constellation of a situation, correlates it, and out of that correlation emerges the correct response."[18]

We can now understand why, in a recent article in *Science*, two expert systems builders, Richard Duda and Edward Shortliffe, who assume rather cautiously but without evidence that "experts seem to employ rule-like associations to solve routine problems quickly,"[19] are nonetheless finally forced by the phenomenon to conclude:

The identification and encoding of knowledge is one of the most complex and arduous tasks encountered in the construction of an expert system. . . . Even when an adequate knowledge representation formalism has been developed, experts often have difficulty expressing their knowledge in that form.[20]

Likewise, we should not be surprised that in the area of medicine we find doctors concluding:

The optimistic expectation of 20 years ago that computer technology would also come to play an important part in clinical decisions has not been realized, and there are few if any situations in which computers are being routinely used to assist in either medical diagnosis or the choice of therapy.[21]

We predict that in any domain in which people exhibit holistic understanding, no system based upon heuristics will consistently do as well as experienced experts, even if those experts were the informants who provided the heuristic rules. According to the media, however, many systems already outperform experts and so falsify our prediction. We shall therefore now deal with each alleged exception in turn.

The Exceptions That Prove the Rule

The first supposed exception is a system, called MACSYMA, developed at M.I.T., for doing certain manipulations required in algebra and calculus. MACSYMA began as a *heuristic* system. It has evolved, however, into an *algorithmic* system, using procedures guaranteed to work but involving so much calculation people would normally not use them. Perhaps that is why MACSYMA is not on Feigenbaum's list of expert systems in *The Fifth Generation.* So the fact that MACSYMA, as far as we know, now outperforms all experts in its field does not constitute an exception to our prediction.

DENDRAL was one of the first and most touted expert systems, which, according to Feigenbaum, "began AI's shift to the knowledge-based viewpoint." It has a history similar to MACSYMA's. Feigenbaum, stockholder in and director of an expert systems company, however, gives the impression that DENDRAL is still based on heuristic rules gleaned from experts and that it is widely used in industry. He says that "DENDRAL has been in use for many years at university and industrial chemical labs around the world."[22]

When we called several universities and industrial sites that do mass spectroscopy, we were surprised to find that none of them use DENDRAL. The resolution of this apparent contradiction turned out to be revealing. DENDRAL was the name of the original research project, which developed several quite different programs. One of those, Heuristic DENDRAL, uses heuristic rules operating on the spectrum produced by a mass spectrometer to infer various molecular structures that might produce the observed spectrum. It then tests to see how well the spectra of the candidate structures match the actual mass spectra observed, and ranks the candidates based on this matching. Heuristic DENDRAL is, indeed, an expert system, but it is not commercially available. David Smith, director of engineering at Finnigan Corporation in San Jose, California, the world's largest manufacturer of mass spectrography equipment, explained: "There are no commercial companies that produce mass-spectrometers that have DENDRAL available in their data systems. It does not run on any of the current popular operating systems that are used with a mass spectrometer. It was coded ten years ago or longer, and it just has not been maintained, either by Stanford or by any commercial interest."

An outgrowth of the DENDRAL project, CONGEN, does seem to be in use daily by chemists, but it is not a heuristic-based expert system. CONGEN uses an algorithmic procedure to generate all molecular structures consistent with information based on several sources, including spectroscopy. The program does not heuristically infer constraints from mass spectra, as does Heuristic DENDRAL, but directly accepts constraints provided by human experts.[23]

We asked Bruce Buchanan, a co-developer of DENDRAL, whether the heuristic part of DENDRAL was an expert system that could outperform intuitive experts, and, if so, why it wasn't used in industry. He explained that (1) the system as programmed contained knowledge of only one very specific class of compounds, and for such compounds it outperformed the best chemists, (2) it was not commercially available because apparently the investment required in order to codify the knowledge of the many specific domains that concern industry was prohibitive, and (3) spectroscopy had been chosen as a test bed for expert systems in the first place because chemists doing mass spectral interpretation must rely largely on systematic inference rather than intuitive pattern recognition. Since in spectrographic analysis skilled performance requires calculation, the success of heuristic DENDRAL does not falsify our hypothesis.

R1, another expert system both as good as human specialists and heuristic, was developed at Digital Equipment Corporation to decide how to combine components of VAX computers to meet customers' needs. Like DENDRAL it performs as well as anyone in the field only because the domain in question is so combinatorial that even experienced specialists fail to develop holistic understanding. The experienced "technical editors" who perform the job at DEC depend on heuristic-based problem-solving and take about ten minutes to work out even simple cases, so it is no surprise that an expert system can rival the best specialists.

Chess seems an obvious exception to our prediction, since chess programs have already achieved master ratings. The chess story is complicated and fascinating.

Chess programs have come a long way since Stuart first played against one in 1958. He recalls:

I knew that the program I was playing was experimental and that game programming was in its infancy, but I was not prepared for what happened. To play the computer in those days you entered your move into the computer at a keyboard and its move was shown by printing out a picture of the new position. About five moves into the game, I was surprised to discover on the machine's picture that it had given me an extra castle, which was sitting out in the middle of the board. I didn't feel it ethical to use the phantom castle, so went about my business attacking the computer's king while it proceeded to sneak up on the extra piece it had given me. By the time the program had captured the castle, I had an unstoppable attack on its king. But, just as I was about to mate the machine, it printed out its picture of the position and, lo and behold, it had now given *itself* an extra castle, which prevented my mate. The game was never finished, but no doubt the bug was removed from the program, since it soon played legal, although poor, chess.

Speaking of the poor quality of early chess programs, it is time to lay to rest a silly story about Hubert that has reappeared in numerous books and articles[24] since it was first reported in Alvin Toffler's book *Future Shock* in 1971. Toffler inaccurately interpreted Hubert as predicting in 1965 that computers would *never* play even amateur chess. He then accurately reported that Hubert, who is at best an amateur chess player, was beaten at M.I.T. in 1968 by a chess program named Mac Hack. If you read the full quotation, it is clear that Toffler's interpretation is a distortion. Hubert's assertion was simply a correct report of the state of the art at that time and *contained no prediction:* "According to Newell, Shaw and Simon themselves, evaluating the Los Alamos, the IBM, and the NSS programs: 'All three programs play roughly the same quality of chess (mediocre).' Still no chess program can play even amateur chess."[25]

Programs that play chess are among the earliest examples of expert systems. The first such program was written in the 1950s, and by the late 1960s fairly sophisticated programs had been developed. Master players, as they check out each plausible move that springs to mind, generally consider one to three plausible opponent responses, followed by one to three moves of their own, and so on. Quite frequently only one move looks plausible at each step. After looking ahead a varying number of moves depending on the situation, the terminal position of each sequence is assessed based on its similarity to positions previously encountered. In positions where the best initial move is not obvious, about one hundred terminal positions will typically be examined. Such thinking ahead generally confirms that the initial move intuitively seen as the most plausible is indeed best, although there are occasional exceptions. To imitate human players, the program designers attempted to elicit from the masters heuristic rules that could be used to generate a limited number of plausible moves at each step and evaluation rules that could be used to assess the worth of the roughly one hundred terminal positions. Since masters are not aware of following any rules, the rules that they suggested did not work well, and the programs played at a marginally competent level.

As computers grew faster in the 1970s, chess programming strategy changed. In 1973 a program was developed at Northwestern University by David Slate and Larry Atkin which in effect rapidly searched *every* legal initial move and every legal response to a depth determined by the position and the computer's speed, generally about three moves for each player. A clever procedure in the program actually eliminated certain sequences of moves that could not possibly be best without examining them, thereby greatly speeding up the search. Although the roughly 1 million terminal positions in the look-ahead were still evaluated by rules, plausible-move-generation heuristics were discarded. The resulting program looked less like an expert system, and quality of play greatly improved. By 1983, using those largely brute-force procedures and the latest, most powerful computer (the Cray X-MP, capable of examining about 10 million terminal positions in choosing each move), a program called Cray-Blitz became world computer chess champion and achieved a master rating based on a tournament against other computers that already had chess ratings.

Such programs, however, have an Achilles' heel. While they are perfect tacticians when there are many captures and checks and a decisive outcome can be found within the computer's foreseeable future (now about four moves ahead for each player), computers lack any sense of chess strategy. Fairly good players who understand that fact can direct the game into long-range strategic channels, thereby defeating the computer, even though those players have a somewhat lower chess rating than the machine has achieved based on play against other machines and human beings who do not recognize the strategic blindness. The ratings held by computers and reported in the press accurately reflect their performance against other computers and human players who do not exploit the computer's weakness, but greatly overstate their skill level in strategic play.

A Scottish International Master chess player, David Levy, is a computer enthusiast and chairman of a company called Intelligent Software in London. Levy, ranked as roughly the thousandth best player in the world, bet about $4,000 in 1968 that no computer could defeat him by 1978. He collected, by beating the best computer program at that time 3.5 games to 1.5 games in a five-game match. He was, however, impressed by the machine's performance, and the bet was increased and extended until 1984, with Levy quite uncertain about the outcome. When the 1984 match approached and the Cray-Blitz program had just achieved a master-level score in winning the world computer championship, Levy decided to modify his usual style of play to exploit to a maximum the computer's strategic blindness. Not only did he defeat the computer decisively, four games to zero, but more important, he lost his long-held optimism about computer play. As he confessed to the *Los Angeles Times:*

> During the last few years I had come to believe more and more that it was possible for programs, within a decade, to play very strong grandmaster chess. But having played the thing now, my feeling is that a human world chess champion losing to a computer program in a serious match is a lot further away than I thought. Most people working on computer chess are working on the wrong lines. If more chess programmers studied the way human chess masters think and tried to emulate that to some extent, then I think they might get further.

Levy summed up his recent match by saying: "The nature of the struggle was such that the program didn't understand what was going on."[26] Clearly, when confronting a player who knows its weakness, Cray-Blitz is not a master-level chess player.

We could not agree more strongly with Levy's suggestion that researchers give up current methods and attempt to imitate what people do. But strong chess players seem to use the holistic similarity recognition described in the highest of our five levels of skill, so that imitating them would mean duplicating that pattern recognition process rather than returning to the typical expert system approach: "The great chess player does not see squares and pieces. . . . He internalizes a very special sense of 'fields of force.'. . . What matters thus is not the particular square, nor even piece, but a cluster of potential actions, a space of and for evolving events."[27] Since similarity for a strong chess player means similar "fields of force" and since no one has yet succeeded in describing such fields, there is little prospect of duplicating human performance in the foreseeable future.

The only remaining game program that appears to challenge our prediction is Hans Berliner's backgammon program, BKG 9.8. There is no doubt that the program used heuristic rules obtained from masters to beat the world champion in a seven-game series. But backgammon is a game involving a large element of chance, and Berliner himself is quite frank in saying that his program "did get the better of the dice rolls" and could not consistently perform at championship level. He concludes: "The program did not make the best play in eight out of 73 nonforced situations. . . . An expert would not have made most of the errors the program made, but they could be exploited only a small percent of the time. . . . My program plays at the Class A, or advanced intermediate, level."[28]

These cases are clearly not counter-examples to our claim. Neither is a recent SRI contender named PROSPECTOR, a program that uses rules derived from expert geologists to locate mineral deposits. Millions of viewers heard about PROSPECTOR on the "CBS Evening News" in September 1983. A special Dan Rather report called "The Computers Are Coming" showed first a computer and then a mountain (Mount Tolman) as Rather authoritatively intoned: "This computer digested facts and figures on mineral deposits, then predicted that the metal molybdenum would be found at this mountain in the Pacific Northwest. It was." Such a feat, if true, would indeed be impressive. A brief interview with us was shown on the same program. Viewers must have felt that we were foolish when we asserted that, using current AI methods, computers would never become intelligent. In reality, the PROSPECTOR program was given information concerning prior drilling on Mount Tolman where a field of molybdenum *had already been found.* The expert system then mapped out undrilled portions of that field, and subsequent drilling showed it to be basically correct about where molybdenum did and did not exist.[29] Unfortunately, economic-grade ore was not found in the previously unmapped area; drilling disclosed the ore to be too deep to be worth mining. One cannot conclude, therefore, that the program can outperform experts. Up to now there are no further data comparing experts' predictions with those of the system.

Among other programs we know of that meet all the requirements for a test of our hypothesis are MYCIN, mentioned earlier; INTERNIST-I, a program for diagnosis in internal medicine; and PUFF, an expert system for diagnosis of lung disorders. They are each based exclusively on heuristic rules extracted from experts, and their performance has been compared with that of experts in the field.

A systematic evaluation of MYCIN was reported in the *Journal of the American Medical Association.* The program was supplied with data concerning ten actual meningitis cases and asked to prescribe drug therapy. Its prescriptions were evaluated by a panel of eight infectious disease specialists who had published clinical reports dealing with the management of the ailment. The experts rated as acceptable 70 percent of MYCIN's recommended therapies.[30]

The evidence concerning INTERNIST-I is even more detailed. In fact, according to the *New England Journal of Medicine,* which published an evaluation of the program, the "systematic evaluation of the model's performance is virtually unique in the field of medical applications of artificial intelligence."[31] INTERNIST-I is described as follows:

> From its inception, INTERNIST-I has addressed the problem of diagnosis within the broad context of general internal medicine. Given a patient's initial history, results of a physical examination, or laboratory findings, INTERNIST-I was designed to aid the physician with the patient's work-up in order to make multiple and complex diagnoses. The capabilities of the system derive from its extensive knowledge base and from heuristic computer programs that can construct and resolve differential diagnoses.[32]

The program was run on nineteen cases, each with several diseases, so that there were forty-three correct diagnoses in all, and its diagnoses were compared with those of clinicians at Massachusetts General Hospital and with case discussants. Diagnoses were counted as correct when confirmed by pathologists.

The result: Of "43 anatomically verified diagnoses, INTERNIST-I failed to make a total of 18, whereas the clinicians failed to make 15 such diagnoses and the discussants missed only eight."[33] The evaluators found that the "experienced clinician is vastly superior to INTERNIST-I in the ability to consider the

relative severity and independence of the different manifestations of disease and to understand the temporal evolution of
the disease process."[34] Dr. G. Octo Barnett, in his editorial com-
ment on the evaluation, wisely concluded:

> Perhaps the most exciting experimental evaluation of INTERNIST-I
> would be the demonstration that a productive collaboration is
> possible between man and computer—that clinical diagnosis in real
> situations can be improved by combining the medical judgment
> of the clinician with the statistical and computational power of a
> computer model and a large base of stored medical information.[35]

The Proper Use of Competent Systems

We have found that in domains where a person can function
without calling upon the full range of his natural language understanding, common sense, know-how, and ability to adjust to unanticipated changes, expert systems can competently perform
tasks that would normally be described as requiring judgment
and wisdom. But rather than improving on human performance,
we have seen in detail that the computer falls short of expert-
level human skill.

In areas where competence is sufficient or where their limitations are well understood, expert systems can be appropriate.
Consider medicine, where expert systems development has been
extensive enough to prompt speculation on its social consequences. For several reasons PUFF, which diagnoses lung disorders, is an instructive example. PUFF uses thirty heuristic rules
given to it by Dr. Robert Fallat, the chief of pulmonary medicine
at the Pacific Medical Center in San Francisco, yet it agrees
with him only 75 percent of the time. Why it cannot do better
is a mystery, if one believes, as Robert MacNeil put it on the
"MacNeil–Lehrer News Hour," that researchers "discovered
that Dr. Fallat used some thirty rules based on his clinical expertise to diagnose whether patients have obstructive airway disease." But the machine's limited ability makes perfect sense if
Fallat does not in fact follow those thirty rules or any others.

Still the system is useful. As Dr. Fallat states: "There's a lot
of what we do, including our thinking and our expertise, which
is routine, and which doesn't require any special human effort

to do. And that kind of stuff should be taken over by computers. And to the extent that 75 percent of what I do is routine and which all of us would agree on, why not let the computer do it and then I can have fun working on the other 25 percent."[36]

Yet Dr. Fallat's apparently simple suggestion may be complicated in practice. Just for starters, will the machine screen the cases, bumping the difficult ones to human experts, or vice versa? In the case of PUFF the answer is straightforward. Fallat is able quickly to review PUFF's output and tell with close to 100 percent accuracy whether or not it is acceptable, because the data on which PUFF bases its diagnosis are entirely quantitative and can be displayed graphically for Fallat to "take a gestalt on."[37] PUFF screens all the cases and generates reports on them. Fallat reviews the reports, and if he agrees with PUFF, his paperwork is already done, for the reports are detailed enough to be sent to the doctors for whom he is consulting.

Dr. Fallat's interpretive skills approach 100 percent accuracy, so he can correct PUFF in those 25 percent of cases where PUFF is inadequate to the task. His expertise is what allows him to use PUFF effectively, to save on the labor of paperwork, and to help train students. All in all, Fallat's relationship with PUFF seems a healthy one in which the machine is being used as an aid to, and not a substitute for, the human mind. Unfortunately, most branches of medicine are not so tidy. Few offer so convenient a method of riding herd on mechanical diagnostic assistants as the graph, which Fallat can interpret at a glance. Without a simple way of checking the decisions of the machine, the human expert will have to do as much work as before or else hand over real decision-making to the machine.

Dubious as we are about the benefits of expert systems, we emphatically *do* believe that sophisticated computation has its place in medicine. To begin with, there are "diagnostic prompting systems" like RECONSIDER, which we discussed in our Preface. These systems work by encouraging the doctor to consider alternatives and not jump to conclusions. And there are the new scanning technologies, from computer-enhanced x-ray imaging to CAT scanning to nuclear-magnetic resonance, all based on computerized data processing. Here we would only warn against attempts to automate the *interpretation* of the scan data, replacing virtuoso human beings with merely competent computer programs.

Feigenbaum himself admits in one surprisingly frank passage

that expert systems are very different from experts: "Part of learning to be an expert is to understand not merely the letter of the rule but its spirit. [The expert] knows when to break the rules, he understands what is relevant to his task and what isn't. . . . Expert systems do not yet understand these things."[38] But because of his philosophical commitment to the rationality of expertise and thus to underlying unconscious heuristic rules, Feigenbaum does not see how devastating his admission is.

Once one gives up the assumption that experts must be making inferences and admits the role of involvement and intuition in the acquisition and application of skills, one will have no reason to cling to the heuristic program as a model of human intellectual operations. Feigenbaum's claim that "we have the opportunity at this moment to do a new version of Diderot's *Encyclopedia*, a gathering up of all knowledge—not just the academic kind, but the informal, experiential, heuristic kind,"[39] as well as his boast that Knowledge Information Processing Systems (KIPS) will soon result in "machine intelligence—faster, deeper, better than human intelligence,"[40] can both be seen as a late stage of Socratic thinking, with no rational or empirical basis. In that light those who claim we must begin a crash program to compete with the Japanese fifth-generation intelligent computers can be seen to be false prophets blinded by Socratic assumptions and personal ambition—while Euthyphro, the expert on piety, who kept giving Socrates examples instead of rules, turns out to have been a true prophet after all.

Where does that leave expert systems? Recall that knowledge engineering looked like the way out of the impasse posed by the problem of commonsense knowledge. But, as one might suspect, since both the commonsense problem and the expertise problem are just different manifestations of the general problem that computers cannot capture skills by using rules and features, knowledge engineering is finally forced to confront, on its own turf, the unsolved problems of AI. Thus Richard Duda and John Gaschnig end a generally optimistic article with the realization that the knowledge acquisition problem is a version of the general AI problem of knowledge representation:

> The problem is that although inference networks of rules do much to codify the reasoning process that an expert uses in solving a problem, there's still much that goes on inside an expert's head that doesn't appear in the networks. . . . One of the problems is

that it is difficult for experts to describe exactly how they do what they do, especially with respect to their use of judgment, experience, and intuition.

This is often called the knowledge-acquisition problem. Despite several concentrated efforts, it remains a bottleneck. Past efforts to speed knowledge acquisition have been along three lines: (1) to develop smart editors that assist in entering and modifying rules, (2) to develop an intelligent interface that can interview the expert and formulate the rules, and (3) to develop a learning system that can induce rules from examples, or by reading textbooks and papers.

Somewhat ironically, to do anything ambitious along these lines seems to require fundamental advances in our understanding of two core AI topics—the representation of knowledge and the use of knowledge![41]

But one can refrain from the overly ambitious and still accomplish something practical. Those who are most acutely aware of the limitations of expert systems are best able to exploit their real capabilities. Dr. Sandra Cook, manager of the Financial Expert Systems Program at SRI International, is one of those enlightened practitioners. She cautions prospective clients that expert systems should not be expected to perform as well as human experts, nor should they be seen as simulations of human expert thinking. Cook lists eight reasonable conditions for successful applications (meaning that fairly high-quality performance can be made generally available within a company employing few if any true experts):

1. No algorithmic solution to the problem should exist, so that expertise is indeed required. (Recall that an algorithmic solution procedure is one that is guaranteed to find the demonstrably best solution to a problem.)
2. The problem can be satisfactorily solved by human experts at such a high level that somewhat inferior performance is still acceptable. (Stock market prediction, for example, would be an inappropriate area because human experts themselves perform erratically.)
3. There is a significant likelihood of a poor decision if made by a nonexpert. (Processing business credit applications is a reasonable area for expert system design, because inexperienced beginners have little ability to recognize nonroutine cases.)

4. Poor decisions must have significant impacts. (Expert systems are expensive to create and maintain.)
5. The problem must remain relatively unchanged during the time it takes a user of the system to solve the problem interactively. (Any expert system advice concerning the control of a nuclear reactor during a crisis would come too late to be of use. Only human experts or self-contained computer programs are fast enough to influence events.)
6. The knowledge domain must be relatively static. (Otherwise the system would require expensive continuous updating.)
7. A patient and cooperative expert must be available to the project to answer hypothetical questions which at best reveal the reasoning process he or she may once have used but has discarded since becoming an expert. This exercise can be frustrating, especially if the conclusion generated by the rules the expert articulates frequently fails to match his intuitive responses.
8. The political climate of the business must be conducive to the introduction of a new tool substituting certain user skills (such as furnishing information, sometimes judgmental, to a computer) for others (such as decision-making).

It is hard to believe that the company or government that has such systems dealing competently, but not expertly, with suitably selected problems will dominate all competition, as claimed by enthusiasts for Japan's fifth-generation project and for an expensive American response in kind. The most that can be expected is that expert systems may someday take their place alongside planning charts, management information systems, and professional training programs as useful tools for improving overall performance.

A genuine danger, however, faces the company or government going that route. To the extent that junior employees using expert systems come to see expertise as a function of large knowledge bases and masses of inferential rules, they will fail to progress beyond the competent level of their machines. With the leap beyond competence to proficiency and expertise thus inhibited, investors in expert systems may ultimately discover that their wells of true human expertise and wisdom have gone dry.

CHAPTER 5

COMPUTERS IN THE CLASSROOM: TOOLS, TUTORS, AND TUTEES

[T]rue computer literacy is not just knowing how to make use of computers and computational ideas. It is knowing when it is appropriate to do so.

Seymour Papert
Mindstorms (1980)

WHILE THE GENERAL PUBLIC exhibits an intense yet detached interest in the future of intelligent computers, much as it does in the space program, medical research, and other scientific developments, the subject of the role of computers in education arouses in many parents an almost visceral reaction of protective instinct for their young. Knowing that, computer companies exploit the anxiety of parents in advertisements warning that a computer deficiency in the educational diet of their offspring can lead to serious impairment of their mental growth and later intellectual health. Without any clear idea of what the damage will be or what computers can do to avoid it, frightened parents spend millions of dollars purchasing home computers for their children and clamor at the doors of their children's schools demanding the introduction of computers in their classrooms.

Appropriately offended by the commercial exploitation, critics of the computer are fighting back. In a recent article in the *Los Angeles Times,* for example, Jonathan Kellerman, a child psychologist and associate professor of pediatrics at the University of Southern California, likened computer salesmen to those hucksters of the late 1940s who traveled throughout Appalachia showing pictures of grotesquely injured babies to promote the sale of expensive, and allegedly safe, infant highchairs. Perhaps an even closer analogy would be between computer sales techniques of today and those of the door-to-door encyclopedia salesmen of a generation ago, who contrived to frighten insecure parents into outlays of hundreds of dollars for books that in themselves contributed little to their offspring's education and were already available in school libraries. Without any serious discussion of how the computer could and should be used in education, Kellerman condemns the computer as a provider of "instant gratification," an "interloper," and "an electronic baby sitter." Such irate responses, while understandable, do our children almost as great a disservice as the emotionally unsettling ads hawking the machine.

Advocates and critics alike all too often fail to make clear what the proposed use of the computer they are praising or condemning is, and why such a use is or is not a good idea. Detailed discussion is both time-consuming and space-consuming, and makes more difficult reading than do the snappy ads and retorts, but more of it is needed if the proper role of computers in education is to be established. That is our purpose here, for while we feel there is a proper place for computers in education, we feel as well that most of the educational software available today is inappropriate and, indeed, that computers are today being used in ways that may eventually prove detrimental.

Opposed as we are to efforts to assign human-like roles to computers or computer-like roles to human beings in the classroom, we are not among those skeptics who demand "scientific" documentation of success before adopting any innovation. Nor would we believe such evidence were it produced. Documentation of failures also leaves us unconvinced. The human mind is much too subtle a subject for "scientific" treatment. A child obviously can learn useful things while interacting with a computer that various tests will fail to uncover, and he also can verifiably learn lessons, intended or otherwise, that are either irrelevant or useless because they cannot be made to work in real situations. Furthermore, an experiment involving the computer may appear to have enhanced learning when it is really the attention generated by the experiment that produced the results. (We are reminded of the famous study by the industrial psychologist Elton Mayo on the effect of illumination upon performance. The original lighting in a factory was modified, and production improved. Several further modifications suggested by industrial engineers produced further improvements in performance. Excited by their findings, the engineers returned the illumination to its original state and hastened away to write up their recommendations to improve the factory lighting, only to be informed that the reversion to the initial situation improved production still further. The only conclusion to be drawn was that the attention induced by change produced temporary improvement, and the effect of the actual lighting tested was obscured by those effects.) For such reasons it would be a mistake to shy away from an educational innovation until it has been conclusively "proved" effective or to accept change based on nothing more than observed improvements.

What is needed is an understanding of the learning processes of children, an understanding textured and nuanced enough to distinguish between different types of skills. Only then should we come to commonsense conclusions about the potential role for computers. We shall review here various arguments in favor of a variety of uses of computers in education advanced by articulate advocates and, when appropriate, shall present our contrary views.

Let us look then at what computers can offer. Perhaps the least controversial way computers can be used is as *tools.* Teaching aids, from paintbrushes and typewriters to chalkboards and laboratory demos, can sometimes be replaced to everyone's great advantage by suitably programmed computers.

Besides its use as a tool the computer has the potential to perform tasks usually asked of teachers; for example it can conduct drills in such subjects as spelling, and do so in a more versatile, interesting, and interactive way than any book. The computer can also help students practice applying what they have learned. Not only can an almost endless number of subtraction problems be presented, but they can be put pictorially, graphically, verbally, and in other formats not usually present in books. Distinct from drill and practice is the hoped for use of computers as coaches, the role dearest to the heart of conscientious teachers. As coach, the computer would develop an understanding of the individual student, of his or her strengths and weaknesses, and would tailor instruction accordingly. It would even provide advice and hints and pose problems at the appropriate speed and in the best pedagogical order. Sometimes the two uses of computers—as overseers of drill or practice and as coaches—are lumped together and termed the use of computers as *tutors,* which is the usage we have adopted. In many publications the various attempts to use the computer as teacher are referred to as Computer Aided Instruction (CAI).

Of increasing interest, thanks to a computer language and learning environment called LOGO now being widely marketed, is the use of the computer as *tutee.* The ingenious theory behind the development is that children will learn to think more rigorously if they are put in the role of teacher of a literal-minded, but patient and agreeable, student—the computer.

We shall now take up in turn the computer's role as tool, tutor, and tutee.

The Computer as Tool

The use of computers as tools is the easiest to describe and evaluate. Computer simulations are generally good learning tools. They do, however, raise some problems and must be put into perspective. On the positive side, it is easy to see that they can give children the opportunity to take an active and imaginative part in the study of domains that are otherwise difficult or impossible to bring into the classroom: Evolution is too slow, nuclear reactions too fast, probability too counter-intuitive, factories too big, much of chemistry too dangerous.

If a teacher is explaining how money grows at a given interest rate, for example, the computer can simulate the growth, compressing each year into a second, and graphically exhibit the outcome. By changing a number the student can vary the interest rate and immediately observe the effect. Simulations of biological and environmental systems have also been developed. As regards the teaching of physics, Alfred Bork writes:

> Our most widely used student–computer dialogue is MOTION, an "F = ma" world for the student to explore freely. Students control, in a highly interactive manner, the force laws, equation constants, and initial conditions. Thus, they can examine many more situations than they can in the "real" world, with much more control. Further, they need not view the systems only in configuration (x-y) space, but can plot any two or three physically meaningful variables, thus

moving toward viewing the system as existing in a wide variety of spaces normally unavailable. The very wide use of this dialogue by students *not* enrolled in physics classes testifies to its success.[1]

In the future such simulations will surely become more common, helping students of all ages in all disciplines develop their intuition. Simulations can also help to develop the problem-solving skills students now learn through traditional instruction. Such skills include hypothesis formulation and testing, control of variables, estimation, logical deduction, combinatorics, data collection, data organization, decision-making, and pattern identification.[2]

Twila Slesnick, former director of mathematics and computer education at the Berkeley Lawrence Hall of Science and now senior editor of *Classroom Computer Learning,* notes:

> [R]esearchers suspect that using simulations will help students understand the concept of modeling. This includes being able to distinguish between a model and reality, being able to identify the limitations of a model, being able to evaluate the information the model presents, and being able to distinguish between the *real* consequences of actions and the *hypothetical* consequences of interaction with a model.[3]

Of course, there are pitfalls. Since learning skills require *concrete* cases, it seems only common sense to stick to the world of real objects when there is no compelling reason to use simulations: Basic electricity should be taught with batteries and bulbs. Also, since the social consequences of decisions are difficult to quantify, they are often missing from simulations.[4] The first difficulty can easily be avoided, however, and the second is not serious in cases where the social consequences are well understood. For example, a Stanford anthropology professor has programmed a model of the marriage practices and land inheritance traditions of societies in the Himalayas. The students can vary the marriage laws, from one man marrying several women, through monogamy, to the other extreme, and they can read off the result in land distribution several generations down the line. By manipulating the variables in the system students can see both the immediate and the long-term effects of changing marriage customs.

There may, however, be an attendant risk. The attraction of simulations could lead disciplines outside the sciences to stress their formal, analytic side at the expense of subdisciplines based on informal, intuitive understanding. The sciences are domains that in principle are understandable in mathematical terms, while the humanities, such as literary criticism and traditional history, make no attempt to put their understanding into numbers. The social sciences, however, have both formal and informal aspects, and the existence of the computer as simulator may reinforce the tendency of the social sciences to imitate the natural sciences even when it is not appropriate. The educational success of interactive simulations, for example, may tempt political science departments to emphasize mathematical models of elections at the expense of political philosophy, which asks questions about the nature of the state and of power. Similarly, economic history might be pushed aside by econometrics with its mathematical models. Not only is there danger of undue emphasis on quantifiable aspects of a field, but a more serious danger is that the student will focus on the particular assumed relationships between variables made precise and explicit in a simulation and overlook the real relationships stated more vaguely in a qualitative, historical treatment of a subject. That would be a grave mistake in the social sciences, where no one can state the dynamic relationships governing elections or economies with anything resembling the accuracy or completeness of the laws of physics. Every election campaign or economic swing offers vivid reminders of the inadequacy of predictions based on simulation models. Such risks of distorted emphasis on the formalizable aspects of a field are not inherent in the use of computer simulations. However, those dangerous pressures will grow in direct proportion to the value of computer modeling in the natural sciences.

Along with simulation, another promising use of computers is in the creation of learning environments. Here, rather than teaching some particular goal or skill, the computer serves as a tool kit for coping with events in a micro-world. In the course of using the tools the user figures out how to solve problems in the micro-world and so learns the conceptual structure of the domain.

One of the most promising developments in that area is the merging of learning environments and computer games. Dr. Ann Piestrup, founder of The Learning Company, describes her goals as follows:

The idea was to create a world where failure is impossible, success is rewarded with power, and mastery of knowledge leads to greater challenges. We wanted to build an environment that is always controlled by the learner, in which the game itself provides a landscape of concepts for students to discover. Risk-taking is encouraged. There is feedback, but it is gentle. Finally, mastery of the game also achieves a curricular goal.[5]

That ideal was approached in The Learning Company's highly acclaimed game *Rocky's Boots* and realized in *Robot Odyssey I.* The objective of the latter is to get out of a futuristic city called Robotropolis. The player must struggle through five levels of sewers, skyways, and subways by designing robot vehicles. These friendly robots come equipped with sensors, thrusters, bumpers, and grabbers, which the learner programs to make the robot do his or her bidding. The programs consist of sequences of logical operations such as "and," "not," and "or" that are "wired" into simulated logic chips by the player and which control the robots. Dr. Piestrup explained to us that such games

> . . . require very intricate problem solving skills. The player must remember a lot of things and how they fit together. A player may have to map areas containing dozens of rooms, intertwining pathways, and many layers. Developing logical strategies, the player might discover that he or she can pick up an object in one part of the game world, and leave it in a place where it will be useful later, for example.

There is no doubt that a child interacting playfully with this software learns the conceptual structure of the game domain. It seems clear too that the child acquires problem-solving skills such as the ability to break down a problem and solve it step by step and to formulate strategies that can be used to organize and chose among the available step-by-step procedures. Such a game would presumably take a beginner as far as competence.

It even encourages the kind of involvement required to progress to proficiency. Hubert's son, Stéphane, was deep into Robotropolis ten minutes after loading the game. Rather than standing outside the maze as one does when solving a maze problem in a book, he was so bodily and mentally immersed in the world of the game that Robotropolis overflowed the screen into the living room. He pointed to the closet on the left to explain where he had been and to the fireplace on the right to warn of the guardian robots lying ahead.

What needs to be asked is: Does the game take advantage of involvement to encourage the learner to go on to proficiency and expertise in its world? Does the child learn an approach to situations that will facilitate the passage from problem-solving to holistic similarity recognition in the future? Does the child learn what we and Dr. Piestrup have in our discussions come to call "grokking?"[6]

Unfortunately game designers seem to think that mastery consists in grasping more and more complex conceptual domains by means of more and more sophisticated *problem-solving* skills. That leads to games in which the learner solves progressively more difficult problems, where "more difficult" means problems that require going beyond the previous solution. That sort of game may well lead to ever increasing competence, but it inhibits crossing the line to intuitive expertise, since as soon as one begins to perfect a skill one finds oneself in a more complex environment and hence back in the role of a beginner.

Dr. Piestrup agrees that the ideal learning environment would teach not only logical problem-solving skills but intuitive grokking skills as well. A grokking game would begin like a problem-solving game, requiring the learner to discover a procedure for arriving at the solution to a problem. That would enable the student to arrive at competence while fostering the sort of involvement required for going further. But then, once the learner had the procedure well in hand, the program would encourage the student to forget the procedure and leap directly to the solution. Finally, the program would lead the learner to jump intuitively to the solution in situations that were similar to the one with which he or she was already familiar.

An elementary game of that sort might be an estimation game. Here the player would measure the length of an object by seeing how many times a unit measure can be laid end to end beside it. The goal is not to measure more and more complicated objects under increasingly difficult conditions, but rather to develop a repertoire of typical objects with known lengths so that one can judge immediately the length of a given object without having to measure it. After the player has measured several objects of differing lengths, he would be shown objects he had already measured and be rewarded for speed of response or, what comes to the same thing, shown objects so briefly that he does not have time to measure them in a procedural way. Next would come unfamiliar objects of the same length as objects already measured. Winning would put a premium on rapid intuitive estimation of the length of those unfamiliar objects.

A more advanced game in the spirit of *Robot Odyssey* would teach the recognition of functional similarity required for expertise. An expert chip designer can see at a glance that two chip diagrams are functionally similar even though many gates are different, or that two diagrams are functionally different even though only one logic gate is changed. That may seem like an amazing feat, and it is, but you are using a similar expertise this very minute. Words you see and understand almost instantly would have an entirely different meaning if only one letter were changed; you understand other words as synonymous even though all the letters are different. Being an intuitive reader, you grasp words as a whole rather than figuring them out on the basis of the letters that make them up. Experiments show that you are able to recognize whole words faster than you are able to recognize single letters.[7]

The budding chip designer engrossed in *Robot Odyssey* should be motivated to develop the same sort of intuition. After designing many chips for a range of purposes, let us suppose he could attend a chip fair where he could choose among chips wired according to a variety of chip diagrams. However, each chip would be displayed only briefly. At first he would see diagrams of chips he had already constructed. He would presumably be able to remember their function without figuring it out from scratch. Later he would be shown diagrams of functionally equivalent chips. Getting ahead in the game would depend on how quickly he could spot the sort of chip he needed without figuring out its function the way a computer would. The speed pressure would be intended not to encourage anxiety but to promote confidence in intuitive leaps. In this it would play rather the same role as high-speed practice does in learning speed reading; the student must be pushed to see that holistic intuition is possible.

Learning environments that are also games are a great idea, and we envy the children brought up on them, but the concepts they teach are not easily integrated into the curriculum as it now stands. Perhaps someday that will change, but for the time being it seems important to design learning environments that can be used in the classroom as part of the existing curriculum. Judah Schwartz, director of the Educational Technology Center at Harvard, has this goal: "The ideal piece of software is a tool program that focuses on a well-defined curricular content while also being totally open-ended and flexible. What's more, it puts the student in control—the student leads the 'conversation' with the computer and the computer simply displays the consequences of the student's actions."[8] To show how that can be done, Schwartz has developed *The Geometric Supposer,* a limited domain tool that aids the student in grasping geometric relationships. He explains:

> The program allows the user to make any construction on any triangle that he or she wishes. . . . It therefore becomes a simple matter to explore whether the consequences of a given construction on a given triangle are dependent on some peculiar property of the triangle or if there is a possibility of a more general result obtaining. Needless to say, neither possibility nor plausibility constitutes proof. But conjecture, in this instance with the aid of *The Geometric Supposer* as intellectual amplifier, can assume its proper supporting role.[9]

In conversation Schwartz told us that "in the past two years we've had three new theorems from tenth graders."

In addition to their use in simulation and as intellectual tools, computers function as classroom tools in many other ways. As efficient electronic chalkboards distributed throughout the classroom, computers enable several students to work together on a problem or essay displayed on the screen and to store their result instead of having to erase it before turning to the next problem. Thanks to computer networking, students can share their chalkboard with students in other schools, even schools in other areas. Thus the computer need not isolate students, each before his own terminal, but opens up exciting new possibilities of social learning. The computer is without a doubt a wonderful tool permitting many things never before possible.

The Computer as Tutor

On balance, the use of the computer as a tool is relatively unproblematic. The use of the computer as tutor or tutee, however, presents a picture of success in limited domains, along with the same tendency to base extravagant claims on those successes as is found in fields claiming computer intelligence. Attempts to use computers as tutors suffer from exactly the same difficulties that have beset the attempt in AI to make computers generally intelligent; the psychological assumptions underlying the use of the computer as tutee are the same assumptions that give rise to the unjustified belief that expert systems will someday outperform the experts. Unqualified optimism must always be tempered by a careful look at what has been done and what more can be done. In education that means asking what sorts of skills and what levels of skill can and should be taught using computers.

Failure to raise the question of the proper place of the computer as tutor and tutee rests on the deep unquestioned assumption expressed, as if self-evident, in the "Introduction" to a recent influential anthology, *The Computer in the School: Tutor, Tool, Tutee:* "Despite the extensive innovation in computing, much remains the same—particularly in the way computer logic structures are related to human thought structures."[10] Since nothing more is said of the way human and computer thought structures *are* related, one gets the impression that they are unproblematically similar. That view is not new. As we have already seen, once the Greeks invented logic and geometry, the idea that all expertise might be reduced to some kind of calculative reasoning has fascinated most of the Western tradition's rigorous thinkers. So we arrive at the self-evident claim that computers and people alike are rule-following, symbol-manipulating, rational beings. One assumes what has come to be called the information processing model of the mind and proceeds from there. That is just what people have done for some time in the fields of AI and knowledge engineering—and are now doing in their attempts to use the computer as tutor or as tutee.

Behind the hope that computers can aid or even replace teachers is the idea that the teacher's understanding of both the subject being taught and of the profession of teaching consists in knowing facts and rules, the job of a teacher being to make the domain-specific facts and rules explicit and convey them to the student, either by drill and practice or by coaching, depending on the complexity of the subject to be taught. If that were indeed the way the mind works, the teacher could transfer his facts and rules to the computer, which could replace him as drill sergeant and coach. But since understanding doesn't consist of facts and rules, the hope that the computer will eventually replace the teacher is fundamentally misguided.

That is not to say that computer tutors have no proper place in the classroom. It follows from our description of skill acquisition that, contrary to current avantgarde opinion, there is indeed nothing wrong with using computers as drill sergeants. There is no reason to sneer when the computer is used as "a 'teaching' machine programmed to put children through their paces in arithmetic and spelling"[11] or to think of the use of the computer for drill and practice, as Seymour Papert, the creator of LOGO, does, as an instance of the QWERTY phenomenon—getting stuck like the typewriter keyboard in an early and inappropriate use of a new technology.

Wherever procedures are learned, computers can serve as diagnostic aids. John Seely Brown's use of the computer to tutor subtraction, and to diagnose and classify more than ninety subtraction bugs, shows the power of the computer to facilitate the acquisition of procedural skills that involve following and debugging strict rules.[12] Brown and his co-workers at Xerox have developed subtraction bug hunting into such an art that they have been able to pinpoint the locations in the United States where particular subtraction bugs thrive. They have suggested that students introduce such buggy rules when they try to account for their mistakes, and they have even been able to correlate students' use of a particular aberrant rule with his or her absence from school on the particular day when a certain application of the rule was taught.

As in the case of simulation, the only danger in the use of the computer for drill and practice and for diagnosis arises from the temptation to overemphasize the sort of training in which the computer works, precisely because it works so well. The efficiency of the computer—the way it provides tireless and non-judgmental repetition, instant feedback, different problems for each student, updated records of student progress, and, at least for the present, high motivation—encourages the expansion of that part of the curriculum where drill and practice are appropriate. Under such pressure mathematics might degenerate into addition and subtraction, English into spelling and punctuation, and history into dates and places. *This* is all that is sinister about the success of computers in managing drill and practice.

Drill and practice seem a counterproductive use of computer

technology to Papert only because he thinks of intelligence as simply getting the rule. If our minds were like computers they would first acquire a perhaps slightly erroneous rule, next get the rule debugged, and then use it accurately thereafter. Thus, if minds were machines, it would be incomprehensible that drill and practice are needed at all. The simple fact that even brilliant students need to practice to acquire the ability to do grammar or subtraction and that athletes and performers have to continue to practice even after they have mastered a domain suggests that something fundamental has been left out of Papert's Platonic position. In fact, *four* different functions of repetition have been ignored. First, even in subjects like spelling, drill is required simply to fix the rule in memory. Computers, by contrast, remember instantly and perfectly. Second, in subjects like subtraction, the beginner has to learn what differences are irrelevant (for example, that all cases of having to borrow 1 from the next column are the same no matter which numbers are involved) and which differences make a difference (that, for example, one cannot borrow from the next column if it is zero). That amounts to debugging the rules. Third, students must learn that some features in the context, such as the physical size and the orientation of the numbers, are irrelevant, while others, such as position, are crucial. They must practice to decontextualize, whereas computers have no context to worry about. Finally, as our skill model makes clear, practice is necessary even for the expert, since by continually exercising his skill the expert, who isn't employing rules at all, develops a more and more refined repertoire of experiences to draw upon.

Thus there is no reason to denigrate drill and practice as opposed to learning by acquiring and debugging rules. If computers can put students through their paces more painlessly than traditional methods, more power to them—provided, of course, that the cost of the hardware and especially the software is justified by the improvements the computer offers over conventional workbooks, and that the subject matter can be appropriately presented in a drill and practice format.

A step beyond drill and practice, but still committed to the rule-following view of mind, we find branch and test systems. These systems, perhaps best exemplified by Control Data's appropriately named PLATO system, assume that acquiring knowledge consists of learning prespecified rules and data. At each point the user is presented with a multiple choice situation and, depending on his response, is sent either forward to new material or back to relearn a fact or rule.

Branch and test systems can be very effective, for upon their highly structured substrate powerful graphics and intellectual tools can be laid. That is true of PLATO, the paradigm computer teaching system and a candidate for widespread use in the computerized classroom of the future. But branch and test systems like the core of PLATO, Micro-PLATO—the part of PLATO that runs on microprocessors—are highly ordered and choice-oriented environments that encourage the organization of knowledge and curricula into static patterns. PLATO, in spite of its other potentials, is used primarily to arrange and impart curricula in such a structured manner.

The problem with such systems is not that they don't have a place—they are often very appropriate means of conveying information—but that their place may be more in training than in education. In the words of Harvard's Judah Schwartz: "Although computer-assisted instruction is no longer thought to be a promising route to a golden age of education (except by some thoughtless and greedy purveyors of software), it does seem to have many uses for training."[13] Most critics agree that what is lost in such environments is the process by which the student learns to see connections and similarities for himself and to make his own choices. All that we then have is a program used to shape the student's mind to conform to a prespecified body of knowledge.

The military appears to recognize an important feature of branch and test, which we in the civilian world should clearly understand. The distinction between education, a process aimed at drawing out the abilities of the student, and training, in which the student is learning to negotiate a structured domain, is crucial. We'll illustrate the difference by comparing two videodisk-based branch and test training systems, both designed for the army by Litton Industries.

The first, intended only as a demonstration system but nevertheless a good example, uses the interactive branch and test capacities of a computerized videodisk to train soldiers to a minimum level of competence in diagnosing jeep malfunctions. Competence, in this case, means the ability to find and repair simple problems that would prevent a jeep from running. The designers of the system do not presume to impart the expertise of a master mechanic.

In the second, the army is using the same sort of interactive videodisk technology to teach "leadership and counseling from a platoon leader's standpoint." Film vignettes, the interactive capabilities of the disk, and branching are used to create a simulation in which the trainee is able to make decisions from a pre-specified set of alternatives at prespecified "choice points" and receive immediate feedback on the adequacy of his selected choice. In this case the student is being "trained" in an aspect of human relations—leadership and counciling—that cannot, like jeep repair, be partially abstracted from the everyday unstructured world. The system will teach the student to respond with one of a preprogrammed set of canned responses. That may be desirable in the army, where the leadership being constructed is a subordinate and merely competent bureaucratic leadership, but it is hardly desirable in the larger unstructured world of democratic society.

More flexible kinds of computer tutors, based upon attempts to represent the student's perspective, are called coaching systems. Such systems are being developed by John Seely Brown's AI group at Xerox PARC. We asked Richard Burton, an associate of Brown, to explain the current state of research at Xerox. He replied:

> You could view the coaching system as an extension of the help key. . . . What the intelligent coach is trying to do is to develop a model of what the student is doing so that, when he pushes that key, it has a better idea of what to tell him.

> *OK. How do you proceed?*

> There are several ways to track the student. The more complicated way is to try to intuit what the student's goals are, and you can do that by having a model of what general goals are and trying to parse his actions into a general goal plan and infer his goals. And once you infer his goals you can try to give help.

> *As you know, little progress has been made in the construction of systems that can infer goals within unstructured areas, for that progress would presuppose a satisfactory model of background understanding. Where, then, has progress been made?*

> Where you win . . . is where you know what the student is trying to do because you assigned it in the problem, so you don't have

to infer his goals, so that makes it a little bit easier. Like in geometry, you know he's trying to prove a particular theorem. In general, inferring someone's intentions is hard, and it helps a lot to know ahead of time what kind of things are likely.

Xerox's coaching successes have been in closed and predictable domains. Consider their best-known coach, designed to help students improve their play on a PLATO game called *How the West Was Won*. The game forms a closed micro-world. The coach can simply wait to interject its advice until the student uses a less than optimal strategy or misses an opportunity. At Xerox the same strategy is being used in teaching LISP, a programming language.

But will the same strategy work here, in the open-ended environment of a general-purpose programming language like LISP?

It's certainly harder. The idea is that you could build it incrementally, so it would know about parenthesis errors and the names and uses of certain basic functions. If I happen to make a mistake which it knows about it'll at that point come in, and all the rest of the time it'll just sit there and I won't know it's there.

A LISP tutor that understands the syntax of the language and corrects the programmer whenever he attempts to violate it is, as Burton has said, "just an extension of the help key." But the step from parenthesis errors to the kind of tutoring that requires a model of the student's intentions is a step outside the closed domain of the micro-world. It is not a matter of "increments," and there is no reason to believe that a full-scale LISP tutor will ever be built.

Still, with tools and machines becoming increasingly complex, there are ever more ways of using them incorrectly, or simply in a less than optimal fashion. It would certainly be valuable to have coaching systems that could engage their users in a sort of on-the-job training. Word processors, for example, could perhaps help their users become more expert in their operation. An intelligent "help" facility might note that the user always deleted by using the backspace key and infer that he didn't know how to delete by words, lines, and sentences.

That is the short-term goal at Xerox, where, Burton told us, researchers are looking forward to working coaching into "all kinds of training machines and instrumentation. Tanks maybe. . . . Right now we're worried mostly about copiers." But a recent study of human–machine communication argues that even the relatively tractable problems of automated coaching for users of machines like copiers may be incredibly difficult, for the machines do not share the real-world *situation* of their users. A copier, for example, has no way of understanding what its user is trying to do. It may be programmed to expect the user to put an entire manuscript into the input hopper, and may give advice accordingly. But the user, thinking of more primitive copiers unequipped with such hoppers, may have in mind a one-sheet-at-a-time operation. In such cases, far from aiding the inexperienced user, coaching systems may only initiate a "dialogue of the deaf" that further confounds the confused human being.[14]

Yet because computers are so powerful and so logical, it seems there must be a way to use them to foster sophisticated understanding and high levels of skill. It is that hope which makes both those who want to use the computer as tutor and those who want to use it as tutee condemn current software as too conservative. Our five-stage model of skill acquisition, however, enables us to understand why progress in teaching higher levels of skill acquisition has not taken place and to cast a cold eye on such hopes.

First, let us look more comprehensively at the use of computer as tutor. The assumption behind CAI is that the success of computerized instruction should be extensible to areas where what is required is a real understanding of the student and the domain to be taught. The success of AI programs, it is claimed, makes such an extension possible. A recent report commissioned by the National Academy of Sciences is based on the assumption that AI has been a success and will continue to forge ahead. The report begins:

> [W]ork in artificial intelligence and the cognitive sciences has set the stage for qualitatively new applications of technology to education. What is required to move forward is increased support for basic interdisciplinary research, focused by the development of advanced learning systems employing the methodologies and equipment of artificial intelligence.[15]

Such claims should give us pause. If using AI to help tutor copier use is difficult, imagine the problems with making a machine tutor a real-world subject. It would require giving the computer not only an understanding of the domain to be taught but an understanding of what the student already knows and a way of inferring how he is conceptualizing the problem. Lacking such real understanding, the computer, like a talentless teacher, will fail to pinpoint the student's confusions and will not be able to draw on the student's background understanding to achieve breakthroughs.

For example, if one wishes to educate, not simply train, a student in physics, one has to share the commonsense physics the student brings to the learning situation. Commonsense physics is our understanding of why things bend or break, move or don't, bounce or shatter, and so on. That everyday understanding has turned out to be extremely hard to spell out in a set of facts and rules. When one tries, one either requires more common sense to understand the facts and rules one finds or produces formulas of such complexity that it seems unlikely that they are in a child's mind. In fact, there may be no theory of commonsense physics at all. By playing with all sorts of liquids and solids for several years the child may simply have built up a repertoire of typical cases of solids and liquids and typical skilled responses to their typical behavior in typical circumstances. When that experience is coupled with what seems to be an innate human ability to recognize a case at hand as similar to a learned typical case without decomposition into features and rules, commonsense physics is the result. Anyone skilled at getting around in the world has learned that to keep something moving you have to keep pushing it. The teacher naturally appeals to such intuitions when diagnosing a student's difficulty with problems in which, for example, momentum is conserved.

Papert and Minsky give an excellent example of the sort of know-how that makes up commonsense physics:

> Many problems arise in experiments on machine intelligence because things obvious to any person are not represented in any programs. One can pull with a string, but one cannot push with one. One cannot push with a thin wire, either. A taut inextensible cord will break under a very small lateral force. Pushing something affects first its speed; only indirectly its position! Simple facts like these . . . have not been faced up to until now.[16]

And now, even though such problems have been faced up to for a decade, no one in AI has a clue how to deal with them.

Spelling out a teacher's understanding of physics—an under-standing partly conceptual and partly embodied in his or her mastery of skills for functioning in the physical world—would seem a hopeless task given the years of experience that have gone into the teacher's understanding of the field, not to mention the time the teacher spent as a child developing an intuitive feel for such things as solids and liquids. But the Socratic assumption is invoked, usually as self-evident, to save AI and CAI researchers from despair. After all, if the child can come to understand commonsense physics, one ought to be able to specify the facts the child knows and the rules he uses to relate them, and so make a model of the child's knowledge—which, of course, could then be updated with more and more sophisticated rules as the child learns to debug his earlier hypotheses. Likewise, the physics teacher, since he understands physics, must already have a program for that domain, which we simply have to extract and put into the teaching system.

Researchers admit that extracting and representing common-sense understanding will be difficult. Minsky noted ten years ago:

> Just constructing a knowledge base is a major intellectual research problem. . . . We still know far too little about the contents and structure of commonsense knowledge. A "minimal" commonsense system must "know" something about cause-and-effect, time, purpose, locality, process, and types of knowledge. We need a serious epistemological research effort in this area.[17]

But perhaps the problem is more than difficult. Philosophers from Plato to Piaget have carried on serious epistemological research in this area for two thousand years without notable success. That, plus the fact that no significant progress in AI has been reported since the commonsense knowledge problem surfaced a decade ago, suggests that, as our five-stage model of skill acquisition predicts, there is a limit to how far one can go with a model of everyday know-how based on the sorts of rules and features people can report.

The work of Patrick Suppes of Stanford University provides a cautionary tale of high hopes, disappointing results, and finally an appeal to traditional philosophical assumptions to sanction further research in CAI. Twenty years ago Suppes was one of the pioneer researchers in, and an outspoken enthusiast for, CAI. On the basis of his development of some of the earliest successful drill and practice programs for arithmetic he predicted that "in a few more years millions of school children will have access to what Philip of Macedon's son, Alexander, enjoyed as a royal prerogative: the personal services of a tutor as well informed and responsive as Aristotle."[18] But, as is often the case in fields related to AI, that optimism turned out to be another instance of the first-step fallacy. As an authority on CAI recently remarked: "The revolution predicted for education 25 years ago— when it was thought that computers soon would replace teachers as the primary source of instruction—remains elusive."[19]

During the two decades since his prediction, Suppes has developed highly successful programs in a discipline ideally suited for sophisticated drill and practice: mathematical logic. In recognizing and constructing proofs, there are clearly right or wrong answers, errors are easy to recognize, and commonsense physical knowledge, not to mention the social dimension of human life, is irrelevant. But even in this area the programs never cross the gap between drill and practice and coaching, between training in logical techniques and understanding the conceptual structure of the field. There is an art to writing short and elegant proofs, and intuition is required to know when to attempt to write one. Suppes's programs do not even attempt to teach that art. They tell the student when his proof is valid and when it is incorrect, and give hints as to what rule to use next. They also give tests and determine from the scores when the student is ready to go on to more difficult material. However, as they do not take into account situational elements but only objective features, and in no way illuminate relevant issues or appropriate strategies, they remain drill sergeants, not coaches. And even in this very restricted subject, which reminds one of the narrow domains of expert systems rather than the broad areas addressed by AI, limits on the computer's capabilities gradually became obvious. An Aristotle-like tutor turned out to be far out of reach.

In a recent article Suppes acknowledged that computers will not be first-rate teachers unless researchers can solve four fundamental problems: the need to talk, to listen, to know, and to coach. Those desiderata reveal why computerized coaches must remain a dream as long as computers cannot develop skills and cannot share the human form of life. We must look at each difficulty in detail if we are to understand why it is futile to hope to use the computer tutor as more than a drill sergeant.

The first problem Suppes lists is that of getting computers to talk:

> We have the capacity for the computer to talk. What we need, however, is a better theory about what is to be said. For example, when I serve as a tutor, teaching one of you, or when one of you is teaching me, intuitively and naturally we follow cues and say things to each other without having an explicit theory of how we say what we say. We speak as part of our humanness, instinctively, on the basis of our past experience. But to get a computer to talk appropriately, we need an explicit theory of talking.[20]

Unfortunately, there is no such theory and no reason to expect one to exist. Suppes acknowledges that conversational skill is intuitive, based on past experiences. Thus it is at level five of our five-stage model. No wonder the search for a formalizable theory of dialogue—the kind Suppes's project requires—has been conducted without notable progress for more than a decade by linguists attempting to produce a theory of pragmatics, that is, of the way language is used.

The second problem is one of continuous speech understanding. As Suppes puts it:

> The aspect of dialogue that is technically difficult for us at the present time, even more than talking, is that of listening. Without any question, the problem of defining computer hardware and software that can listen to a student talk is much more difficult than having the computer talk to the student.[21]

Understanding continuous speech is certainly a skill in which we are all intuitive experts. As one might expect, the attempt to find a formal theory that would enable a computer to exhibit this skill has been an outstanding disappointment in a field riddled with disappointments. Continuous speech recognition seems to be a skill that resists analysis into features and rules. What we hear does not correspond to the features of the sound stream. Depending on the context and on expectations, one hears a certain stream of sound as "I scream" or "ice cream," and so hears a space or pause in one of two different places, although there is no pause in the sound stream at all. One expert effectively emphasized the different ways the same stream of sound can be heard: "It isn't easy to wreck a nice beach."[22]

The most successful attempt to use a computer for continuous speech recognition was that of Newell and Simon's group at Carnegie–Mellon, and it was not a great success. As is usual in the field, no one tried to analyze or document the reason, but it is generally agreed that although HEARSAY, the CMU continuous speech recognition system, did manage to meet the stipulated condition of recognizing a limited number of words uttered by a speaker to whom the computer had been pretuned, the techniques used pushed computer capacity to the limit and did not show promise that further work in the same direction on bigger and faster machines would lead to much improvement.

The efficient and relevant representation of commonsense knowledge is essential in almost any domain outside of logic and grammar. So we find Suppes next noting:

> To have an effective computer-based system of instruction, we must transcend mindless talking and listening and learn to understand and use a large knowledge base. For example, if we were simply to require information retrieval from a knowledge base, it would be relatively simple in the future to put the entire Library of Congress in every elementary school. . . .
>
> A different and more difficult question is how to get the sizable knowledge base to interact with the student. As we come to understand how to handle such a knowledge base, the school computer of the future should be able to answer any wayward question that the student might like to ask.[23]

If the computer could do that, it would have solved a version of the frame problem, that is, ability to see the relevance of each part of its knowledge base to the rest of its knowledge. But as we saw in our discussion of AI, no such solution is in sight.

Finally, Suppes arrives at coaching, without which a computer could hardly substitute for an inexperienced teacher, let alone an Aristotle:

> The fourth problem, and in many ways the least-developed feature of this technology, is the theory of learning and instruction. Even if you can make the computer talk, listen, and adequately handle a large knowledge data base, we still need to develop an explicit theory of learning and instruction. In teaching a student, young or old, a given subject matter or a given skill, a computer-based

learning system can record anything the student does. It can know cognitively an enormous amount of information about the student. The problem is how to use this information wisely, skillfully, and efficiently to teach the student. This is something that the very best human tutor does well, even though he does not understand at all how he does it, just as he does not understand how he talks. None of us understands how we talk and none of us understands how we intuitively interact with someone we are teaching on a one-to-one basis.[24]

What is interesting about Suppes's acknowledgment of all four areas of difficulty is his mixture of respect for our intuitive expertise based on experience and the typical philosopher's assumption that a formal theory underlies our intuitive skill, or at least that a theory spelling out such a skill in terms of features and rules must be possible. That assumption sustains his optimism that these difficulties are opportunities in disguise—opportunities to apply for more grants to push forward with the perennial philosophical task of making explicit the rules or theories underlying our skillful and intuitive capacities. Thus in the face of the unsurmounted and apparently insurmountable difficulties that have brought AI to a standstill, Suppes is full of hope: "We are sitting on the edge of a revolution in the way in which instruction is delivered to students of all ages and varieties. . . . I hope that the Federal government will provide strong support for this constructive direction of change throughout the rest of this century."[25]

The report commissioned by the National Academy of Sciences echoes that misleading optimism. In proposing further research into "expert coaching systems," the report acknowledges that "effective coaching . . . requires knowledge about how and when to intervene"[26] but then goes on to make the characteristic assumption that such knowledge consists of unconscious rules: "Although such knowledge is usually held tacitly, even by master teachers, existing computer-based coaching systems have begun to characterize this kind of knowledge as a collection of rules that govern computer intervention."[27] The report also repeats the unfounded prediction that "parallel research in cognitive science and artificial intelligence is within reach of developing intelligent diagnostic, coaching, and discovery learning systems for a variety of subjects."[28]

Our model of skill acquisition predicts and explains both the impasse in building computer tutors and AI optimism. The optimism arises when one takes the first step: a successful use of the computer for drill and practice to teach beginners some subject. But as soon as one gets to level two, where situational elements and judgment are involved, one runs into a stone wall. If our experience of skill acquisition is to be trusted—and we have nothing else to trust—our everyday expertise is not "stored" in our mind in terms of facts and rules at all, but in our memories of past situations we have already successfully confronted.

Since computers used as tutors can successfully implement only drill/practice and branch/test training systems and thus teach novice or, at best, competent performance, they reinforce rather than reduce the danger of producing the sort of expert novices many feel our schools already encourage. As the report commissioned by the National Academy of Sciences notes: "New learning systems themselves can become the carriers of cognitive theory and new principles of pedagogy into classrooms and homes."[29] Thus instead of remedying inadequate education, CAI that attempts coaching could easily become part of the problem.

The real danger of CAI is not that our children will become programmed by drill and practice programs as in *1984*, as Papert prophesied on a recent "Nova" program. The danger is in trying to teach only what can be rationalized rather than admitting that the beginning student can use rules only up to a point, after which he must be allowed to pass beyond analysis to higher stages of skill acquisition, where human tutors can point out prototypes and where apprenticeship and practice alone can produce expertise.

The Computer as Tutee

The same information processing model of the mind that leads people to try to replace teachers with computers supports the idea of using the computer as tutee. Instead of assuming that the teacher's knowledge of a domain is a program that can be made explicit, put into a computer and taught to the student, the student is assumed to acquire knowledge (that is, a program) in the process of programming the computer. Learning and learning to program are the same thing. As Taylor puts it:

To use the computer as *tutee* is to tutor the computer; for that, the student or teacher doing the tutoring must learn to program, to talk to the computer in a language it understands. The benefits are several. First, because you can't teach what you don't understand, the human tutor will learn what he or she is trying to teach the computer. [Note the Platonic assumption that understanding something means being able to state it in explicit rules.] Second, by trying to realize broad teaching goals through software constructed from the narrow capabilities of computer logic, the human tutor of the computer will learn something both about how computers work and how his or her own thinking works.[30]

In that view one learns by constructing and debugging a program. Seymour Papert is the most articulate exponent of such a cognitivist, computational model of human thinking, which he calls the epistemological view. Like Leibniz, he thinks even physical skills are implicit theories. "Our strategy," he tells us, "is to make visible even to children the fact that learning a physical skill has much in common with building a scientific theory."[31]

The microcomputer reinforces the attraction of the cognitivist's model of thinking, and Papert's brilliant insight is that children can master that way of thinking by actually programming the computer, which, since it can deal only with data and rules, is an epistemological engine *par excellence.* Programming the computer would, in Papert's view, require the child to articulate his own program by reflecting on and naming the features he is picking out in his environment and by making explicit the procedures he is using to relate those features to events in the learning domain. Papert says:

> I have invented ways to take educational advantage of the opportunities to master the art of *deliberately* thinking like a computer, according, for example, to the stereotype of a computer program that proceeds in a step-by-step, literal, mechanical fashion. [W]hat is most important in this is that through these experiences children would be serving their apprenticeships as epistemologists, that is to say learning to think articulately about thinking.[32]

Papert is dramatic and convincing when he points out the revolutionary effect that giving the child an explicit grasp of the cognitivist approach to the mind would have on education.

> We are at a point in the history of education when radical change is possible, and the possibility for that change is directly tied to

the impact of the computer. Today what is offered in the education "market" is largely determined by what is acceptable to a sluggish and conservative system. But this is where the computer presence is in the process of creating an environment for change.[33]

And like a true revolutionary, Papert sees that actually implementing his cognitivist ideas would transform our understanding of ourselves and of our whole society:

> In a computer-rich world, computer languages that simultaneously provide a means of control over the computer and offer new and powerful descriptive languages for thinking will undoubtedly be carried into the general culture. They will have a particular effect on our language for describing ourselves and our learning.[34]

Because the stakes are high, it is very important to look at both the power and the limitations of Papert's cognitivist view of education before embracing his educational reform. If our critique is to be constructive rather than carping, it will have to be based on a model of the mind that points up the cognitivists' insights as well as their systematic oversights.

Papert notes that "many people will argue that overly analytic, verbalized thinking is counterproductive even if it is deliberately chosen."[35] But he does not take this "flimsy" objection seriously. Indeed, why should he? In our culture such objections are usually the purview of defenders of mystical intuition, and the battle against them was won long ago by procedural thinkers from Plato to Leibniz. Unless one can provide a concrete alternative to the dominant view that to learn is to acquire a mental program, it follows logically that one should use the computer as tutee to aid the student in perfecting his ability to think procedurally. Moreover, such techniques can and should be generalized to all areas of education, including even the playground.

To see the limitations of that view, we must question the assumption that computers and people have similar thought processes, hence that learning a skill amounts to mastering a step-by-step procedure. Here we fly in the face of a tradition that seems to be based on solid evidence. But the philosophers and psychologists who allegedly possess that evidence have accurately described skills only at the moment when those skills became conspicuous. They have yet to notice that we only become aware of our skills when things are not going smoothly or when someone performing an experiment has given us a task in which we have no prior experience or skill. Then we are indeed dependent on analysis. However, if we let the phenomena of everyday, successful, skilled activity show itself as it is in itself, if we describe what the tradition has passed over, we find we have to abandon the view that a beginner starts with specific cases and, as he becomes more proficient, abstracts and interiorizes more and more sophisticated rules, or, as Papert puts it, that experience in particular situations is necessary only to improve the rules, "to trap and eliminate bugs."[36] Skill acquisition moves in just the opposite direction: from abstract rules to particular cases.

Anyone beginning to acquire a skill in a new domain needs to learn to recognize basic features and rules for combining them and acting on them. So, for example, for learning addition algorithms Papert's model works perfectly: "Learning algorithms can be seen as a process of making, using, and fixing programs. When one adds multidigit numbers one is in fact acting as a computer."[37]

Moreover, there are advantages in getting the child to think about his own reasoning on the model of the computer:

> Trouble with adding is not seen as symptomatic of something else; it is trouble with the *procedure* of adding. For the computerist the procedure and the ways it can go wrong are fully as interesting and as conceptual as anything else. Moreover, *what* went wrong, namely the bugs, are not seen as mistakes to be avoided like the plague, but as an intrinsic part of the learning process.[38]

Another useful concept for educating beginners is the notion of a micro-world. The fact that the micro-world failed as a step toward modeling real-world understanding does not prevent it from being salvaged as a simplified environment in which the beginner can more easily pick out the features he needs to recognize, and in which the procedures he is learning apply automatically. "The use of the micro-worlds provides a model of a learning theory in which active learning consists of exploration by the learner of a micro-world sufficiently bounded and transparent for constructive exploration and yet sufficiently rich for significant discovery."[39]

All this is very persuasive. Still, one must remain critical. At the advanced-beginner stage the micro-world idea can already begin to get in the way of learning. If what the learner was acquiring were more and more sophisticated features and rules, then one could neglect situational elements and gradually complicate the micro-world by adding more features as the child developed greater skill. But if, as our skill model suggests, the learner is acquiring a repertoire of situational elements and of whole, real-world situations, then keeping the learner in a micro-world can actually be counterproductive. For example, it might help a beginner learn some basic ideas of chess if one simplified the rules—by making all exchanges forced as in checkers, let's say. One could still pick out and name features, such as center control and knight forks, but situational elements, such as unbalanced pawn structure, would be different, so that remembering prototypical examples of them would be useless in a real game. Likewise, in playing such games over and over one would not be acquiring a stock of prototypical *whole* real chess situations with their associated successful responses. Or, to take another illustrative example of a skill, driving in a parking lot might help a beginning driver learn to shift, but finally no simplified micro-world can substitute for driving on roads with other cars and pedestrians all around, since memories of concrete events and situations are what is required for expertise.

Although the micro-world approach may well be a dead end even for advanced beginners, the idea of the student as tutor can still be helpful. Since the student needs to learn to recognize situational elements, he or she might well be led to find them by acting as teacher or coach. Nevertheless, while one can name situational elements and recite ways to use them, one cannot *program* them. As we saw in discussing the world of the advanced beginner, situational elements like engine sound and unbalanced pawn structure can be recognized by similarity to prototypes, but no one has any idea how they could be decomposed into the sort of objective features required by a computer program.

Now we can see why naming elements and verbalizing procedures are sometimes but not always helpful. We can agree with Papert that "a fundamental problem for the theory of mathematical education is to identify and name the concepts needed to enable the beginner to discuss his mathematical thinking in a clear articulate way. And when we know such concepts we may want to seek out (or invent!) areas of mathematical work which exemplify these concepts particularly well."[40] Even the advanced beginner, when passing on to competence, still has some use for analysis and verbalization. One can learn the names of specific strategies and the features and situational elements suggesting which strategy to apply. Using programming, if only as a metaphor, might help develop that analytic planning capacity.

Papert's proposals are appropriate up to this point. But he wants to generalize the need for verbalization to all levels of skill:

> I believe in articulate discussion (in monologue or dialogue) of how one solves problems, of why one goofed that one, of what gaps or deformations exist in one's knowledge and of what could be done about it. I shall defend this belief against two quite distinct objections. One objection says: *"it's impossible to verbalize;* problems are solved by intuitive acts of insight and these cannot be articulated."* The other objection says: *"it's bad to verbalize;* remember the centipede who was paralyzed when the toad asked which leg came after which."[41]

Being told that whatever you know can be verbalized or, as Taylor put it, you can't teach what you don't understand and you don't understand something unless you can program it, may remind you of a time in school when you knew something perfectly well but your teacher claimed you didn't know it because you couldn't explain how you got your answer. Of course, sometimes the teacher was right. If you had not yet had experience with a certain type of problem, getting the right answer would have been just a lucky guess, but if you had had considerable experience in a certain type of situation and had a good record for getting the right answer, it was infuriating to be told that because you couldn't explain how you got your answer you didn't understand. You no doubt felt that such intuition should be praised, not ridiculed.

In our rationalistic tradition even Nobel scientists face that sort of problem. The physicist Richard Feynman, for example, had trouble getting his views accepted by the scientific community because he couldn't explain how he got his answers. Freeman Dyson, a fellow physicist who took on the role of Feynman's interpreter, writes:

> The reason Dick's physics was so hard for the ordinary physicists to grasp was that he did not use equations. . . . He had a physical picture of the way things happen, and the picture gave him the

solutions directly with a minimum of calculation. It was no wonder that people who had spent their lives solving equations were baffled by him. Their minds were analytical; his was pictorial.[42]

Papert's cognitivist perspective has no place for such nonanalytical understanding.

Our model explains why, in moving to proficiency, where the learner must see whole patterns and remember them, analysis and verbalization no longer help but actually get in the way. One *could* name issues and whole patterns; there is nothing mystical or ineffable about them. But since there are probably more subtly differentiated patterns in the mind of, say, a chess grandmaster than we have words in our whole vocabulary, pointing them out and naming them is a hopeless task. More important, since pattern storage and retrieval take place without conscious awareness, there is no point in having names for the patterns learned. To see this it helps to remember that in linguistics we have a huge vocabulary for describing grammar, tense, aspect, conjugation, declension, and so on, and that being able to pick out such features and rules does seem to help a beginner learn a second language. For the beginner it might well be helpful to program a computer to produce sentences in a simplified grammar of the language being learned. But, as anyone who has learned a foreign language knows, such knowledge of vocabulary and rules does not create proficiency. One needs experience speaking, reading, and listening. Only then can one finally stop thinking of rules and speak flexibly and fluently—even sometimes breaking the rules—in a wide variety of situations.

Thinking of oneself as a computer acquiring and naming features and procedures might well accelerate the passage from beginner to advanced beginner, and it can still be a useful metaphor in passing from advanced beginner to competence. But it follows from our model of skill acquisition that thinking like a computer will *retard* passage to the higher levels of proficiency and expertise. Since analytic, verbalized thinking is counterproductive at those higher stages, there are solid arguments that the computer running LOGO can be a dangerous tutee.

The Risks of the Machine View of Mind

The debate concerning the benefits and risks of the use of the computer as tutor or tutee can and, given the pressure of time, must be settled independently of the question of whether at some deep level the mind operates according to rules. For education the crucial question is not whether skills are tacit theories, as Leibniz, Piaget, Polanyi, and Papert claim—and we doubt— but whether it facilitates learning to think of skills that way.

Our contention is that whether or not there is a tacit theory underlying expertise, it is counterproductive to base an educational program on such an idea. Even if there are rules underlying expertise, the rules to which the expert has access are not the rules that generate his expertise, and so learning and acting on the rules the expert can formulate will not improve performance. Moreover, trying to find rules or procedures in a domain often stands in the way of learning even at the earliest stages. True to our conviction that an example equals a thousand inferences, we shall use illustrations, rather as parables, to make these two points.

In the Air Force, instructor pilots teach beginning pilots how to scan their instruments. The instructor pilots teach the rule for instrument scanning that they themselves were taught and, as far as they know, still use. At one point, however, Air Force psychologists studied the eye movements of the instructors during simulated flight and found, to everyone's surprise, that the instructor pilots were not following the rule they were teaching.[43] In fact, as far as the psychologists could determine, they were not following any rule at all. If one accepts our five-stage model of skill acquisition, that should come as no surprise. The instructors, after years of experience, had learned to scan the instruments in flexible and situationally appropriate ways.

Now suppose that the instructor pilot's instrument scanning rule is put into a CAI program. The computer tutor now begins, like the instructor pilots, by drilling the beginners in applying the rule. Moreover, the computer tests the beginners by asking them questions and following their eye movements to be sure they have learned the rule and are applying it correctly. So far so good. But eventually the beginner will be ready to make the leap to situational understanding, achieving proficiency by leaving behind any awareness of rules and, like the instructor pilots who abandoned their rule without realizing it, responding immediately to situations perceived as similar to those previously encountered. At that point, since the process by which we recognize similarity cannot be made explicit as rules, and since no one knows how to find any other rules, there is nothing more for the computer tutor to teach. The proficient performer is on his own.

If, however, one insists on extending the CAI method to higher levels of skill acquisition based on its success in teaching beginners, we get an educational horror story. The computer tutor, like the sorcerer's apprentice, continues to check the protocols and eye movements of the student pilot and forces him to return to the rule whenever he starts to violate it. In a slightly more elaborate nightmare, the computer has been programmed with more and more sophisticated rules and features for the student to learn. In either case the student is prevented by the accuracy, relentlessness, and record-keeping powers of the computer tutor from making the transition from rule-following, analytic competence to intuitive proficiency and expertise.

That is no mere bogeyman. Expert systems are actually being developed to teach doctors the huge number of rules that expert system builders have "extracted" from experts in the medical domain. GUIDON is such a teaching system:

> The GUIDON system developed by Clancey at Stanford exploits the MYCIN knowledge base about meningitis and bacteremia to teach both facts and problem-solving strategies. MYCIN's 450 diagnostic rules were not modified, but were augmented by an additional 200 rules that included methods for guiding the dialogue with the student, presenting diagnostic strategies, constructing a student model, and responding to the student's initiative.[44]

One can only hope that someone has the sense to disconnect the doctor from the system as soon as he or she has reached the advanced beginner stage. Otherwise such CAI techniques could become a disastrous educational practice, even in the unlikely case that it turns out that cognitivism is correct and that experts follow unconscious and inaccessible programs.

In most disciplines expertise is possible only if the tutor can allow the student, at the appropriate stage, to quiet the conscious analytic mind and act intuitively, whether the brain is a computer with a program or not. In other fields one cannot even begin to learn if one thinks of oneself as an information processor extracting a rule that describes the structure of the domain.

This is no "flimsy" objection but the conclusion of psychological experiments performed by Lee Brooks and published in an important paper, "Nonanalytic Concept Formation and Memory for Instances."[45] Brooks constructed two complicated artificial grammars and used a computer to generate two lists of strings of letters—one from each grammar. He then divided his subjects into two groups. The first was shown the list generated by grammar A and the list generated by grammar B. These subjects were given the task of abstracting the two sets of rules from the two sets of examples. The subjects in the second group were given the same two lists accompanied by additional information designed to prevent them from thinking that all the items on a list fell into a single category.

Each group was then tested to see what it had learned. The subjects in the first group had learned nothing since they were unable to abstract the arbitrary and complex rules used in generating the grammatical strings. What was surprising was what happened in the second group. These subjects were shown thirty new strings of letters which fell into three categories: Ten of these strings were generated by grammar A, ten by grammar B, and ten by neither grammar.

> Their job was to sort them into these three categories. Their initial response was . . . giggles or irritation together with an emphatic protestation that they didn't know what they were doing. [Yet] they were able to distinguish each of the three categories from one another at a level well above chance.[46]

Brooks concludes that in "the contrast between deliberate, verbal, analytic control processes and implicit, intuitive, nonanalytic processes . . . too loose a use of the word 'rule' has served to submerge the likely fact that much of our knowledge is a loose confederation of special cases in which our knowledge of the general is often overridden by our knowledge of the particular. . . . Stressing the nonanalytic, instance-oriented strategy could . . . under some circumstances allow the learner to deal with more complicated problems than would an analytic strategy."[47]

Brooks's work, among other things, led Donald Broadbent of Oxford University, one of the fathers of information processing psychology, to reexamine his view that skills are based on inference rules. In assessing the implications of his own experiments showing that subjects looking for rules do less well than subjects simply remembering results, he reviews Brooks's work and notes:

Brooks suggests a highly plausible theory. . . . [Subjects] can react on the basis of similarity between the situation now present and others met in the past. . . . Thus action based on matching the current situation to similar ones from the past will give better than chance performance.[48]

Broadbent concludes:

Performance based on verbalizable knowledge, and that which selects action by matching the situation to those in earlier experience, may be alternative modes of performance each with its own advantages.[49]

The moral of Brooks's and Broadbent's work for the use of the computer as tutee is obvious. Whatever the unconscious is doing—whether the brain is abstracting rules or not—thinking of oneself as a computer and therefore looking for rules can prevent the brain from doing its job, and so can stand in the way of learning.

In some areas at least, one must be especially careful *not* to think of oneself as a computer and *not* to think of learning as finding procedures, or one cannot even begin. It is ironic to find Papert claiming to be in agreement with Timothy Gallwey of *Inner Tennis* fame, a most articulate proponent of this point:

Gallwey encourages the learner to think of himself as made up of two selves: an analytic, verbal self and a more holistic, intuitive one. It is appropriate, he argues, that now one and now the other of these two selves should be in control; in fact, an important part of the learning process is teaching each "self" to know when to take over and when to leave it to the other. . . . Gallwey's strategy is to help learners learn how to make the choice for themselves, a perspective that is in line with the vision already suggested of the child as epistemologist, where the child is encouraged to become expert in recognizing and choosing among varying styles of thought.[50]

Papert implies that Gallwey believes one can use either the analytic or the intuitive approach at all levels of learning, whereas in truth Gallwey's method consists in helping the learner achieve mastery by preventing analytic thinking from the very start. *Our* model does suggest that, sometimes at least, the beginner should be encouraged to think like an epistemologist, but Gallwey's whole strategy consists in avoiding the trap of getting stuck in rational procedures, by bypassing the analytic mind and passing directly to proficient performance.

Papert and Gallwey represent two extreme approaches to skill acquisition. Papert tries to create a learning environment in which the learner is constantly faced with new problems and needs to discover new rules; he treats the learner as a perpetual beginner. Gallwey, on the other hand, would like to create a learning environment in which there are no problems at all and so never any need for analytic reflection. Our view is that at any stage of learning, problems may arise that require rational analytic thought, and the learner must discover ways to think them through. That is the value of Papert's computer model. Nonetheless, skill in any domain is measured by the performer's ability to act appropriately in situations that might once have been problems but are no longer problems and so do not require analytic reflection. This is Gallwey's insight. The risk of Gallwey's method is that it leaves the expert without the tools to solve new problems, but the risk of Papert's approach is far greater. It would leave the learner a perpetual beginner by encouraging dependence on rules and analysis, thereby blocking the acquisition of expertise.

GRANTING THAT computer literacy consists in knowing what sorts of skills and what levels of skill can and should be taught using computers, where should the literate educator stand on the question? After one has separated the hopes and grant proposals from the actual successes of such computer education pioneers as Brown, Suppes, Papert, Piestrup, and Schwartz, and after one has mapped their successes and failures upon a description of skill acquisition which predicts that they would occur just where they have in fact occurred, one realizes where to invest one's money and time.

Computers are marvelous tools which, when used as electronic blackboards, interactive simulators, and conjecture testers, greatly improve sociality and intuition in the classroom. Provided one does not narrow one's goal to forcing the student to think procedurally like a computerized problem-solver, there is no limit to the levels of skill that imaginative new learning environments may be able to foster. Computers are also useful as rule-following, literal-minded tutees, as long as one limits oneself to teaching elementary math and programming, as most LOGO users now do.

But the outlook for the computer as tutor is less bright. If one accepts our skill model, one is forced to conclude that the levels of skill appropriately taught using the computer are quite limited. At the beginning level the computer can be useful for drill and practice in subjects requiring nothing more than the memorization of facts, rules, and procedures such as spelling or subtraction. And in restricted areas, where trained competence, not educated expertise, is the goal, computers and interactive media like videodisks may indeed prove useful. However, one should not attempt to tutor any higher level of skill, for that would require giving logic machines skills that have proved to be beyond their capacities.

We have seen that the advocates of computers as tutors and tutees think, like Socrates and Plato, that we cannot teach what we do not understand and that we only understand what we can formulate in the sorts of rules and procedures used by a logic machine. If that were true, teachers could be gradually replaced by computers. But teachers are no doubt aware, and parents must become aware, that expertise in teaching does not consist in knowing complicated rules about their discipline and about coaching—what tips to give, when to keep silent, when to intervene—although teachers may have learned such rules in graduate school. What an expert teacher gains from experience is not more facts about some field plus rules of coaching of the sort he or she once explicitly followed as a beginner; rather, the teacher learns intuitively and spontaneously to draw on the commonsense knowledge and experience he or she shares with the student in order to provide the tips and examples needed by the advanced beginner. The teacher also learns how to motivate the involved practice by which a student gains expertise in any domain.

Chapter 6

Managerial Art and Management Science

The usefulness of decision analysis in making a wide variety of both private and public decisions has now been established.

> Ronald A. Howard
> "An Assessment of Decision Analysis" (1980)

Look, I'll admit it. I was one of the guys teaching all the quantitative methods with such vigor. I was part of the problem.

> Robert H. Hayes
> in "Overhauling America's
> Business Management,"
> *The New York Times Magazine* (1980)

AMERICAN MANAGEMENT has lost its worldwide preeminence. Once seen as the geniuses behind America's international power, our corporate managers are now chastised for America's stagnating productivity, aging and obsolete machinery, inferior but more expensive products. Much heralded books such as *In Search of Excellence*[1] and articles such as "Managing Our Way to Economic Decline"[2] hold that the modern American manager's overdependence on analytic thought and quantitative analysis is a principal cause of our current problems. As the anti-analytic bandwagon has begun to roll, advocates of Zen Buddhism, Jungian mysticism, and extrasensory perception have climbed aboard, and the young student of management must now wonder whether to head for Harvard or the Himalayas.

While analytic management was no doubt oversold in the 1950s and 1960s, when whiz kids with computerlike minds were controlling everything from General Motors to the Department of Defense, we must not now turn our back on detached deliberation and on tools such as mathematical modeling. We must integrate those scientific methods and computational tools into our more traditional, intuitive ways. We must, in short, establish the proper place of analysis and computation in managerial decision-making.

By now, many chroniclers of good management practice have noted that Japanese companies and some of America's most respected and successful companies as well are not heavy users of the modern mathematical and computer tools of management science.[3] Authorities generally do not delve into reasons why analysis is not adopted, other than to argue that effort put into mathematical modeling is expensive and time-consuming and too often replaces, rather than augments, more critical endeavors such as the cultivation of customers and the deepening of worker involvement.[4] This leaves open the possibility that what might be needed beyond those suggested improvements is better and more timely analytic methods, procedures capable of including "soft" considerations that are not easily quantified and that take into account the subjective knowledge of experienced managers. Indeed, propounding this as just the tonic needed to restore the sagging fortune of analytic management, a new breed of management scientist, a sort of knowledge engineer called a decision analyst, has put himself forward as savior of calculative rationality.

A top manager, perhaps already disenchanted with conventional quantitative methods, may suspect that this latest fad is just more snake oil. But he might find himself hard pressed to refute the assertion that by capturing expert knowledge in a mathematical model and then processing it systematically, accurately, objectively, and almost instantaneously—as only a computer can—his decision-making can be improved and made rational. Thus critics of formal models often are unable to justify their skepticism to themselves and their peers. What is needed is not further documentation that calculative analysis has failed but reasons *why* it does not work. Our skill acquisition model provides the explanation. An expert manager, deeply involved in his job and intimately familiar with his company, intuitively understands and decides, based on what has and has not worked in the past. He no longer forms his decisions using formulas applied to the facts, as he did as a novice or even a competent manager, and as is done by conventional mathematical models, nor does he plan the future as in decision analysis.

Detached deliberation and intuition need not be viewed as opposed alternatives, as is all too often the case in simplistic treatments. When properly used, they are productive team-mates. Soon we shall describe a kind of deliberation that smart, intuitive managers already certainly use: deliberation about their intuitive, experienced-based, holistic understanding.

Recognizing the difference between intuitive, experience-based understanding and analytic reasoning helps us understand why Japanese firms are often better managed than American ones. Japanese workers employed by large corporations typically stay with one company throughout their career, rise through the ranks, and, should they reach the top levels of management, are thoroughly familiar with all aspects of the company they manage. American managers, on the other hand, frequently change jobs in order to hasten their climb up the corporate ladder. What does the typical American manager bring with him when he changes companies? Not, unfortunately, much of the know-how he presumably acquired on the basis of concrete experience in his previous job. No two companies are exactly alike in personnel, problems, or philosophy. The manager's experiences in his old job must be translated into facts and general principles before they can be brought to bear in his new position. And, as we have seen, when holistic concrete experience is decomposed and transformed into rules, a great deal of its content is lost. As the transplanted manager consciously applies learned managerial techniques in his new job, he will be regressing to the managerial style of a competent executive, at best. Yet to some degree he has no choice; being unfamiliar with the specific characteristics of his new company, he is compelled to fall back on more abstract knowledge.

Naturally there are benefits associated with bringing in new blood. Traditional and perhaps nonproductive lines of authority can be broken, narrow-minded perspectives can be widened, and new energy can be injected into tired organizations. A newly hired manager can, with time, once more acquire sufficient concrete experience to become an intuitive expert. The period of adjustment depends, of course, on the similarity between situations. A high-ranking executive of an automobile company defecting to a competitor will still know his industry well and will probably even have some sense of the philosophy, style, tradition, and personnel of his new employer. But, at the other extreme, a retired military commander of proven administrative ability taking over the directorship of an art museum would not only have to start almost from scratch but might actually have his adaptation impeded by concrete memories of what worked and didn't work in the army.

To judge from recent American business experience, the costs of job-hopping seem to outweigh the benefits. Businesses with job-hopping executives suffer from management by abstract principle, while a few excellently managed American companies and many Japanese corporations thrive on involved management exhibiting deep understanding based on concrete experience.

A particularly pernicious example of relying on formulas and principles instead of real-life business experience is the current practice of making capital investment decisions through the use of discounted cash flow calculations. If capital investment is postponed for a year it is, in a certain sense, less costly than if made now. Money not spent now can be placed in a safe interest-bearing or profit-making investment, producing sufficient money for the capital expenditure, plus a surplus, a year in the future. As a result, especially when interest rates are high and sales low, capital investments should logically be postponed. This fiscal logic (called discounted cash flow to signify that the importance of money spent or earned in the distant future should be discounted with respect to costs or profits now) has become the dominant consideration in the scientific determination of capital goods investment policy. Valid as that reasoning is, it recognizes only one aspect of the very complex, competitive, uncertain business picture. Short-sighted and overly conservative investment policies result.

While other considerations going beyond the purely financial are sometimes factored into the investment decision calculations, the scientific combination of factors by means of formulas may well be one of the culprits behind our current business woes. What is needed instead is good old-fashioned management by know-how: the experience-gained, intuitive recognition of when the time is right for courageous investment policies, and the implementation of those policies without recourse to rationalization by formula. Such methods are reminiscent of the aggressive management practices that made American industry great in earlier times (and that today are more likely to be found in Japanese management methods). One input into the intuitive decision-making process might well be a discounted cash flow calculation, but the outcome of that calculation should merely be noted along with many other things and not implemented automatically.

Some intuitive managers, wishing to appear scientific, have found a way of using discounted cash flow methods while staying true to their own sense of purpose. The interest rate used in discounted cash flow formulas implicitly weights numerically the future relative to the present. The higher the interest assumed available in a safe investment, the stronger the bias against investments that do not yield large immediate returns. A high interest rate used in discounted cash flow calculations heavily discounts long-term returns relative to quick ones, while a low rate puts relatively more weight on the long-term returns. Certain oil company executives, realizing that without exploration and development of resources (a long-term investment) they will soon be out of the oil business, use a very low interest rate in evaluating long-term decisions, making all such investments relatively attractive but making larger future returns more desirable than smaller ones. Those same companies, when considering the acquisition of a new service station, use a high interest rate, reflecting their belief that the sooner the return, the better.

When discounted cash flow is applied in this manner, the critical choice of the interest rate becomes a matter of intuition about the true significance of the investment for the long-range health of the organization rather than a problem of predicting actual bank interest payments in the future. Accordingly, what passes for science is really managerial art. It seems a pity that a subterfuge such as this is necessary. It wouldn't be if managers fully appreciated their five-stage development from detached calculating novices to involved, intuitive experts.

A second modern scientific management technique has recently been criticized by Thomas Peters, an author of *In Search of Excellence*.[5] It is termed, often with reverence, long-range, strategic, or corporate planning. Thinking ahead might seem beyond reproach. But a comparison of what is involved in strategic planning with the way we behave in everyday life when facing situations where the future is clearly important yields vital differences. In daily life we do *not* stand back and consciously plan ahead. Instead, intensely involved in the present, we perform that action which experience has proved will work out satisfactorily in the long run. Coordinated behavior is assured through the medium of a unified style or what in business is sometimes called a philosophy.

In athletic competition, for example, one exploits a weakness without foreseeing exactly what the gain might be. Likewise, when we start to speak a sentence we generally do not know its conclusion, but experience shows that one will present itself when needed. When driving we rarely think explicitly about what might be beyond the next bend; we simply approach the curve at what experience has shown to be a prudent speed allowing safe adaptation to almost any contingency. The more skilled we become, the more we live in the present, recognizing that if we keep sensitive fingers on the pulse of current events and respond well now, the future will take care of itself. There is no reason why top management, in any but the most unusual and unfamiliar situations, should behave differently from other skilled individuals. For centuries managers coped with uncertainty about the future without using computer models.

Well-managed companies establish a guiding philosophy, which, accompanied by a vigilant assessment at all times of the present situation, suggests various decisions having long-range impacts. Flexibility and consistency are emphasized. It is interesting that, according to *Business Week,* "neither Johnson and Johnson, nor TRW, nor 3M—all regarded as forward thinking—has anyone on board called a corporate planner."[6] Strategic planning, which had its genesis at General Electric, has been abandoned there. The company's planning department, now down to eight people from thirty just four years ago, calls the concept of formal strategic planning archaic.[7]

Deliberation in Management

Experienced intuitive managers do not attempt to understand familiar problems and opportunities in purely analytic terms using calculative rationality, but realize that detached deliberation *about the validity of intuitions* will improve decision-making. Common as it is, little has been written about that conscious deliberative buttressing of nonconscious intuitive understanding, probably because detached deliberation is often incorrectly seen as an *alternative* to intuition.

The same experience-based recognition of similarity that produces the expert's intuitive understanding may also alert him to differences between the current situation and similar previous ones. Rarely will all salient features of a complex business situation exactly match those seen before. The intuitive decision-maker would like somehow to change the situation or else adjust his decision to take account of those perceived differences. He wonders: How important are these differences? What should I do about them?

A struggle commences, with two ways out. The decision-maker can reduce his current understanding to facts about the situation and then calculate, based on this decomposition, what to do about the differences. Management scientists embrace that calculative rationality, eagerly offering their mathematical and computational assistance. But, as our skill model shows, to follow that route is to degrade managerial understanding to competent at best.

Wishing to resist that reductionist temptation, the wise manager focuses upon the intuitively seen discrepancies between the current situation and one with which he would feel completely comfortable. He hopes to find ways of changing the situation that will keep all intuitively desirable options open while decreasing his uneasiness. That may not be possible if some disturbing elements are beyond his control, for example, abnormally high interest rates. If changing the situation is impossible, focusing on disturbing differences can awaken a further intuitive conceptualization of the situation, with its own associated decision. Should that happen, the manager would invent new options balancing the original intuitive decision and the newly conceived one. Thus a choice can be made with deliberation, yet without turning one's back on intuitive, holistic understanding.

Even when an intuitive decision seems obvious, it may not be right. Experts are fallible, and there are deliberative methods for protecting against errors that result from being too deeply enmeshed in a situation. When deeply involved, one views a situation from one perspective. One sees certain elements as salient, holds certain expectations, and makes decisions accordingly. With the passage of time, the perspective changes. A businessman content with the *status quo,* for example, may only dimly perceive a potential problem. As the problem develops, disturbing elements of the situation gain prominence; as those elements change, the nature of the difficulty takes shape. Finally the decision-maker clearly grasps the problem and knows what must be done. His clear-sightedness is the result of a long chain of events, each gradually modifying his understanding. If any event in the chain had been interpreted slightly differently, subsequent events would have been viewed differently also, and a whole different chain of interpretations culminating in an entirely different "obvious" decision might have resulted. For that reason two experts, even though they share a common background, can come to very different conclusions.

Aware that his current clear perception may well be the result of a chain of perspectives with one or more weak or questionable links and so might harbor the dangers of tunnel vision, the wise intuitive manager will attempt to dislodge his current understanding. He will do so by rethinking the chain of events that led him to see things the way he does, and at each stage he will intentionally focus upon elements not originally seen as important to see if there is an alternative intuitive interpretation. Generally, of course, there isn't, but sometimes that contemplative exercise will result in a reassessment of the current situation. Even if current understanding cannot be dislodged in this way, the wise manager will ask trusted aides for their perceptions of the situation and, should theirs differ from his own, will give their views a sympathetic hearing. For that reason, no conscientious manager wants to surround himself with "yes men." Should the process described above fail to undermine the manager's confidence in his own perceptions, the initially conceived decision can be implemented with increased assurance.

The management consultant, but not the management scientist, can play an important role here. While the scientist would seek facts and formulas about the problem, the consultant can serve as a facilitator for the exchange of intuitive ideas. Furthermore, he can offer his own perspective on the situation and recount relevant experiences from companies he has helped.

An intuitive manager will sometimes sense that nothing he has tried or experienced in a particular type of situation has turned out as well as he had hoped. Then he will talk to other experts to see if any of them have tried something different that worked out well in a similar situation.

Sometimes, but not often, an intuitive decision-maker finds himself torn between two equally compelling decisions. Presumably that occurs when the current situation resembles two prior experiences with differing associated decisions, and both come to mind. We have already discussed the possible compromise between those decisions, but sometimes they are incompatible. For example, an executive may be torn between a decision to act decisively or not to act at all, and a halfway measure may clearly be worse than either. Only a better understanding of the current situation can break the tie, so the decision-maker will delay if possible and seek clarification. More reports and data, within reason, cannot hurt, but much more important are real-life stories meaningful to the manager. Much of an executive's daily time, according to Henry Mintzberg's careful observations of managerial behavior, is spent seeking just that. Mintzberg observes that businessmen prefer concrete information, even gossip, speculation, and hearsay, to the abstracted summary information contained in routine reports flooding their offices.[8] His perception has been confirmed by Peters.[9] If a manager can afford the time, the decision will be put off until something is learned that leaves only one action intuitively compelling.

Suppose a manager's intuitive assessment of a situation still remains unshaken. Should it be trusted? Not necessarily, for the manager's experience-based intuitive understanding may conceivably depend on experience that is insufficient or no longer relevant. The manager may then have to discount his own intuitions as based on too little evidence, particularly when important matters must be decided. Or perhaps the manager will conclude that, while he has considerable experience with similar problems, events in the outside world have changed sufficiently to render those experiences of doubtful worth. In energy-intensive industries, for example, no amount of business experience prior to the energy crisis of 1973 would justify responding intuitively after that event. If the intuitive manager has reason to discount his expertise in a particular situation, he can fall back on the rational calculative approach of management science and anticipate at least a competent decision.

The modeling result, however, should be treated as just one

more possibly relevant input bearing on the problem, and certainly not as its definitive solution. Since models represent novice or, at best, competent understanding of unstructured problems, unquestioned acceptance of the recommendations of a mathematical model would degrade decision-making.

The kind of detached *deliberative rationality* that we have been describing is quite different from the detached *calculative rationality* of novice, advanced beginner, and competent managers. Those three levels of skill are all characterized by the conscious description of one's situation in terms of isolable component elements and by decisions arrived at by rule. The expert, consciously deliberating rationally about a decision as described above, is thinking about *the process and product of his intuitive understanding.* There may even be experts at thinking about their intuitive thinking, who would then have intuitions about the validity of their intuitions. A good management consultant is an expert facilitator of a manager's deliberative rationality. A good management scientist, on the other hand, attempts to replace it.

We could go on exploring the rich subtleties of expert deliberation, but we have already said enough to make our point clear. The creators of artificial intelligence, expert systems, and management science models totally fail to recognize what experts *really* think about. That is not surprising, since the kind of thinking we have been describing, while detached and rational, is not calculative and cannot be captured in the features and rules of information processing models.

Learning Business Expertise

If expert managers are expected to know their businesses intimately, to be deeply involved in their companies' problems and opportunities, and to act largely on the basis of their prior concrete experiences, what does this tell us about the education of such managers? This question raises an interesting issue concerning our five-stage model of skill acquisition. Can one get to stage five without first passing through the previous four?

The answer cannot be a categorical no, for at least in the case of physical skills like bicycle riding one does not begin with rule-based exploration but with trial-and-error learning. But in

learning most skills, one *studies*, rather than learning by trial
and error, and therefore passes through the stages we have out-
lined. Bombarded by things to see, hear, and feel, we wouldn't
know without instruction what was relevant to the skill being
learned and what should be regarded as inconsequential background. When a novice watches a master chess player, gymnast,
improvisational jazz pianist, or business manager, he doesn't
know enough about what constitutes the meaningful elements
of the situation to imitate successfully. He must learn those elements by passing through the initial stages of skill acquisition.
Then he is ready to act on the basis of his own observation or
experience. So what should business schools teach?

Many of the important elements in business situations are
what we earlier called "situational": They are learned by advanced beginners through examples and not by means of formal
definition in terms of context-free features. Such aspects must
be taught by means of illustrations. For example, various cases
of successful product positioning can be presented, as well as
examples of poor positioning. (Well-positioned products meet
an unfilled need in terms of price, quality, and other characteristics.) Attempts at precise definition of situational aspects should
be avoided, because in the future such elements will be learned
from experience based only on examples, and because there
will always be situations where the definitions do not apply.
The future manager should be encouraged from the very start
to develop his innate similarity-recognition abilities, which will
ultimately be the key to his success.

Next, the importance of perspective, required in stage three
of skill acquisition, should be taught. That seems to be best done
by means of case studies, but not cases of the kind now used
in various business schools. Current cases too often present context-free facts, each of which is assumed to be relevant, and
require a decision along with a justification in terms of those
facts. Well-constructed cases of the sort we advocate might be
called *situational* and should

1. Contain historical information about the company and
   about the problematic situation
2. Establish a rich current context, including what is described in the statement of the case as hearsay and gossip,
   as well as information from current business magazines

and newspapers and discussion of general economic conditions

3. Include situational aspects as well as cold, hard facts
4. Contain much information of doubtful relevance
5. Encourage student involvement by referring to the decision-maker in the case description as "you," e.g. "Your company has just. . . . What would you do?"

Furthermore, and this is perhaps our most radical proposal:

6. Each case should be part of a *sequence* of cases concerning the same hypothetical company. In some of the cases a reasonable response might be to note a potential problem area that should be watched, but to do nothing. After a case has been discussed, the teacher should report to the students what actually was or was not done and what happened as a result. Students should then be strongly encouraged to incorporate that knowledge in their analyses of future cases concerning the same company.

Case discussion should focus on the choice of perspective as much as on the decision flowing from it. No student's perspective should be summarily dismissed as wrong. Rather, interpretations should be judged as more or less consistent with the described situation. The student should be expected only to justify his perspective or suggested action by fitting it into a narrative based on the previous experiences of the company, rather than to explain the logic behind his conclusion.

Conventional case studies now encourage a decomposed, analytic approach to problems, thereby establishing thinking habits that may cause the student later to reach a plateau at the competent manager stage. Situational case studies, on the other hand, establish habits of thought that, with concrete experience, will facilitate a student's transition from competent analytic manager to intuitive expert. To encourage the student to use intuition, cases should sometimes be discussed immediately after they are presented, allowing no time for analysis and reasoning.

That is about as far as classroom education in decision-making can go. If possible, the student should now be immersed in real business situations and deliberations. His involvement would increase if he were allowed to participate in discussions, and if feasible he should track the situation until the results of actions become known. He should be encouraged to ask experts about history, philosophy, and interpretation rather than for explanations in terms of rules.

Next would come an apprenticeship during which the learner would not only participate in major decisions but be responsible for minor ones. Like the residency period of a doctor, the young businessman, steeped in theory, would begin to acquire actual situated experience.

Throughout the whole process, educators should stress that the decompositions involved at each stage are only a step toward a higher and more holistic understanding, and that true business expertise is heavily dependent on concrete experience in real situations.

Limits of Conventional Mathematical Models

During his early job experiences the manager will be subjected to many temptations. One of them is the desire to explain— that is, rationalize—all of his acts. Another is the urge to abstract from experiences new and more subtle rules for making decisions, rather than merely to remember the outcome so he can recognize and make the correct response to similar situations in the future. A third temptation concerns us here, pressure to rely on "scientific decision-making."

To understand what the mathematical models of management science can and cannot offer, we shall first review briefly the history of the field. Unlike the case of artificial intelligence, in which grandiose initial expectations have, under the weight of repeated failures, gradually contracted into modest proposals for narrowly focused expert systems, management science started with humble aims and has gradually expanded its pretensions. Calling their field "operations research" when it began during World War II, mathematicians attempted to describe in quantitative terms such logistical problems as the optimal provision of supplies and such tactical problems as the optimal way to hunt for enemy submarines. After the war many of the theoretical mathematicians conscripted into that practical effort continued to be interested in the modeling of real-world phenomena. Their attention turned to problems of industrial production and distribution. Armed with the newly developed

digital computer, they attacked questions like the sequencing
of tasks on production lines, the timing of the replacement of
obsolete equipment, and the determination of inventory replacement policies. Those were all fairly well-structured problems.
The choice of the facts relevant to the problem, the decisions
open to determination, the relationships describing how the decisions altered the situation, and the goal or criterion in terms
of which the desirability of outcomes should be measured all
needed little or no interpretation. Many of the problems proved
to be too difficult given current mathematical techniques or computer power, but in the remaining cases mathematical models
produced useful results.

Flushed with their triumphs in solving the structured problems typically faced by industrial foremen, management scientists then turned their attention to the policy-level problems
confronted by business executives. Marketing, product diversifi-
cation, resource allocation, and other entrepreneurial decisions
became the target of mathematical modelers. Those problems
were all unstructured, but management scientists presumed that
experienced managers could provide the structuring necessary
for modeling. With only a novice's knowledge of the problem
areas they were addressing, problem description in terms of
isolable elements, relationships among those elements, and explicit criteria for decision seemed to management scientists the
obvious strategy. What was thereby overlooked, of course, was
the extent to which know-how, based upon concrete experience,
replaces that kind of decomposed understanding as a manager
acquires expertise in his job.

More recently mathematical modelers have offered their
wares to the public sector, claiming to be able to model various
governmental policy problems. Those problems are characterized by all of the difficulties of unstructured business managerial
problems plus the additional difficulty of specifying an acceptable criterion for comparison of policies. The goals of one segment
of society are generally at variance with those of others, the
present must be balanced against the future, and considerations
of political expediency as well as equity enter the picture.[10]

We shall now treat in detail each of the steps involved in
creating management-science mathematical models and the way
in which intuitive know-how is replaced at each stage by isolable
facts and figures. When you see how this works you will under-

stand why mathematical modelers are out of their depth dealing with problems faced by business executives and government policy-makers.

If a single, perhaps very complex, decision is to be studied, the management scientist constructs his model by first identifying important facts (often called state variables) about the problem, then identifying what is under the control of the decision-maker (decision or control variables). Next, since not all decisions are possible in all situations, the modeler identifies constraints that limit the admissible decisions when the state variables are known. Finally, he specifies a criterion, expressed by a numerical index of merit to be assigned to each admissible decision. Mathematics, usually implemented on a digital computer, then determines the admissible decision that has associated with it the best possible index of merit.

For example, consider the simplest sort of structured one-item and one-time-period inventory control problem. The inventory on hand constitutes the only state variable, the additional inventory to be procured is the single decision variable, the available warehouse capacity may constrain the sum of inventory on hand and that added through ordering, and the criterion to be minimized is the expected sum of the ordering and storage costs, plus the shortage cost should demand exceed the supply on hand.

Somewhat more complex models are required in dynamic situations where decisions affect not only the present but the future as well. Since the first decision influences the future, the subsequent situations must be modeled along with the present. The automobile replacement problem is of this dynamic type. If only the costs and benefits in the current year were considered, rarely would it pay to replace your car. But the purchase of a new car decreases upkeep cost in the future, and if those savings are to be calculated, a dynamic planning model must be constructed. For dynamic models, formulas must be provided that describe the way in which current decisions determine future values of the state variables (called dynamic equations), so that decisions both in the present and in the future will together optimize an index of merit throughout the entire duration of the process.

To return to our simple inventory problem, suppose that demand for the product being stored is expected to occur during each week for the next fifty-two weeks and that weekly procurement decisions must be made after noting the inventory on hand at the start of the week. The dynamic equation in this case relates the state variable (inventory level) at the end of a week to three quantities: inventory level at the beginning of the week, the quantity procured during the week, and the demand incurred during the week. Expressed in words, the inventory balance equation states: Inventory at week's end equals inventory at its beginning plus the amount procured during the week minus the demand incurred during the week. The criterion is the expected sum of ordering, storage, and shortage costs for the duration of the process. As we have said, inventory problems are structured, meaning that the choice of state, decision, constraint, dynamic equation, and criterion is fairly obvious and requires little or no judgment. The inventory balance equation above is beyond dispute.

In sum, management science models, since they almost invariably concern the future as well as the present, require the determination of what will constitute state variables, decision variables, constraints, dynamic equations, and criterion.

Mathematical models used for purposes of prediction but not control—for example, in economic forecasting—require the same modeling process, except that no decision variables or constraints are present and no criterion is needed. The two key decisions in constructing a forecasting model for an unstructured situation are the choices of what will constitute the state variables and of what to use as the dynamic equations, which predict the values of state variables in the future as functions of their values in the present. For example, government forecasting models used to predict inflation include various arbitrarily defined economic indices as state variables. They may include variables describing international political events (such as military buildups and trade agreements), labor's inclination to strike, and consumers' propensity to spend. All forecasting models must contain formulas that explicitly relate future values of those variables to current ones. The equations concerning inflation are not objectively verifiable like the relationships in physics and chemistry, or the inventory balance equation of our earlier example, but must be invented, presumably by experts on such matters. The predictions by these models will be no more reliable than the weakest of their component equations and no more wise than the choice of which indices and events to include and which to exclude. No amount of computation can begin to compensate for a poor choice of variables or relationships among the variables. Unfortunately, as we shall see in the sections to follow on state variables and dynamic equations, expert forecasters are not experts at supplying good information to modelers.

We'll examine each of the elements of a dynamic optimization model to see to what extent the model captures a manager's understanding. Assuming an unstructured situation and an available expert, we ask to what extent a model can capture the expert's understanding. We'll then turn our attention to decision analysis, which decomposes the problem not into state variables, decision variables, constraints, dynamic equations, and criterion, but into alternating decisions and chance events, and preferences among alternative holistic outcomes. This new method of modeling, the subject of a recent enthusiastic article in the *Harvard Business Review*,[11] avoids certain pitfalls of conventional mathematical modeling. Unfortunately, this attempt at circumventing some of the shortcomings of conventional modeling runs into subtle and unsuspected difficulties of its own.

State Variables

The typical state variables in mathematical models are context-free facts—quantities such as production levels, demands, dollar costs, and interest rates, which are recognizable by novices without benefit of concrete experience. Sophisticated models also include quantities describing the current situation that depend on context and are recognized on the basis of a businessman's concrete experience, such as measures of economic climate and the probabilities of specified economic or political events. Those are aspects used by advanced beginners. Thus, should an expert act as consultant in the construction of a model, he must unfortunately regress to the detached analytic viewpoint of the beginner in order to answer questions about what context-free and situational elements to include and what values to assign to those elements. His decision-making know-how is of no avail. If the model is dynamic, future events hypothesized in the model may change the decision-maker's perspective, and his assessment of what state variables describing a future situation to include in the model may change as a result. So to build a model that reflects changing perspectives, a decision-maker has to imagine not only the new situations that might occur in the future but also their effects. Such hypothetical reasoning about future perspectives is typical of the competent decision-maker. Current management science models do not address the issue of evolving perspectives at all. Thus models, while they might in principle capture competent understanding, actually represent at best the understanding of an advanced beginner.

Decision Variables

Decisions to be included in a model must be explicitly identified. Given the current situation, an expert decision-maker can probably provide a set of alternative decisions, although the intuitive expert does not generally think in those terms, seeing only those decisions that need to be made without explicitly examining all possible alternatives. If the model is dynamic, the set of decisions to be evaluated and compared at future times must also be stipulated. Since models do not currently account for evolving perspectives, that set is generally taken to be the same as the present set, thereby possibly ignoring what a decision-maker would intuitively choose to do if immersed in some actual future situation.

Constraints

The expert may intuitively know what are acceptable and unacceptable whole concrete situations. But to provide constraints for mathematical models the knowledge must be rationalized in the form of acceptable and unacceptable combinations of state variables and decisions. Here again, any expert contributing to the construction of a model will be forced to regress to thinking like an advanced beginner to furnish the sort of information required.

Dynamic Equations

An expert may have a strong experience-based, intuitive sense that if he takes action A, result B will follow. A model, however, requires an explicit rule, expressed in terms of its state and decision variables, that replicates the expectation. An expert knows no such rule. If the prediction involves the implications of actions taken in the present, an *ad hoc* rule may be constructed to fit various of the expert's explicitly stated intuitive expectations. But since the usual intention of a model is to extrapolate knowledge beyond those cases that a decision-maker can explicitly handle, it must remain an act of faith that the rule accurately reflects the decision-maker's intuitions in *all* cases. If the decision-maker's intuitions are experience-based, not rule-based, there is no reason to anticipate the universality of any rule. Worse yet, dynamic equations must also predict the outcomes of actions taken in hypothetical future situations with the future described only in terms of the values of state variables. In such cases no expert intuition is available, since intuition presupposes involvement in real situations.

Criterion

Conventional optimization models frequently use weights, or tradeoffs, to combine their isolated elements into a single quantitative index of merit. If not, some other means of combination must be found. But experienced decision-makers do not think in those decomposed terms, at least until after they have intuitively chosen their decision and are attempting to rationalize it. Consequently, the model's measures of relative importance of various aspects of a situation must be contrived without recourse to the concrete lessons of experience.

Many public policy decisions involve financial costs, increase or reduction of risks to life and health, and changes in the quality of life, all differing for different groups of citizens, as well as effects upon both the current generation and future ones. For a decision to be assigned an index of merit, all of those impacts must be rendered commensurate and combined. The most common unit of measurement is dollars, meaning that lives themselves as well as the quality of life must be assigned dollar values, with either all citizens treated equally or with the value depending upon such factors as age, sex, and race. The future must be explicitly valued with respect to the present. It hardly needs saying that nowhere is the inadequacy of models so evident as in social policy.

IN SUMMARY, every step of the conventional mathematical modeling process requires that the expert informants, whose expertise is supposed to be captured in the model, provide the sort of decomposed and decontextualized information that concerns beginners but not true experts. Hence, to participate in the construction of a model, an expert must regress to seeing the world like an advanced beginner or, in some cases, a novice. If experts fail to appreciate the extent and importance of their unrationalized know-how, they may not realize how seriously their own understanding is being degraded; they may even be flattered into believing that the model constructed on the basis of their answers to the model builder's questions captures and amplifies their expertise. If so, and if they act on the basis of the model, business and social decision-making will suffer.

Limits of the Decision Analysis Alternative

A relatively new mathematical technique called decision analysis claims to capture the experienced manager's understanding of his problems more faithfully than the conventional modeling approach. A decision analysis is conducted in three stages. At stage one the analyst constructs a decision tree (for an example see Figure 6–1) representing the problem. The tree comprises, first, the enumeration of all initial decisions being considered by the manager, then an enumeration of the most significant chance events that might occur if each of the decisions were taken, next an enumeration of responsive decisions open to management should each of these possible chance events occur, and so on as far out into the future as desired.

We shall use a greatly oversimplified problem of the type faced by oil wildcatters to illustrate this procedure. (One of the earliest applications of decision analysis, a Harvard Business School doctoral dissertation by C. Jackson Grayson, concerned more realistic wildcatting situations.[12] Grayson later became Wage and Price Commission administrator under President Nixon. After his Washington experience, Grayson noted in a

1973 article in the *Harvard Business Review* that he had *not* used quantitative modeling when making governmental decisions and speculated upon the reasons.)[13] Assume that a wildcatter owns a piece of property on which he may choose to sink a well. Should he do so, assume that one of three results will occur: a very productive well, a mediocre well, or a dry well. The wildcatter also has the opportunity, at a small cost compared with the cost of drilling, first to commission a seismic sampling. If he avails himself of that, suppose that one of three possible underground rock structures with differing implications for the existence of oil will be identified: very encouraging, noncommittal, and very discouraging. The wildcatter can then base his drilling decision on the nature of the structure observed.

In this example, there are three possible initial decisions: drill, don't drill, or sample the structure. Drilling will result in one of three chance events: very productive well, mediocre well, or dry well. The result of not drilling is certain: The *status quo* remains unchanged. Sampling has the three possible outcomes enumerated above, and each can be followed by either the decision to drill or not to drill. If drilling is chosen after sampling, the amount of oil discovered is a chance event with the same three possible outcomes as for immediate drilling.

All of those options are diagramed in Figure 6–1, which looks something like a tree or perhaps a bush. Decision points are depicted by squares, chance events by circles, and the passage of time corresponds to moving from the bottom toward the top of the figure.

The second phase of a decision analysis requires the assignment of probabilities to the various chance events. That is generally done by the decision-maker himself or by his designated expert surrogate. Since, in general, those probabilities are not objectively known quantities like those governing the outcomes of tossing a coin, they are termed subjective probabilities. While these probabilities may reflect personal biases, they are the biases of the decision-maker himself, so the decision ultimately produced by the procedure will be the one that he, but perhaps not someone with a different impression of the probabilities, should find most desirable.

In our example, the wildcatter would be expected to provide what he thought, prior to any sampling, the chances of each of the three outcomes were: very productive well, mediocre

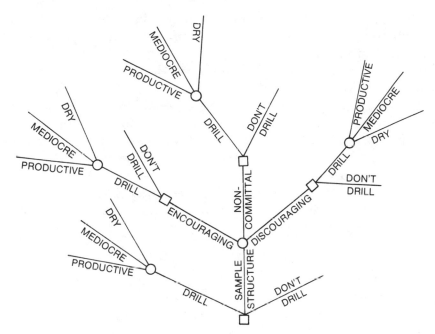

Figure 6–1   Wildcatting Decision Tree.

well, and dry well. He must also assess the probabilities of a seismic samplings being very encouraging, noncommital, or very discouraging. Finally, he would furnish his assessment of the chances of each of the three drilling outcomes in the case of each of the three sampling results. Those assessments must be consistent. There are various techniques for eliciting the probabilities, but they need not concern us here.

At stage three of the formulation, the decision-maker must state his preferences for each of the possible sequences of decisions and events that he has foreseen. That preference is revealed, for each particular sequence, by the decision-maker's answer to the question: At what probability p would it be a matter of indifference to you between (1) the sure occurrence of the particular sequence being assigned a preference and (2) a comparison lottery in which with probability p the best possible foreseen outcome occurs and with probability $1-p$ the worst one results? The comparison lottery is called the basic reference lottery and is always used as the basis for determining how much the decision-maker likes any particular outcome sequence. The p chosen by the decision-maker in answer to the question is called his utility of the particular sequence of events. Utility, which measures strength of preference, is always between 0 and 1. A utility of 1 is assigned to the best possible foreseen outcome, 0 to the worst, and the more the decision-maker likes the outcome, the larger the utility.

After establishing utilities for each possible sequence of alternating decisions and chance events, a computation determines the initial decision that is best for the decision-maker, as well as the decisions that he should make further down the line, depending on what chance events occur.

How well does such a model capture a manager's experience-based understanding? Let us examine, in order, each step of the modeling procedure.

The Enumeration of Possible Decisions in the Construction of a Decision Tree

In a decision analysis, the decision-maker is asked to provide plausible future decisions that he would consider if he were to find himself in a situation described by the sequence of decisions and chance events leading up to it. In a real-world situation, decisions based on prior experience intuitively present themselves to the mind of the involved decision-maker. The abstract and skeletal nature of a possible future condition in a decision analysis, however, forces the decision-maker to reason out plausible decisions rather than invoke experience. But that puts him in a situation analogous to that of an experienced driver who is capable of almost automatic response to a wide variety of real situations but is unable accurately to reason out how he would respond in a hypothetical situation skeletally described by information concerning velocity, visibility, and road condition. Even Rex Brown, the author[14] and co-author[15] of *Harvard Business Review* articles extolling decision analysis, has recognized this problem in his less well-known writings. He points out that in real life decision-makers often do not choose any of the acts they listed as plausible decisions in possible futures when the analysis was performed, because subsequent events have changed their perspective in a way that they did not foresee.[16]

The Enumeration of Chance Events in the Construction of a Decision Tree

When making a decision, the intuitive decision-maker does not explicitly think about all of the chance events that might occur, either in the present or in the future. He has come to realize from experience that there is no way such a list could possibly be complete. Having been the victim of unexpected events, he has learned to choose decisions that will work out in almost any case, even cases not explicitly foreseen. Of course, although decision analysis requires that chance events be made explicit, one could include "the unexpected" as one of the outcome events. But when constructing the decision tree, one must list plausible alternative responses to chance events, and that cannot be done for an event no better defined than "the unexpected." If "the unexpected" occurs at the end of a sequence in the tree, no response is required, but a utility must be assigned to the sequences ending in an "unexpected" way. Again, this is impossible. If the possibility of the unexpected's occurring is ignored, not only is reality distorted but, as the decision analyst Rex Brown has pointed out, the calculation of the optimal decision policy through the use of the tree will be unfairly biased against decisions that introduce delays in order to await unexpected events.[17]

Eliciting Subjective Probabilities Describing the Present

A decision analysis usually characterizes each possible future situation as the current situation (as understood by the decision-maker at the time the analysis is performed, without any attempt at an explicit description) followed by a particular sequence of hypothetical decisions and events. Hence one avoids the abstract characterization in terms of state variables required in the conventional management science model.

The current situation as experienced by a decision-maker generally includes uncertainties about the actual situation. The decision-maker contemplates actions that will reduce those uncertainties. (In the case of the oil wildcatter, a seismic sampling is an attempt to learn about the amount of oil.) In that case the actual situation is sometimes thought of as being one of several possible specified situations, with the decision-maker not knowing for sure which one it is. Then, to model the process of the decision-maker's learning about reality, probabilities, called prior probabilities, are subjectively assigned by the decision-maker to the various possible true situations at the time the analysis is being performed. Those probabilities are adjusted, generally by a formula called Bayes's Law, on the basis of hypothesized observed events. Should that be the approach taken in our oil wildcatting example, the decision-maker would assign prior probabilities to the three possible situations: very productive well, mediocre well, and dry well.

If prior probabilities of the actual situation are used in the analysis, they play the role of state variables, and the decision-maker is asked to provide estimates of quantities about which he normally never explicitly thinks as he makes intuitive decisions. Here is an example that is perhaps closer to home than oil wildcatting: If you were asked to provide the probability of the presence of criminals at certain spots in New York's Central Park, you could not accurately do so, yet experience may have taught you that you should not walk in the park at night.

Eliciting Subjective Probabilities of Chance Events

Chance events play the role in decision analysis of dynamic equations, specifying the future given the present. Hence providing the probabilities of those events replaces the stipulation of the equations. Since intuitive know-how transcends the beginner's calculation of decisions based on enumeration of possibilities and consideration of their probabilities, it does not encourage learning from experience the probabilities of chance events. A New Yorker need not know the frequency of crimes in Central Park to know that it is sufficiently high for him to stay out.

We have conducted several decision analyses for real-world planners in conjunction with courses we have taught on the subject. While the planners will describe their problems with involvement and emotion, they grow uneasy when probability information is elicited. They draw back, contemplate, and usually respond: "Well, I suppose the chances are . . . ."

Eliciting the Decision-Maker's Utilities

In decision analysis, no tradeoff assessment is explicitly required as it is in the construction of conventional criterion functions, although a special decision analysis methodology, called multiattribute utility theory, involves generating such questionable data. All that is really needed, in principle, is a utility assessment of a "whole situation," which is described as the present followed by a particular hypothetical sequence of alternating decisions and chance events. Here, however, we encounter the same difficulty that we described in our earlier section on the enumeration of possible decisions. A future so described, like the micro-worlds suggested as learning tools by cognitivist educators, is necessarily only a skeletal caricature of the real situations in which we live, no matter how many events and decisions are explicitly included. Consequently the decision-maker cannot draw upon the intuitive experience that only a real-world situation can evoke. He is reduced to reasoning out how he believes he might feel about a hypothetical future situation and thereby loses all contact with the feelings that would be elicited by real situations.

Once we have reached this stage in performing decision analyses, answers to our questions almost always begin, "Well, I guess that . . .". When we debrief clients after an analysis, they invariably feel that the formulation of their problem as a tree of decisions and events helped clarify their thinking, but they were uncomfortable when furnishing probability information and even more uneasy with quantifying their preferences for skeletally described situations.

How, then, can advocates of decision analysis like Professor Ronald Howard at Stanford claim that its usefulness has been established?[18] The simple answer is that they can't. No systematic studies of when or why decision analysis is helpful have ever been undertaken. The psychologist Baruch Fischhoff has addressed this dearth of critical reflection,[19] drawing an interesting analogy between decision analysis and a better-known helping profession, psychotherapy. He points out that psychologists annually produce more than three thousand books, chapters, and journal articles on assessment and still know very little about the efficacy of their methods. Efforts of a similar magnitude are needed before any claims for the established usefulness of decision analysis should be taken seriously. The procedure doubtless has a proper place, but it is premature to assert that one has been established. When one is, we believe decision analysis will be found useful on novel problems but inferior to human intuition for problems with which experts have ample experience.

In general, all formal models of decision-making ask the expert questions which place him in a detached objective position and so fail to tap his intuitive expertise. They suffer, just as does conventional AI and expert systems engineering, from the impossibility of replacing involved knowing how with detached knowing that. The same problem reappears in attempts to automate factories and offices.

The Place of Automation

The microcomputer-controlled industrial robots coming into use today are vastly superior to the automatic machines of the previous generation, for with the power and storage capacities of even microcomputers many new possibilities open to the industrial engineer. For example, programs for performing a great variety of tasks can be stored in a robot's control computer. That in turn allows great flexibility in the capabilities of a single robot and rapid change in production procedures without reprogramming. The easy respecification of the robot's programs is a process certain to advance in the near future. GM, for example, is working on a system called Roboteach, which will integrate the programming of the shop floor computers with the central machines within which design is done, and even automate the process by which the robot's programs are generated. Further, computational power gives robots some measure of artificial intelligence: Systems already available endow robots with limited vision and a modicum of tactile discrimination. Those senses in turn permit response to small variations in the position of the product under production or the location of tools used by the robot to do its job. They also allow a computer to perform some quality control functions during production.

While the problems of programming vision and touch are intellectually very challenging and have inspired much research at our universities, it is questionable whether in those areas much progress can, or need, be made. In most cases there are no inherent reasons why each item cannot come down a production line in exactly the same position or why tools to be used by a robot cannot always lie in exactly the same place and position. If vision is used, one should not seek human flexibility. In such areas as microfabrication, where accuracy to within a minute fraction of an inch is required, the vision system could pick out predetermined, well-specified cues. If a robot arm in a production line repeatedly grasps components of a given shape but does not do so with the extreme accuracy required in the placement of the component in an assembly, a computer-based vision system could exactly locate a prespecified edge of the grasped component and the computer could then guide the arm to an accurate placement. The same holds for quality control. If certain possible failures can be precisely characterized, a vision system can look for those failures and the computer can be programmed to take appropriate actions.

People, we have argued, learn to respond flexibly to a changing environment by experiencing and remembering thousands of concrete cases and what to do in each. But robots use prespecified rules and principles, an approach that has shown itself incapable of achieving human capacities. No program can deal flexibly with components of arbitrary shapes or with unanticipated failures that a human being would easily detect. It seems wiser, then, to abandon the goal of human flexibility and seek engineering solutions consistent with the limited capacities of present-generation robots. Better methods of standardization can obviate the need for human flexibility, and they have the advantage of working!

As for mobile robots, the situation is even less promising. David Grossman, manager of automation research at IBM's Thomas J. Watson Research Center, has this to say about inflated dreams of automation: "There is this immense contrast between some people's notion of what will happen and the harsh realities of what is actually here now. When you're in the area of speculative mobile robots—androids—you have left the field of what might go wrong and have entered areas where nothing has gone right yet."[20] The moral is that an intelligent, mobile robot has no place in a factory, and although desperately desired by the military, it is a completely unrealistic goal.[21]

With respect to robots, one finds signs of a repetition of the sad history of artificial intelligence. Expectations are initially too high, and while the research is challenging, little of practical value results. Eventually more modest goals are accepted, and, as with expert systems, useful aids are developed. It is interesting that in both machine intelligence and robotics, the Japanese seem to have the more realistic view. They virtually ignored AI until the recent flowering of expert systems, and their robots, while less exciting, have more commercial applications than ours.

While with suitable standardization the repetitious, unskilled aspects of production lines are being more and more successfully automated, attempts to automate skilled labor have run into problems. Tacit abilities, though long overlooked by students of the labor process, have become more obvious as automation has proceeded.[22]

Skilled machining is a good example of an occupation replete with tacit skills. Due to those skills the field has long resisted full automation. Despite nearly a century of engineering effort since Frederick Taylor, there is still no guaranteed scientific way of accounting for and fully anticipating variations in tool wear, the machinability of various materials, actual machine performance, or changing conditions. Yet such problems are readily and routinely dealt with by machinists and machine operators, relying on their skills and accumulated experience. Only if the production process is rationalized to the point where irregularities are fully defined and contained, thus eliminating the need for the invisible interventions that keep today's factories going, can total automation hope to work. Listen to a skilled operator describe machine wear:

> Cars are basically the same, but every car is different. . . . At first when you're learning, you just learn rules about driving. But as you get to know how to drive, you get the feel for the car you're driving—you know, things like how it feels at different speeds, how well the brakes work, when it's going to overheat, how to start it when it's cold . . . when you put [a skilled operator] on a new machine she knows these machines so well, she's got a feel for it, she picks up right away what she's got to do different on this new machine than she was doing on the other one.[23]

It is into the complexity of the commonsense world that factory automation is introduced. With its introduction, of course, come concerted efforts at modernization and rationalization, but they don't always do the job. Discussing the shortcomings of numerically controlled machine tools, the historian David Noble quotes a skilled machinist at a large aerospace plant:

> It's hard to say whether the program is bad or not. I think it's more probably that the principle behind programming is somewhat erroneous. If you were a time study engineer and went into a machine shop the two things you would observe the machinist doing would be making calculations—he sits down, looks at a blueprint, does the calculations—then putting the part on the machine—he's mostly positioning it, moving something from part A to part B, or moving a cutting tool. If you look at it superficially, that's what's involved in machining and you should be able to duplicate it. Computers will do calculations. And you can fix up the machine tool itself with servomotors and logic circuits. . . .
>
> The problem is that there are a lot of subtle things in machining. If you didn't have any experience with woodworking, you could watch somebody making a dovetail with a router and it looks real simple. But when you try it, it turns out to be a bunch of splinters.[24]

If unskilled production line labor can be automated and skilled labor such as machinists' can't, where does that leave white-collar workers? That is no simple question. One has to weigh limited advantages against limited costs. The advantages are, of course, reliability, uniformity, and efficiency. The cost is more subtle. Those who, like the white-collar labor union in Sweden, have recognized a danger and are seeking legislation against it have begun to call the problem "deskilling." Deskilling does not refer to the obvious and harmless fact that if we replace some group of skilled operators with competent systems, soon there will be no one left with that skill. No one bemoans the loss of elevator operator skills resulting from the introduction of automatic elevators. There was no high-level elevator expertise, and automatic elevators are as good as or better than those run by human beings. Deskilling refers to the loss of expertise in an area where the computer is merely competent. A loan company will be able to use a competent loan approval system to enable beginners to make routine loans, whereas normally beginners in the loan business will need years of experience at dealing with whole situations and getting involved feedback before those with the necessary talent and commitment can pass from novice to competent to expert. If, however, the beginner is given immediate access to competence by answering a list of queries from the system, the company will have to pay for its easy entry into competence later when none of its staff develop into experts who can deal with difficult cases.

The Swedes discovered that problem when they tried to computerize their forest evaluation system. "[F]oresters began to feel worried about the possibilities of maintaining the professional competence necessary to ensure a high quality of work. One forester commented: '. . . New foresters never learn the theoretical and practical foundations of forest evaluations. . . .' "[25] The same problem arose in the Swedish national insurance adjusting office. The question becomes whether the employee should be an unskilled servant answering the preformulated questions of a competent system or whether the computer should be a tool that does not try to replace the worker's experience in making decisions but rather serves as a data storage and calculation aid. In the first case the worker would be able to deal almost immediately with simple, routine cases but would lose or never develop the capacity to deal with difficult and unusual ones. In the second case expertise would come more slowly, but the resultant combination of expert and computer would be able to deal with a much wider range of problems.

Society as a whole will have to decide in which areas it can tolerate mere competence and in which areas it wishes to practice old-fashioned training and apprenticeship so as to preserve old-fashioned expertise. In our judgment companies that allow those who show talent to rise to the top the hard way—passing through the stages from rule-using novice to intuitive expert—will have an advantage over companies that rely heavily on competent systems. Many companies will no doubt learn the hard way, and those that set their sights too high, reaching beyond the achievable to the pie-in-the-sky of total automation and mechanical expertise, will be forced to recognize reality. In the end, when the expert systems euphoria fades, we shall see competent systems finding restricted use in isolated areas. They are useful in highly combinatorial areas in which there are no intuitive experts, such as VAX configuration, and in providing advice and services to those in need of fast assistance who cannot obtain the ministrations of human experts.

Mind-over-Machine Approaches

It turns out, then, that at every level of business from the factory floor to the board room, wherever skills are involved, formal models fail to capture human expertise. Once that is recognized, new possibilities open up for machine aids to the human mind. Some management scientists themselves have recognized the inadequacy of both the conventional and the decision analysis models of the way a manager decides. They see that intuition plays an important role, especially when managers face unstructured, but not wholly unfamiliar, problems. Decision support systems (DSSs) represent the most recent attempt by those management scientists to save computer and mathematical modeling. Designers of those systems wisely acknowledge that traditional management science stand-alone systems are too ambitious. They therefore develop systems that use computer-run models to *support*, not replace, the activities of the intuitive decision-maker. To offer timely advice to the busy executive with pressing problems, DSSs are designed to be used easily and directly by the decision-maker without the intervention of either the professional model builder or computer programmers. The models that the decision-maker includes in his DSS are used to answer "what if" questions, describing what the future will look like should certain decisions be made, or sometimes determining which decisions will produce a desired future that has been specified by the user.

When a decision-maker knows intuitively what he does and does not like but finds it impossible to reduce his understanding to rules and formulas, DSSs have considerable merit—but only if the "what if" models incorporated in the computer system are objectively valid at the time the program is being run and if the decision-maker is fairly certain they will remain valid during the forecast period of the model. Examples of such objective descriptions are financial models that compute cash flows in the future that would result from hypothetical current decisions such as across-the-board pay increases, where all other inflows and outflows are assumed known, or production-inventory models that predict such things as inventory, raw materials, and overtime levels as a function of production decisions. Such models can be very complex, using historical probability data to predict demand and producing, by means of the simulation of a great many randomly generated possible futures, probability distributions for future inventory, raw materials, and overtime levels. These models are of value since even the most experienced manager would probably lack good intuitions about the details of such probability distributions.

If the models used to answer the "what if" questions are *not* objectively obvious but must be produced by choosing arbitrarily what are to be considered the important state variables and the relationships governing their evolution, all the problems mentioned in our discussion of conventional management science models and decision analysis raise their ugly heads. For example, in marketing one might want to use a DSS to assess the impacts of various hypothetical advertising campaigns and then use one's intuition to pick the most desirable proposal. But no one really knows what variables enter into the public's initial response to a certain campaign or how those variables, the initial public response, and further ads mold future behavior. A model of this process would invent such variables as loyalty to product, propensity to spend, and perceived need, and would manufacture formulas for predicting how the variables would change as a function of advertising. Such a model would represent novice or, at best, competent understanding, while the decision-maker, if experienced, may be able to intuit public response much more reliably. In that case a DSS would degrade performance. The intuitive decision would be supported by an analytic foundation built on sand.

So DSSs must be used with extreme care. They have much to offer when the future can accurately be predicted using a model, but whether that future is acceptable can best be assessed intuitively. They offer nothing but regressive thinking cloaked in the illusion of scientific precision when the decomposed, analytic model used to answer "what if" questions represents an understanding inferior to an expert's holistic, involved intuitions. DSS is neither a panacea nor merely a new buzz word invented to save a discredited pseudoscientific approach. Just as traditional management science has its proper place but risks extinction if its pretenses continue to outstrip what it can produce, DSSs will take their rightful place as limited, but useful, tools of management if, and only if, their designers understand and acknowledge their limitations.

WHAT, THEN, is the proper place of modeling? First, modeling has proved a useful methodology for handling structured problems. Many of the production, distribution, and scheduling problems confronted by manufacturers are far too complex for good intuitive decision-making but are sufficiently structured to be described mathematically and solved by computers. Others cannot be *solved* but can be modeled as part of decision support systems, which can indeed support intuitive decision-making. Likewise for queueing problems such as those faced by traffic engineers. Problems involving the reliability of complex systems are currently the subject of very useful mathematical modeling.

Second, modeling has been useful in coping with novel problems—ranging from nuclear reactor and MX missile siting to hurricane seeding, large-scale reforestation, space mission planning, and the overhaul of the tax system—that, being new, fall into no existing domains of expertise.[26]

Third, while a problem may not be novel, if the decision-maker lacks sufficient experience with the type of problem, the understanding supplied by a model may be superior to his own model-like novice, advanced beginner, or competent understanding.

And last, certain problems that are unstructured, and about which intuitive expertise exists, come up regularly at the operational levels of industry. Then computerized models, even if they do not deal with the problems as well as an expert might if he had the time, make possible the generation of decisions that are at least acceptable, routine, fast, and economical. For example, the computerized assignment of workers to jobs in certain job-shop situations is rapid, reasonably efficient, and normally free of egregious error. Models of that sort are really examples of expert systems and, like expert systems, can be expected to render competent, if not expert, decisions. The use of models in such cases can be seen as a well-justified step toward routinization, since it allows human decision-making expertise to be directed toward more important problems.

As long as management scientists restrict their modeling efforts to these four kinds of situations, the field is destined to flourish. Management scientists might even go further and offer the experienced expert facing a familiar unstructured situation the opportunity of discovering what sheer computational power can deduce from distinctly inferior understanding. But if their field is to maintain (or regain) its legitimacy, claims of the decisional and predictive superiority of models must be assiduously avoided. Here the expert must be made aware of his own uniquely human capabilities and the corresponding deficiencies of any formal model. In short, practitioners of management science must acknowledge its inherent limitations and inform their clients of them. The experienced manager can then use this knowledge, and that provided by any models that he still chooses to commission, as he sees fit.

Some computer system designers have already seen the limits on the use of computers in managerial decision-making and have moved in a different direction. They envision a role for computers in managerial practice other than the reproduction of human capacities. For example, "coordinators" is the name given to a new family of microcomputer tools developed by Fernando Flores of Action Technologies, a San Francisco company, Terry Winograd of Stanford University, and others. Their idea is that managerial action is necessarily social and involves people interacting verbally. Coordinators are designed to facilitate actions of people working with each other. Using a coordinator, the manager conducts his business by inquiring, instructing, ordering, questioning, requesting, proposing, inviting, promising, and reporting. As he does, the coordinator automatically sends his messages to others and elicits communication from others. Of course, the computer has no understanding of the messages it is sending. Still, by keeping track of them the tool facilitates the ongoing conversations that are essential to management.

Management information systems of some years back were capable of regurgitating vast quantities of data but were difficult to use and could not respond flexibly to a manager's needs. Modern decision support systems are beginning to deal with those shortcomings. Other new tools, such as coordinators, are based on the recognition that decision-making is only one part of a manager's activities and are providing computer-based support for the manager's conversations and communications. Electronic mail is coming into its own. Along with these developing tools, the computer continues to provide file maintenance, word processing, and accounting services. There are encouraging signs that, after several false starts, computers are finally taking their proper place as aids to managers' intuitive minds.

CONCLUSION

PEOPLE THAT (*Sic*) THINK

People in every field will start asking themselves AI-type questions about how they . . . model the knowledge in their field in the form of an understanding system. . . . AI will change the questions people ask and the methods they use.

Roger Schank
The Cognitive Computer (1984)

There are two equally dangerous extremes—to shut reason out and to let nothing else in.

Pascal
Pensées (1670)

AN UNCRITICAL ARTIFICIAL INTELLIGENCE ENTHUSIAST entitled her book on the subject *Machines Who Think.*[1] The intended implication, of course, was that artificial intelligence had advanced to the point where computers could be programmed to think like people. We have seen that computers do indeed reason things out rather like inexperienced persons, but only with greater human experience comes know how—a far superior holistic, intuitive way of approaching problems that cannot be imitated by rule-following computers. The title of this chapter calls attention to the dangers we face as the misunderstanding of human skill that pervades the AI community spreads to society as a whole.

The assumption of calculative rationality implies that society can be improved by teaching children to think more analytically and by requiring adults who wish to advise us to justify their thoughts and actions in a supposedly rational manner. That is an idea introduced at the beginning of Western thought by Socrates and Plato. Why, if it has been with us for two thousand years, is it suddenly so important that this idea be confronted and corrected? At least three events have recently moved the

193

rationalistic view of man out of the relatively harmless domain of philosophy into the public arena. They are massive organizational changes in society, the tremendous impact on our lives of modern science, and the invention of the high-speed digital computer.

As recently as the last century, almost all businesses were small or medium-size and were owned and operated by a single entrepreneur. As a consequence a decision-maker needed to justify his decisions to no one, and he could rely on the intuitive understanding produced by his prior experience. Large bureaucratic structures change all that. Almost every employee has a boss to whom he or she is responsible and who in turn is responsible to someone else. Even the president or chief executive officer of a company is responsible to a board of directors, and members of that board must convince their peers of decisions they support. The choice is between justification by calculative rationality, that is, inferences drawn from isolated, objective facts describing the problematic situation, and consensus-based intuitive shared understanding, derived from concrete experiences, which defies precise verbalization. In our Socratic tradition of precise definition and dialectical argumentation, when there is a choice between intuitive consensus and rationalistic argumentation the latter wins out. Indeed, the hierarchical organization of decision-making, the increasingly bureaucratic nature of society, and the pervasiveness of economic metrics of success and failure encourage an excessive reliance on calculative rationality. Since wisdom and judgment prove too hard to defend, information, decontextualized facts, and contrived numerical certainties are substituted. If the model doesn't work out right, change the assumptions. If the spreadsheet brings unpleasant news, hide unwarranted optimism in its formulas.

A similar story can be told about political life. The constant presence of the mass media encourages political leaders to justify every decision publicly with explicit reasons and statistics. Are we winning the war? Look at the body count. Is the economy healthy? Look at the GNP. With the demand for logical and numerical justification, plausible sounding reasons are contrived, and aggregations and statistics pass from useful guides to tokens of false rationality and empty reassurance. In 1964, when Barry Goldwater ran on the slogan "In your heart you know he's right," the ridicule he received demonstrated the tenor of the times.

From now on, political rhetoric would have to be glossed with the legitimacy of calculative reason and statistics.[2]

With the explosions at Hiroshima and Nagasaki in 1945, the power and potential of science burst upon the public. The scientific method, characterized by the description and prediction of observable phenomena through the use of formal models specifying the interactions of context-free elements, had yielded power beyond all prior imagining. Then, a mere decade later, the launching of Sputnik 1 by the Soviets again magnified the prestige of science and scientists. True, scientific progress had brought with it great problems, but it also brought the confidence to face those problems and attack them with the same detached, objective, testable procedures that had proved so successful in explaining and controlling the physical world. Ideas that had begun with the eighteenth-century Enlightenment and gone on to transform production with the Industrial Revolution and scientific management now became the common currency of public discourse.

But merely aspiring to be rational about the organization of society was not enough; the problems were tremendously complex and beyond the calculative ability of the human brain. The desire to rationalize society would have remained but a dream were it not for the invention of the modern digital computer. Science had produced a device that seemingly mirrored and tremendously amplified human reason: a "brain" that could cope with man's problems. A truly rational society suddenly seemed not only necessary and attractive, but possible. The organization of work, politics, medicine, and law, to name only a few domains, has felt the impact of that aspiration. While much has been made of the virtues of rational discussion drawing upon a vast data base of instantaneously available information, too little has been said of the dangers inherent in the trend.

The increasingly bureaucratic nature of society is heightening the danger that in the future skill and expertise will be lost through overreliance on rationality. Today, as always, individual decision-makers understand and respond to their situation intuitively as described in the highest levels of our skill acquisition model. When time permits, they further validate and fine-tune their intuitions using what we have called deliberative rationality. But when more than one person is involved in a decision, the success of science and the availability of computers have led more and more toward that explicit, detached mode of problem description and alternative evaluation we have called calculative rationality.

All this sounds enlightened and progressive until one realizes that genuine know-how, wisdom, and good judgment are sacrificed in the process. Any attempt to be explicit and logical, allegedly so that rational discussion can be directed toward the relevance and validity of isolated elements used in the analysis, limits "judgment" to the choice of those elements. But with experience comes a decreasing concern with accurate assessment of isolated elements, so in the area in which their response is demanded experts have no expertise.

It is often desirable that experts defend their recommendations against other experts, or in some way be cross-examined so that those affected can question their presuppositions. If this is taken to mean that the expert must articulate his values, rules, and factual assumptions, examining becomes a futile exercise in rationalization in which expertise is forfeited and time is wasted. But the alternative need not be the imposition of unquestioned authority. In Japan consensus seems to be reached through discussion without reducing intuition to rationalization. The cross-examination of competing experts in an intuitive culture might take the form of a conflict of interpretations in which each expert is required to produce and defend a coherent narrative which leads naturally to the acceptance of his point of view.

Demanding that its experts be able to explain how they do their job can seriously penalize a rational culture like ours, in competition with an intuitive culture like Japan's. Indeed, intuition, not Fifth Generation Expert Systems, may be Japan's most powerful secret. Take, for example, how the Japanese almost took over the poultry industry. According to *American Scientist:*

> With the depression at its lowest point in the early 1930s . . . one of America's big industries, that of producing eggs and raising chickens, was faced with an important question: 'What was to be done with the Leghorn cockerel?' . . . Egg producers who bought chicks wanted pullets only, and, as a result, hatcheries were always swamped with unwanted cockerels. Some of the producers had heard of the practice of chick sexing, developed in Japan. This new technique of accurately determining the sex of the day-old chick sounded like one of the mysteries of the Orient . . . Nevertheless, the hatcheries felt that, perhaps, here was the answer that

would save their industry. Five young Japanese experts were sent for. . . . They gave an amazing demonstration; the American investigators were astounded at the accuracy of the Japanese sexors. One expert, Hikosoboro Yogo, during the demonstration, reached a speed of 1,400 chicks an hour with an accuracy of 98 percent.[3]

Had the poultry farmers insisted on an explanation of how the task was accomplished before they adopted the technique, the industry would have been ruined. Even poultry men cannot distinguish male from female organs in a day-old chick, so the chicken sexors bypass the rule-following stage altogether. They watch while an expert takes a box full of assorted chicks as they come from the incubator, picks up the chicks, turns them back side up, takes a quick look, and releases them into two other boxes marked "pullets" and "cockerels," respectively. After three months of apprenticeship trainees are able to begin sorting on their own. With long experience, a chicken sexor does not even have to look at the chicks' sexual organs. "Yogo claimed to be able to determine the sex of a chick immediately, even before he looked at the genitals. This was hard to believe. But by this time, Yogo had sexed three to four million chicks, and he proved he could do it."[4]

The secret is not in Japanese fingers but in a culture that trusts intuition. Luckily, American poultry farmers were desperate enough to care only for results, not reasons. Without insisting on rules, but after handling several million chicks, Americans showed that they too could perform fantastic feats. "Ben Salewski, who learned to sex chickens in 1936 in Washington, claimed that he could sense the sex of the chick by touch . . . and no doubt there are other experts who use similar intuition in sexing. He has developed an accuracy of 99.5 percent and cruises along at the rate of 900 to 1,000 chicks per hour."[5]

With that striking example in mind, let's now examine the inroads and associated costs of so-called rational decision-making. Granted that formal analysis, if properly viewed as a useful tool, has a place in the overall decision-making process, we shall be critical, for such criticism is needed to balance today's tendency to assume, without evidence, the virtues of the rationalistic approach.

Under the auspices of the National Academy of Sciences, renowned scientists are frequently impaneled to investigate and then prepare advisory reports on matters of serious national concern. The reports, it is assumed, will tell administrators of government agencies what scientists know about the situation under study. For example, the introduction of a new insecticide or the removal from use of a current one raises ecological, epidemiological, and economic issues. Traditional science clearly bears on at least the first two domains, and economics would like to see itself in the same mold. Professor Howard Raiffa of the John F. Kennedy School of Government at Harvard, who is a respected mathematician and a leader in the modern rational decision-making movement, has described to us his experiences as chairman of such National Academy of Sciences advisory panels.

While the methods of science are fairly rigorous and standardized, Professor Raiffa says, the *application* of science is not. Each scientist-consultant must decide subjectively what he or she is going to study, what are the variables to be treated as relevant and therefore scientifically controlled, and how to interpret the results, since a study only assures one that if x is done in a certain specific situation, y will occur. Consequently, the various relevant studies in each subdomain of the problem area frequently pull in different directions regarding overall recommendations. As such, the conflicting studies are of little use to administrative decision-makers. The question of which studies are most relevant and safely generalizable is, unfortunately, no longer a scientific matter. For example, no one knows for sure what significance the number of cancers produced in rats by very large doses of a particular product has for the long-term health of human beings if the product is used in very small quantities as an insecticide.

Professor Raiffa reports that as a panel chairman he speaks informally with appropriate senior scientists of high repute and no known bias about the proper interpretation of the superficially conflicting evidence. Since those people are wise, intuitive synthesizers of evidence and good judges both of people and of scientific practice, he often gets a good sense of the real significance of the various experiments. But in the same breath those informants will frequently warn him that their judgments are strictly off the record and must not be included in the panel's report, since they are subjective, not verifiable, and therefore unscientific. Needless to say, it is those judgments that really could help in the decision-making process. If scientists could acknowledge that deep understanding can never be completely explained and objectively defended but nonetheless is valid, wiser decisions that affect all of our lives might well result. Otherwise, at every level of the process of synthesizing scientific studies into real understanding of the problem, expert wisdom is lost and what remains is at best a competent appraisal.

But the issue goes deeper than the reticence of scientists. Judges and ordinary citizens serving on our juries are likewise beginning to distrust anything but "scientific" evidence. A ballistics expert who testified only that he had seen thousands of bullets and the gun barrels that had fired them, and that there was absolutely no doubt in his mind that the bullet in question had come from the gun offered in evidence, would be ridiculed by the opposing attorney and disregarded by the jury. Instead, the expert has to talk about the individual marks on the bullet and the gun and connect them by rules and principles showing that only the gun in question could so mark the bullet. If he is experienced in legal proceedings, he will know how to construct arguments that convince the jury, but he does not tell the court what he intuitively knows, for he will be evaluated by the jury on the basis of his "scientific" rationality, not in terms of his past record and good judgment. As a result some wise but honest experts are poor witnesses, and lesser authorities who are experienced at producing convincing legal testimony are much sought after. The same thing happens in psychiatric hearings, medical proceedings, and other situations where technical experts testify. Form becomes more important than content.

It is ironic that judges hearing a case will expect expert witnesses to rationalize *their* testimony, but when rendering a decision involving conflicting conceptions of what is the central issue in a case and therefore what is the appropriate guiding precedent, judges will rarely if ever attempt to explain their choice. They presumably realize that they know more than they can explain and that ultimately unrationalized intuition must guide their decision-making, but lawyers and juries seldom accord witnesses the same prerogative.

Some recent environmental legislation embodies the rationalistic view that only formal explanations are acceptable. The ecologist who knows from experience that a proposed dam will critically damage a certain species of wildlife is credible only if he can make up a mathematical model entailing that conclusion. The talent for inventing scientific-looking explanations is becoming more valued than the talent for being right.

Doctors are among the most highly skilled of human experts,

and we would expect that they would recognize the intuitive factors in their decision-making. Yet the very nature of their skill, the fact that it constantly requires them to "play God," seems to predispose them to think of their decisions as being rule-based. Doctors who must decide, for example, whether to continue an attempt at resuscitation or whether to recommend a patient for a kidney transplant may be tempted to appeal to rules of thumb and rational procedures as means of managing their anxiety.

Doctors are tempted to rationalize their intuitive decisions not only to justify them to themselves and their peers, but also in order to explain them to their patients. Yet there is a danger of overvaluing explicable forms of knowledge if the patient makes the ultimate decision regarding treatment, based on the facts furnished by the doctor. While patient involvement certainly has merit, since the doctor can never know the patient's innermost feelings about such matters as life, health, disability, and pain, the patient's decision suffers from the fact that the doctor can never factually explain *his* innermost feelings about the preferred therapy based on a lifetime of experiences with similar cases. Every case is unique, so statistics about likelihoods of outcomes of various possible treatments based on all previous cases are of little value. As we have seen, the frequency with which a particular procedure yielded a particular outcome observed in *all* previous sufferers from a disease or injury differs from the statistics for victims of the patient's age, sex, general health, mental outlook, and so on, and there is no scientific way of knowing what reference group should be taken as relevant. In reality, a patient is viewed by the experienced doctor as a unique case and treated on the basis of intuitively perceived similarity with situations previously encountered. That kind of wisdom, unfortunately, cannot be shared and thereby made the basis of a patient's rational decision.

Teaching too is endangered by rationalization. The well-known aphorism "Those who can't do, teach" unfairly maligns many dedicated educators who enjoy teaching but could be successful practitioners should they choose. Yet, like most sayings, it contains more than a grain of truth. The difference between teaching and doing was strikingly and amusingly demonstrated in a recent experiment.[6] It was based on videotapes of six exemplars—five students and one experienced paramedic—as they gave cardiopulmonary resuscitation to patients. The videos were then shown to students, to experienced paramedics, and to CPR instructors, and each was asked which of the exemplars he would choose to *save his own life* in an emergency. The results were revealing. In the paramedic group, nine out of ten selected the experienced paramedic. The students chose the paramedic five out of ten times, and the instructors were correct even less often, only three times out of ten. The instructors, attempting to find the paramedic by looking for the individual closely following the rules they taught, failed to find the expert because an experienced paramedic has passed beyond the rule-following stage!

Teachers of a skill are frequently articulate dispensers of helpful facts, procedures, and principles. As such, they may well hasten the student's progress from novice to advanced beginner to competent performer. But if, like expert systems, all they know are facts and rules of inference, such teachers cannot possibly be successful doers or guides on the way to expertise.

Society must clearly distinguish its members who "know how" from those that "know that." It must encourage its children to cultivate their intuitive capacities in order that they may achieve expertise, not encourage them to become human logic machines. And once expertise has been attained, it must be recognized and valued for what it is. To confuse the common sense, wisdom, and mature judgment of the expert with today's artificial intelligence, or to value them less highly, would be a genuine stupidity.

Epilogue

Rational Animals Are Obsolete

SOCRATES STANDS AT THE BEGINNING of our tradition as the hero of critical, objective thought. There is something to be said for his sort of detached calculative rationality, but we have seen that it should be appealed to only by a beginner or an expert who, having left his domain of experience, can no longer trust his instincts. Nietzsche, who wrote at what he considered the end of our Western philosophical tradition, had a view of Socratic rationality similar to our own. For Nietzsche, Socrates was not the hero of our culture but its first degenerate, because Socrates had lost the ability of the nobles to trust intuition. "Honest men do not carry their reasons exposed in this fashion," Nietzsche maintained.

Of course, Socrates' "rationality" was not a personal sickness. Athenian society was coping with monumental changes, not the least of which was the transformation of Athens into an imperial power. Deliberative reflection no doubt served as a device for evaluating the continued relevance of traditional ways. But Socrates seems to have overreacted and tried to call all traditional wisdom into question. As Nietzsche saw it, Socrates was symptomatic of a whole culture that, having lost its intuitive sense, desperately sought rules and principles to guide its actions:

> Rationality was at that time divined as a *saviour;* neither Socrates nor his "invalids" were free to be rational or not, as they wished— it was *de rigueur,* it was their *last* expedient. The fanaticism with which the whole of Greek thought throws itself at rationality betrays a state of emergency: one was in peril, one had only *one* choice: either to perish or—be *absurdly rational.*[1]

Aristotle, living a generation after Socrates, occupied an ambiguous position as the opponent of Socrates and Plato. He realized that even if, as Socrates and Plato had believed, people were continuously following rules, they needed wisdom or judgment in order to apply those rules to particular cases. But Aristotle nonetheless seems to have thought that before one could act, one had to deduce one's actions from one's desires and beliefs. The basis of action was, for Aristotle, the practical syllogism: If I desire S and I believe that A will bring about S, then I should do A. Both Aristotle's sense of the importance of judgment and his problem-solving view of intelligence were compatible with his definition of man as *zōion logon echon,* the animal equipped with *logos,* for when Aristotle thought of man as an animal equipped with *logos,* the word *logos* could still mean speaking, or the grasping of whole situations, as well as logical thought. But when *logos* was translated into Latin as *ratio,* meaning "reckoning," its field of meaning was decisively narrowed. It was a fateful turn for our Western tradition: man, the logical animal, was now he who counted, he who measured.

All that was necessary to complete the degeneration of reason into calculation was to equate concepts with collections of objective features, e.g. house = object, shelter, for man; man = thing, living, thinking. By the time Hobbes wrote, around 1600, it was possible to claim not only that reasoning meant reckoning, but that reckoning was nothing more than "the addition of parcels." Four centuries later we so consider reckoning our essence that, trying to create machines in our own images, we see only the problem of creating machines that can make millions of inferences per second.

We have gone farther than Aristotle and Hobbes could have imagined, generalizing Aristotle's model of intelligence to all skills, even physical skills, so that even the animal part of man, which Aristotle understood as animated, that is, self-moving, is thought to function by unconscious calculation. At Wright State University Dr. Roger Glaser and Dr. Jerrold Petrofsky have performed ground-breaking research using computer-controlled electrical impulses to exercise the paralyzed limbs of spinal-cord-injured individuals. Yet that amazing therapy is surrounded by heated debate. Dr. Petrofsky, who apparently believes that man's animality is rational, has begun to make extraordinary claims, predicting that the new techniques will eventually lead to computer-controlled free walking for the paralyzed—a strikingly literal example of the first-step fallacy that has buttressed faith in AI for years. He has begun to search for facts about muscle condition, limb position, and terrain that can be combined by rule to produce flexible walking. In a conversation with us, Dr. Glaser opposed that optimism as unrealistic and as cruelly raising false hopes: "We have no idea how the subconscious process that replaces the conscious step-by-step procedure used by beginners works," he said. "We might walk by using sophisticated subconscious rules, but how can we find them? Or walking might involve some process of direct pattern recognition followed by a learned response."

We sometimes work out solutions to problems in our heads, but we rarely "figure out" how to move our bodies. Thus thinking looks like a better candidate for computerization than walking. And if thinking *is* reckoning, then it is reasonable to expect that, as futurists have been telling us for years, the computer as logic machine is the next stage of evolution, which will someday not only excel us but replace us.

That is an appalling vision of the future. Yet there is no disputing computers have fundamentally and permanently transformed our relationship to our technologies. Soon we shall live in a world of extraordinarily rich, subtle, and powerful tools. Will they remain our servants, helping us to our human ends? Or will they outstrip our humanity, and cast us aside?

To the already anxious swirl of modern life a final element of anxiety has been added, fear of obsolescence. And anxiety drives us in several desperate directions. Luddites reappear, warning not against the improper uses of computers, but against computers in general, offering, as Jerry Mander did in the "computer-as-poison" issue of the *Whole Earth Review,* six sweeping reasons for doing away with computers altogether. Mystics emerge too, and warn that technology is cutting us off from our intuitive capacity to commune directly with other minds and with nature. Finally, romantics rebel against rationality as they did in the days of Goethe and return to his old slogan, "Feeling is everything."

From our point of view the problem with those reactions is not that they are wrongheaded but that they are misdirected. The enemies of technology focus valuable attention on the fact that computers are no panaceas, but such opposition can at best slow their proliferation. A real victory over the improper application of advanced technology—a victory of mind over machine—can come only with the recognition that technology has many proper as well as improper uses and with a widely cultivated ability to tell the difference. Computers are perhaps the most powerful, and certainly the most flexible, devices we have yet built. They have many positive, indeed many wonderful uses. The question is not how to eliminate them but how to make the most of their powers.

Likewise, nostalgia for what is being lost is a healthy reaction to the glorification of the "hacker culture." The back-to-nature mystics, however, confuse the supposed dangers of technological devices with the real danger of the technological mentality. In opposing computers they miss the real problem: total dependence upon calculative thinking and a loss of respect for the less formalizable powers of the mind. They fail to see that computers properly used need not alienate us from our everyday experience-based intuition or whatever other intuitive powers we may possess.

Of the computer opponents only the romantics are on the right track. They oppose not technology but technological rationality. But by rejecting *all* rationality, they fail to see that calculative rationality is appropriate for beginners and in novel situations and that deliberative rationality is not opposed to intuition but based upon it. Put in its proper place rational deliberation sharpens intuition.

The question is whether we are going to accept the view of man as an information processing device, or whether we are still enough in touch with our pre-Platonic essence to realize the limits of the computer metaphor. With our mechanical contrivances now able to solve certain problems more effectively than we can, we are being forced to rethink some very old and by now very basic elements of our self-image. It is our hope that the rethinking will lead to a new definition of what we are, one that values our capacity for involved intuition more than our ability to be rational animals.

What we do now will determine what sort of society and what sort of human beings we are to become. We can make such a decision wisely only if we have some understanding of what sort of human beings we already are. If we think of ourselves only as repositories of factual knowledge and of information processing procedures, then we understand ourselves as someday to be surpassed by bigger and faster machines running bigger and more sophisticated programs. Those who embrace that limited conception of intelligence welcome the change with enthusiasm.[2]

Should we become servants of expert systems and, demanding of our experts their rules and facts, become careless of the intuitive powers that fall outside our stunted vision, we will in one generation lose our professional expertise and confirm those expectations. Our children brought up on LOGO and our *competent* specialists crammed with procedures will indeed be inferior to the systems they have been trained to imitate.

But fortunately there are other possibilities. We can use computers to track the vast array of facts and law-governed relationships of our modern technological world, yet continue to nurture the human expertise that inference engines cannot share by encouraging learners to pass from rule following to experience-based intuition. If we do so, our experts will be empowered by their computer aids to make better use of their wisdom in grappling with the still unresolved problems of technological society.

The chips are down, the choice is being made right now. And at all levels of society computer-type rationality is winning out. Experts are an endangered species. If we fail to put logic machines in their proper place, as aids to human beings with expert intuition, then we shall end up servants supplying data to our competent machines. Should calculative rationality triumph, no one will notice that something is missing, but now, while we still know what expert judgment is, let us use that expert judgment to preserve it.

NOTES

Preface

1. *Strategic Computing, New Generation Computing Technology: A Strategic Plan for Its Development and Application to Critical Problems in Defense,* Defense Advanced Research Projects Agency, Oct. 28, 1983, p. 1.

2. Marvin Minsky in *Omni* magazine, April 1983 (italics ours).

3. Joseph Weizenbaum, *Computer Power and Human Reason: From Judgment to Calculation* (W. H. Freeman, 1976), p. 207. At a time when books glorifying the computer revolution have finally begun to be joined by books focusing on its "dark side," it should be noted that Weizenbaum's book was among the first. For a more recent review of the topic, see Siegel and Markoff, *The High Cost of High Tech* (Harper & Row, 1985). For an excellent exploration of the forces behind industrial automation, many of which also lie behind the attempt to automate intelligence, see David Noble, *Forces of Production* (Knopf, 1984).

4. "Luddite" has come in recent years to signify those who oppose technological development of all kinds. The original Luddites were not mindlessly antitechnology, as they have been caricatured for almost two hundred years. They opposed only technologies that

destroyed their livelihoods. The use of the name "Luddite" as slur reveals a common tactic by which the technology boosters gain advantage over their opponents—portraying them as blind humanist enemies of science and technology. We expect Ned Ludd's name to be hurled against us. However, such name-calling does not reflect the needs of society for balance, evaluation, and reflection in the face of what we all agree is a monumental technological revolution.

Prologue
"The Heart Has Its Reasons That Reason Does Not Know"

1. Leibniz, *Selections,* ed. Philip Wiener (Scribners, 1951), p. 48 (our italics).

2. See Hubert Dreyfus, ed., *Husserl, Intentionality, and Cognitive Science* (Bradford Books, MIT Press, 1982), pp. 1–27.

3. Herbert A. Simon and Allen Newell, "Heuristic Problem Solving: The Next Advance in Operations Research," *Operations Research,* 6 (January–February 1958): 6 (italics in original).

4. *Ibid.*

5. The history of science is full of examples of theoretical junctures in which advance came by acknowledging that a fundamental assumption was untenable. Consider the famous Michelson–Morley experiment. It was, after all, only one experiment, and little was more central to the world view of nineteenth-century physics than the ether theory, which it endangered. Michelson himself was never happy with it, for he had set out not to disprove, but to prove the ether theory. Still, the experiment was refined, repeated, and recognized for what it was, proof that the ether theory was flawed; it was from that failure that Einstein's special theory was born.

6. Hubert L. Dreyfus, "Alchemy and Artificial Intelligence," The RAND Corporation Paper P-3244, December 1965.

7. *Strategic Computing, New-Generation Computing Technology: A Strategic Plan for Its Development and Application to Critical Problems in Defense,* Defense Advanced Research Projects Agency, October 28, 1983.

8. *Information Technology R & D: Critical Trends and Issues* (U. S. Congress, Office of Technology Assessment, OTA-CIT-268, February 1985), pp. 95–96.

Chapter 1
Five Steps from Novice to Expert

1. P. N. Johnson-Laird and P. C. Wason, "A Theoretical Analysis of Insight into a Reasoning Task," in Johnson-Laird and Wason, eds., *Thinking: Readings in Cognitive Science* (Cambridge University Press, 1977), pp. 143–45 and 151–53.

2. Patricia Benner, *From Novice to Expert: Excellence and Power in Clinical Nursing Practice* (Addison-Wesley, 1984).

3. *Ibid*, p. 23.

4. *Ibid*.

5. Such a player, if he participated in organized chess tournaments, would have a rating of approximately Class A, which would rank him in the top 20 percent of tournament players.

6. Herbert Simon, "Studying Human Intelligence by Creating Artificial Intelligence," *American Scientist*, May–June 1981, p. 308.

7. Such players are termed masters, and the roughly four hundred American masters rank in the top 1 percent of all serious players.

8. About two dozen players hold this rank in the United States. They, as well as about four dozen slightly less strong players called International Masters, qualify as what we call experts.

9. Quoted in Richard Restak, *The Brain* (Bantam, 1984), pp. 85–86.

10. Herbert A. Simon, *Models of Thought* (Yale University Press, 1979), pp. 386–403.

11. Our view that experts directly associate situations and actions should not be confused with the situation → action rules which form the basis of Allen Newell's production systems. In the production-system formalism the situation must be defined in terms of a set of objective features, and if the current situation exactly matches the stored description the associated action is called up.

   In his recent work Newell has used the production system approach in a model of the acquisition of skill. Newell sees, as we do, that in acquiring a skill a person passes through a competent stage in which he sets goals and solves problems. In problem solving, sub-goals are set and the system may learn that given a certain initial condition a certain sub-goal can be achieved. Skill improves when this fact is remembered as a production rule and used thereafter.

   As productions are used to by-pass complicated chains of reasoning, speed of performance improves. Once the system had learned the solution to an entire problem given a certain set of inputs, the direct relation between the problem situation and the solution would be stored as one production rule. The move to a single situation-action correlation would dramatically speed up performance. This is as near as the formal models of AI have approached our model of the final step to expertise.

The model, however, fails to capture our notion of expertise. First, in the Newell model the situation must be described in terms of objective features, rather than being stored as an unanalyzable whole. Second, the action is triggered by an exact match between the current situation and a stored description, rather than by an overall similarity. Those differences account for Newell's tendency to understand increased skill as merely increased speed, whereas true expertise is characterized by a discontinuous move to letting the issues in a situation elicit a fluent and flexible response.

12. Benner, *From Novice to Expert*, p. 32.

13. *Ibid.*

14. Quoted in Gerald Holton, *Thematic Origins of Scientific Thought: Kepler to Einstein* (Harvard University Press, 1973), p. 357.

15. Maya Bar-Hillel, "The Base-Rate Fallacy in Probability Judgments," *Acta Psychologica,* 44 (1980): 211–33.

16. P. Slovic and S. Lichtenstein, "Comparison of Bayesian and Regression Approaches to the Study of Information Processing in Judgment," *Organizational Behavior and Human Performance,* 6 (1971): 668.

17. R. M. Dawes, "A Case Study of Graduate Admissions: Application of Three Principles of Human Decision Making," *American Psychologist,* 26 (1971): 180–88.

18. This example comes from M. Allais, a French economist. See H. Raiffa, *Decision Analysis* (Addison-Wesley Publishing Company, 1968), pp. 80–82.

19. For a detailed discussion of the dubious nature of conclusions drawn from experiments, see Robert L. Winkler and Allan H. Murphy, "Experiments in the Laboratory and the Real World," *Organizational Behavior and Human Performance,* 10 (1973): 252–70. For a balanced presentation of this issue and a good list of references, see Hillel Einhorn and Robin Hogarth, "Behavioral Decision Theory: Processes of Judgment and Choice," *Annual Review of Psychology,* 32 (1981): 53–88.

20. Almost all the field experiments conducted thus far that are cited as evidence for poor human predictive performance, such as those mentioned in P. Slovic, B. Fischhoff, and S. Lichtenstein, "Behavioral Decision Theory," *Annual Review of Psychology,* 28 (1977): 15–17, suffer flaws. Sometimes what the subject is asked to predict in an experiment is not something that the subject normally ob-

serves or explicitly predicts during his real-world skilled performance, even though it may be related to the area of subject expertise. For example, security analysts certainly think about future
behavior of stocks, but their work does not require precise probabil-
istic predictions about performance at the end of two weeks, as
did one of the experiments reported in Slovic *et al.* Frequently
there are real-world incentives for less than accurate prediction.
Military intelligence predictions, cost predictions, and others fall
into this category.

21. S. C. Lichtenstein, B. Fischhoff, and L. Phillips, "Calibration of
Probabilities: The State of the Art," in Jungermann and de Zeeuw,
eds., *Proceedings of the Fifth Research Conference on Subjective
Probability, Utility and Decision Making*, 1976, pp. 280–85.

Chapter 2
Logic Machines and Their Limits

1. For an account of the experiments showing that human beings
can actually rotate, scan, and otherwise use images, and the unsuc-
cessful attempts to understand those capacities in terms of programs that use features and rules, see Ned Block, ed., *Imagery*
(M.I.T. Press/Bradford Books, 1981). Also Ned Block, "Mental Pictures and Cognitive Science," *The Philosophical Review*, October
1983, pp. 499–541.

2. This example is taken from John Haugeland, *Artificial Intelligence:
The Very Idea* (Bradford/MIT, 1985). Haugeland's book gives a
clear account of the digital computer as a general symbol-manipulating device and deals in depth with the philosophical issues raised
by AI.

3. Douglas Hofstadter, "Metafont, Metamathematics, and Metaphys-
ics," *Visible Language*, XVI, No. 4 (1982): 326.

4. *Ibid.*, p. 310.

5. Marvin Minsky, "Artificial Intelligence," *Scientific American*, September 1966, pp. 251–52.

6. David L. Waltz, "Artificial Intelligence," *Scientific American*, October 1982, p. 133.

7. Avron Barr and Edward A. Feigenbaum, *The Handbook of Artificial Intelligence* (William Kaufmann, Inc., 1981), I: 7.

8. See references in "The Nature and Plausibility of Cognitivism,"
in John Haugeland, ed., *Mind Design: Philosophy, Psychology, Artificial Intelligence* (MIT Press/Bradford Books, 1981), p. 267.

9. Karl H. Pribram, M. Nuwer, and Robert J. Baron, "The Holographic

Hypothesis of Memory Structure in Brain Function and Perception," in D. H. Krantz *et al.*, eds. *Contemporary Developments in Mathematical Psychology* Vol. 2 (W. H. Freeman, 1974).

10. Eleanor Rosch, "Principles of Categorization," in E. Rosch and B. Lloyd, eds., *Cognition and Categorization* (Lawrence Erlbaum Associates, 1978), pp. 27–48. See also Susan Cary, *Conceptual Change in Childhood* (MIT Press/Bradford Books, 1985).

Chapter 3
Artificial Intelligence: From High Hopes to Sober Reality

1. Marvin Minsky, ed., *Semantic Information Processing* (M.I.T. Press, 1968), pp. 25–26.

2. Jerry Fodor, *Modularity of Mind* (MIT/Bradford, 1983), p. 127.

3. Richard A. Shaffer, "Simulating Human Thought in Computers Proving Elusive," *Wall Street Journal,* August 5, 1983, p. 21.

4. Minsky, *Semantic Information Processing,* pp. 26–27.

5. *Ibid.,* p. 18.

6. *Ibid.,* p. 13.

7. *Ibid.*

8. Daniel G. Bobrow, "Natural Language Input for a Computer Problem Solving System," in Minsky, *Semantic Information Processing,* p. 183.

9. Minsky, *Semantic Information Processing,* p. 26.

10. *Ibid.* (our italics).

11. Terry Winograd, "A Procedural Model of Language Understanding," in Roger Schank and Kenneth Colby, eds., *Computer Models of Thought and Language* (W. H. Freeman Press, 1973). SHRDLU is an anti-acronym whose letters don't stand for anything. It was picked up by Winograd from *Mad Magazine,* which uses this traditional typesetter's test as the name of mythical monsters and the like.

12. Terry Winograd, "Understanding Natural Language," *Cognitive Psychology,* No. 3, 1972, pp. 8–11.

13. Winograd, "Procedural Model of Language Understanding," p. 167.

14. Marvin Minsky and Seymour Papert, draft, July 1970, of a proposal to ARPA for research on artificial intelligence at M.I.T., 1970–1971, p. 39.

15. *Ibid.*

16. *Ibid.*, p. 48.

17. *Ibid.*, pp. 50–52.

18. *Ibid.*, p. 52.

19. Terry Winograd, "Artificial Intelligence and Language Comprehension," in *Artificial Intelligence and Language Comprehension* (National Institute of Education, 1976), p. 9.

20. For a detailed discussion of the difference between universe and world, see H. Dreyfus, *Being-in-the-World: A Commentary on Heidegger's* "Being and Time" (M.I.T. Press, 1986).

21. M.I.T. Artificial Intelligence Laboratory, Memo No. 299, September 1973, p. 96.

22. Patrick H. Winston and the staff of the M.I.T. AI Laboratory, AI Memo No. 366, May 1976, p. 22.

23. Winograd, "Artificial Intelligence and Language Comprehension," p. 17.

24. Roger C. Schank *et al.*, *Proceedings,* Panel on Natural Language Processing, IJCAI-77, pp. 107–8.

25. Marvin Minsky, *Computation: Finite and Infinite Machines* (Prentice-Hall, 1967), p. 2.

26. Gina Kolata, "How Can Computers Get Common Sense?" *Science,* 217 (September 24, 1982): 1237.

27. The exception is the work of Douglas Lenat, merely six years old. *Scientific American* reports with excitement that "recently a program called AM (for automated mathematics) was developed . . . that can formulate new concepts and theorems in mathematics from about 100 elementary concepts in set theory. . . . The program found that the square root of a number with three divisors is always a number with exactly two divisors. . . . In this way AM began to explore the rich pattern of mathematical relations that develops from the concept of numbers with exactly two divisors, otherwise known as prime numbers. In about an hour of running time on the computer Lenat's program went on to reproduce several well-known conjectures about prime numbers and guessed that every natural number is the product of a unique set of primes."

Many hailed that program as a giant step forward in the programming of learning and discovery. But Lenat himself later realized, and announced with impressive integrity, that the program had found prime numbers so easily because of a special property of the language in which it had been programmed. Lenat notes that his "simple-minded" program worked "embarrassingly well" and then adds: "Recently, we have come to see that it is, in part, the density of worthwhile math concepts, *as represented in LISP* that is the crucial factor." "Why AM and EURISKO Appear to

Work," *Proceedings of AAAI* 1983, p. 2. On balance, it should be noted that Lenat's more recent *Scientific American* article, "Computer Software for Intelligent Systems," September 1984, in which he claimed a number of nonmathematical discoveries for EURISKO, mentioned neither this caution about LISP nor the fact that EURISKO made those discoveries during a process in which he, Lenat, helped it to decide which avenues of inquiry to follow out.

28. David L. Waltz, "Artificial Intelligence," *Scientific American*, October 1982, p. 133.

29. Douglas Lenat, "Computer Software for Intelligent Systems," *Scientific American*, September 1984, p. 209.

30. Lars-Erik Janlert, "Modeling Change: The Frame Problem," Department of Information Processing, University of Umeå, Sweden, p. 1.

31. *Ibid.*, p. 7.

32. Marvin Minsky, "A Framework for Representing Knowledge" in P. H. Winston, ed., *The Psychology of Computer Vision* (McGraw-Hill, 1975), p. 212.

33. Roger C. Schank, "The Primitive Acts of Conceptual Dependency," *Theoretical Issues in Natural Language Processing*, obtainable from the Association for Computational Linguistics, Cambridge, Mass., June 10–13, 1975, p. 131 (our italics).

34. *Ibid.*

35. Roger C. Schank with Peter G. Childers, *The Cognitive Computer* (Addison-Wesley, 1984), p. 121 (italics in original).

36. *Ibid.*, p. 117.

37. Lenat, "Computer Software for Intelligent Systems," p. 211.

38. *Ibid.*, p. 209.

39. See Geoffrey Hinton and James Anderson, eds., *Parallel Models of Associative Memory* (Lawrence Erlbaum Associates, 1981).

40. For more details, see Hinton and Anderson, eds., *ibid.* or Janet Metcalfe Eich, "A Composite Holographic Associative Recall Memory," *Psychological Review*, Vol. 89, No. 6 (1982): 627–661, which contains an extensive set of references.

41. See Hinton and Anderson, *Parallel Models of Associative Memory*, and Geoffrey Hinton, "Learning in Parallel Networks," *BYTE* magazine, April 1985, pp. 265–273.

Geoffrey Hinton is one of the most active researchers using this approach. His new computer architecture, in which the computer is used to simulate a holistic system, is called a Boltzmann *Machine*. Again, an important distinction is blurred for lack of a precise vocabulary. A Boltzmann architecture allows a digital computer to simulate not a machine but rather a nonmechanistic system.

For a report on a holistic pattern recognizing device not using a memory trace or distributed representations, but based on directly connecting input patterns to desired outputs which has actually been built out of chips rather than simulated on a computer, see Igor Aleksander and Piers Burnett, *Reinventing Man* (Holt, Rinehart and Winston, 1983).

For a recent magazine report on the difficulties confronting conventional AI and the range of alternative approaches now being explored, as well as their relation to recent brain research, see "Seeking the Mind in Pathways of the Machine," *The Economist*, June 29, 1985, pp. 87–90.

42. T. Kohonen, E. Oja, and P. Lehtiö, "Storage and Processing of Information in Distributed Associative Memory Systems," in Hinton and Anderson, eds., *Parallel Models of Associative Memory*, pp. 123, 124.

43. See Jerome Feldman, "Connections," *BYTE* magazine, April 1985, pp. 277–84, and Jerome Feldman, "A Connectionist Model of Visual Memory," in Hinton and Anderson, eds., *Parallel Models of Associative Memory*, pp. 49–81.

44. Douglas R. Hofstadter, *Gödel, Escher, Bach: An Eternal Golden Braid*, Vintage Books, New York, 1980, p. 691.

45. *Ibid.*, p. 350

46. *Ibid.*, p. 347

47. *Ibid.*

48. *Ibid.*, p. 348

49. Patrick Henry Winston and Richard Henry Brown, eds., *Artificial Intelligence: An MIT Perspective* (M.I.T. Press, 1979), I: 426.

50. Marvin Minsky, "K-Lines: A Theory of Memory," *Cognitive Science*, No. 2, Vol. 4 (1980), p. 118.

51. *Ibid.*, p. 127 (italics in original).

52. David Marr, *Vision*, W. H. Freeman, 1982.

53. Imre Lakatos, *Philosophical Papers*, John Worrall, ed. (Cambridge University Press, 1978).

54. Ned Block, "Mental Pictures and Cognitive Science," *Philosophical Review*, October 1983, and Susan Carey, *Conceptual Change in Childhood*, (M.I.T./Bradford Books, 1985).

55. "The Current State of AI: One Man's Opinion," *AI Magazine*, Winter/Spring, 1983.

Chapter 4
Expert Systems Versus Intuitive Expertise

1. *New York Times*, March 29, 1984, p. 1.
2. Edward Feigenbaum and Pamela McCorduck, *The Fifth Generation: Artificial Intelligence and Japan's Computer Challenge to the World* (Addison-Wesley, 1983).
3. *Business Week*, July 9, 1984, pp. 54–62; *Newsweek*, July 4, 1983, pp. 58–64.
4. Feigenbaum and McCorduck, *Fifth Generation*, p. 56.
5. *Ibid.*, p. 38.
6. *Ibid.*, pp. 76–77 (italics in original).
7. *Ibid.*, p. 18.
8. *Ibid.*, p. 64.
9. *Ibid.*, p. 55.
10. *Ibid.*, p. 79 (italics in original).
11. *Ibid.*, p. 85.
12. *Ibid.*, pp. 79–80.
13. *Ibid.*, p. 82.
14. *Ibid.*
15. *Ibid.*, p. 179.
16. Avron Barr and Edward A. Feigenbaum, *Handbook of Artificial Intelligence*, (William Kaufmann, Inc., 1981), I: 7.
17. These quotations are drawn from an interview with Arthur Samuel released by the Stanford University News Office, April 28, 1983.
18. Daniel Goleman, "Holographic Memory: An Interview with Karl Pribram," *Psychology Today*, 12, No. 9 (February 1979): 80.
19. Richard O. Duda and Edward H. Shortliffe, "Expert Systems Research," *Science*, 220, No. 4594 (April 15, 1983): 266.
20. *Ibid.*, p. 265. Incidentally, we wonder how Duda and Shortliffe can be so confident that their knowledge representation formalism is "adequate," when "experts often have difficulty expressing their knowledge" in it.
21. G. Octo Barnett, M.D. "The Computer and Clinical Judgment," *New England Journal of Medicine*, 307, No. 8 (August 19, 1982): 493.
22. Feigenbaum and McCorduck, *Fifth Generation*, pp. 61, 62.
23. This summary of the facts about DENDRAL is based on Barr and Feigenbaum, *Handbook of Artificial Intelligence*, II: 106–15.
24. A recent version is in Steven Levy, *Hackers* (Anchor/Doubleday, 1984), pp. 78–79.

25. Hubert Dreyfus, "Alchemy and Artificial Intelligence," RAND Corporation, Paper P-3244, 1965, p. 10.

26. *Los Angeles Times,* May 12, 1984.

27. George Steiner, *Fields of Force: Fischer and Spassky at Reykjavik* (The Viking Press, 1974), p. 66.

28. Hans Berliner, "Computer Backgammon," *Scientific American,* June 1980, pp. 64–72.

29. The "CBS Evening News" report is not the only sensationalized and inaccurate report on PROSPECTOR spread by the mass media. The July 9, 1984, issue of *Business Week* reports in its cover story, "Artificial Intelligence: It's Here": "Geologists were convinced as far back as World War I that a rich deposit of molybdenum ore was buried deep under Mount Tolman in eastern Washington. But after digging dozens of small mines and drilling hundreds of test borings, they were still hunting for the elusive metal 60 years later. Then, just a couple of years ago, miners hit pay dirt. They finally found the ore because they were guided not by a geologist wielding his rock hammer, but by a computer located hundreds of miles to the south in Menlo Park, Calif."

There have also been accurate reports in the press. In *BYTE,* September 1981, the caption under the figure on page 262 is accurate, and the *Fortune* article of August 20, 1984, also notes the truth about PROSPECTOR's "strike."

30. Victor L. Yu et al., "Antimicrobial Selection by a Computer," *Journal of the American Medical Association,* 242, No. 12 (September 21, 1979): 1279–82.

31. Randolph A. Miller, M.D.; Harry E. Pople, Jr., Ph. D.; and Jack D. Myers, M.D., "*INTERNIST-I,* an Experimental Computer-Based Diagnostic Consultant for General Internal Medicine," *New England Journal of Medicine,* 307, No. 8 (August 19, 1982): 494.

32. *Ibid.,* p. 468.

33. *Ibid.,* p. 473.

34. *Ibid.,* p. 494.

35. *Ibid.*

36. "MacNeil–Lehrer Report on Artificial Intelligence," April 22, 1983.

37. Personal conversation with Dr. Fallat at the San Francisco Medical Center.

38. Feigenbaum and McCorduck, *Fifth Generation,* pp. 84–85.

39. *Ibid.,* p. 229.

40. *Ibid.,* p. 236.

41. Richard O. Duda and John G. Gaschnig, "Knowledge-Based Expert Systems Come of Age," *BYTE,* September 1981, p. 264.

Chapter 5
Computers in the Classroom: Tools, Tutors, and Tutees

1. Alfred Bork, "Learning Through Graphics," in Robert Taylor, ed., *The Computer in the School: Tutor, Tool, Tutee* (Teacher's College Press, 1980), p. 69 (italics in original).

2. Twila Slesnick and Batya Friedman, "Discovery Learning with Computers: The Simulation Game," *Curriculum Review*, August 1983, p. 1.

3. Twila Slesnick, "Hold It: You're Using Computers the Wrong Way," *The Executive Educator*, April 1983, p. 30 (italics in original).

4. Slesnick and Friedman, "Discovery Learning with Computers," p. 2.

5. Quoted by Howard Rheingold in "Video Games Go to School," *Psychology Today*, September 1983, p. 40.

6. This term was invented by Robert A. Heinlein in *Stranger in a Strange Land.* (Berkley, New York, 1968). We use it here to mean a deep, intuitive understanding.

7. "Directional Letter-by-Letter Analysis and the Word-Superiority Effect," in *Memory & Cognition*, 12, No. 2 (1984): 195–201.

8. Interview with Judah Schwartz in *Classroom Computer Learning*, February 1985, p. 22.

9. Judah L. Schwartz, "Tyranny, Discipline, Freedom and License: Some Thoughts on Educational Ideology and Computers," *Education in the Electronic Age* (WNET, New York, 1983), p. 64.

10. Robert Taylor, ed., *The Computer in the School* (note 1 above).

11. Seymour Papert, *Mindstorms: Children, Computers, and Powerful Ideas* (Basic Books, Inc., 1980), p. 29.

12. For example, here are the first five subtraction bugs:

    1. When a column has a 1 that was changed to a 0 by a previous borrow, the student writes 0 as the answer to that column. (914 − 486 = 508).

    2. When a column has a 1 that was changed to a 0 by a previous borrow, the student writes the bottom digit as the answer to that column. (512 − 136 = 436).

    3. If a column starts with 1 in both top and bottom and is borrowed from, the student writes 0 as the answer to that column. (812 − 518 = 304).

    4. If a column starts with 1 in both top and bottom and is borrowed from, the student writes 1 as the answer to that column. (812 − 518 = 314).

    5. The student adds instead of subtracting but he subtracts the carried digit instead of adding it. (54 − 38 = 72).

Cf. John Seely Brown and Kurt Van Lehn, "Repair Theory," *Cognitive Science*, No. 4, Vol. 4, 1980.

13. Schwartz, "Tyranny, Discipline, Freedom and License," p. 61.
14. Lucy A. Suchman, *Plans and Situated Actions: The Problem of Human–Machine Communication*, Technical Report, Xerox Palo Alto Research Center, January 1985.
15. "Report of the Research Briefing Panel on Information Technology in Precollege Education," *Research Briefings 1984*, (National Academy Press, 1984), p. 19.
16. M.I.T. AI Laboratory, Memo No. 299 (September 1973), p. 77.
17. Marvin Minsky, "A Framework for Representing Knowledge," in John Haugeland, ed., *Mind Design* (Bradford/M.I.T. Press, 1981), p. 124.
18. P. Suppes, "The Uses of Computers in Education," *Scientific American*, Vol. 215, No. 3, 1966.
19. T. Slesnick, "Hold It: You're Using Computers the Wrong Way," *The Executive Educator*, April 1983, p. 29.
20. Patrick Suppes, "The Future of Computers in Education," in Robert Taylor, ed., *The Computer in the School*, (note 10 above), p. 257.
21. *Ibid.*
22. "It isn't easy to recognize speech."
23. Suppes, "Future of Computers in Education," p. 258.
24. *Ibid.*, p. 259.
25. *Ibid.*, pp. 259–60.
26. "Report of Research Briefing Panel" (note 15 above), p. 25.
27. *Ibid.*
28. *Ibid.*, p. 21.
29. *Ibid.*, p. 28.
30. Taylor, *Computer in the School* (note 10 above), p. 4 (italics in original).
31. Papert, *Mindstorms* (note 11 above), p. 96.
32. *Ibid.*, p. 27 (italics in original).
33. *Ibid.*, pp. 36–37.
34. *Ibid.*, p. 98.
35. *Ibid.*, p. 28.
36. *Ibid.*, p. 113.
37. *Ibid.*, p. 152.
38. *Ibid.*, p. 153 (italics in original).
39. Seymour Papert, "Teaching Children to be Mathematicians," in Taylor, *Computer in the School*, p. 208.
40. *Ibid.*, p. 180.

41. *Ibid.* (italics in original).

42. Freeman Dyson, *Disturbing the Universe* (Harper & Row, 1980), pp. 55–56.

43. J. DeMaio, S. Parkinson, B. Leshowitz, J. Crosby, and J. A. Thorpe, "Visual Scanning: Comparisons Between Student and Instructor Pilots," AFHRL-TR-76-10, AD-A023 634, Williams AFB, AZ, Flying Training Division, Air Force Human Resources Laboratory, June 1976.

44. Duda and Gaschnig, "Knowledge-Based Expert Systems Come of Age," *BYTE,* September 1981, p. 255.

45. Lee Brooks, "Nonanalytic Concept Formation and Memory for Instances," in Eleanor Rosch and Barbara Lloyd, eds., *Cognition and Categorization* (Erlbaum, 1978).

46. *Ibid.,* pp. 172–73.

47. *Ibid.,* pp. 207–9.

48. Donald E. Broadbent, Peter FitzGerald, and Margaret H. P. Broadbent, "Conscious and Unconscious Judgment in the Control of Complex Systems," Department of Experimental Psychology, University of Oxford, preprint, p. 21.

49. *Ibid.,* p. 23.

50. Papert, *Mindstorms,* pp. 97–98.

Chapter 6
Managerial Art and Management Science

1. Thomas Peters and Robert Waterman, Jr., *In Search of Excellence* (Harper & Row, 1982).

2. Robert Hayes and William Abernathy, "Managing Our Way to Economic Decline," *Harvard Business Review,* July–August 1980.

3. For example, a study by McKinsey & Company of eight management attributes that are common to the thirty-seven companies often used as examples of well-run organizations emphasizes that none of the attributes depend on modern management tools such as are provided by management scientists. T. J. Peters, "Putting Excellence into Management," *Business Week,* July 21, 1980, p. 196.

4. Proponents of management science are quick to rationalize managerial resistance by claiming that managers "don't understand" analysis. Henry Mintzberg replies: "It is difficult to support the case that managers resist analysis simply because they don't understand it. Perhaps they don't take the time to understand it because

it seems irrelevant to their needs; indeed, perhaps if managers more fully understood all the analyses presented to them, they would be inclined to accept fewer of them." Henry Mintzberg, "Beyond Implementation: An Analysis of the Resistance to Policy Analysis," in *INFOR*, 18, No. 2 (May 1980): 103.

5. Thomas Peters, "The Planning Fetish," in "Manager's Journal," *Wall Street Journal*, July 7, 1980.

6. *Business Week*, June 30, 1980, p. 93.

7. See *New York Times*, Sunday, May 5, 1985, Section 3, p. 1.

8. Henry Mintzberg, *The Nature of Managerial Work* (Harper & Row, 1973), p. 36.

9. T. J. Peters, "Putting Excellence into Management," *Business Week*, July 21, 1980, p. 196.

10. This brings us to an important caveat. Our discussion of managerial expertise should not be misunderstood as support for a society in which expertise justifies power. Many would like to see a society in which the people affected by a decision make that decision, and our defense of human expertise and intuition against codifiable systems of competence should not be read as a defense of expertise against that democratic ideal. These are important questions, but before one can begin to discuss them one must be clear what expertise is, who in any given domain are the experts, and how much expertise one is willing to give up for the sake of the values of democratic participation.

11. Jacob Ulvila and Rex Brown, "Decision Analysis Comes of Age," *Harvard Business Review*, September–October 1982, pp. 130–41.

12. C. Jackson Grayson, *Decisions Under Uncertainty* (Division of Research, Harvard University Graduate School of Business Administration, Boston, 1960).

13. C. Jackson Grayson, "Management Science and Business Practice," *Harvard Business Review*, July–August 1973.

14. Rex V. Brown, "Do Managers Find Decision Theory Useful?" *Harvard Business Review*, May–June 1970, pp. 78–89.

15. Ulvila and Brown, "Decision Analysis Comes of Age."

16. Rex V. Brown, "Modeling Subsequent Acts for Decision Analysis," Technical Report, Decisions and Designs, Inc., Suite 100, 7900 Westpark Drive, McLean, Virginia 22101, July 1975, pp. 7–9.

17. *Ibid.*, p. 12.

18. Ronald Howard, "An Assessment of Decision Analysis," *Operations Research*, 28, No. 1 (January–February 1980): 15. (See this chapter's epigraph.)

19. Baruch Fischhoff, "Clinical Decision Analysis," *Operations Research*, 28, No. 1 (January–February 1980): 28–43.

20. Quoted in Kathleen Stein, "Robo-Shock," *Omni*, April 1983.

21. The current state of the art is not encouraging: "A Stanford University researcher has developed a robot cart that can navigate in a simple environment at a speed of 3 to 5 meters per hour while analyzing one image of its surroundings for each meter of progress using a computer capable of processing a million instructions per second. For such a system to navigate at walking speed would require a computer capable of from 10^9 to 10^{10} instructions per second. Computers of this speed are being developed, but may require facilities as large as a room just to provide cooling for the hardware." From *Information Technology R & D: Critical Trends and Issues* (U. S. Congress, Office of Technology Assessment, OTA-CIT-268, February 1985), p. 101.

22. There is a fairly extensive literature on tacit skills developing within Marxist sociology, by way of commentaries on Harry Braverman's now classic *Labor and Monopoly Capitalism.* This literature questions traditional understandings of scientific management and Taylorism and focuses on the hitherto invisible contributions workers make to the labor process. For a good bibliography, see Tony Manwaring and Stephen Wood, "The Ghost in the Machine: Tacit Skills in the Labor Process," *Socialist Review*, No. 74, March/April 1984, pp. 55–83.

23. Quoted in Manwaring and Wood, "Ghost in the Machine," pp. 61–62.

24. Quoted in David Noble, *The Forces of Production: A Social History of Industrial Automation* (Knopf, 1984), p. 345.

25. Bo Sundin, ed., *Is the Computer a Tool?*, (Almqvist & Wiksell International, Stockholm, 1980), p. 60.

26. Obviously, the fact that modeling *can* help the decision maker to understand, if not solve, such problems is not in any way an argument that they *should* be solved, but if the decision is made to attack them, analysis can prove useful.

Conclusion
People That (Sic) Think

1. Pamela McCorduck, *Machines Who Think* (W. H. Freeman and Company, 1979).

2. President Reagan seems an exception to this trend. He enunciates his political vision while rarely rationalizing it. Isolated facts seem to interest him so little that he occasionally misstates them. He

succeeds in politics by projecting the image of wisdom and sound judgment and by asking the voter to look at his record.

3. John H. Lunn, "Chick Sexing," *American Scientist,* 36 (1948): 280–81.
4. *Ibid.,* pp. 286–87.
5. *Ibid.,* p. 287.
6. Gary Klein and Helen Klein, "Perceptual/Cognitive Analysis of Proficient Cardio-Pulmonary Resuscitation (CPR) Performance," paper delivered at the Meetings of the Midwestern Psychological Association, Chicago, 1981.

Epilogue
Rational Animals Are Obsolete

1. Nietzsche, *Twilight of the Idols,* Aphorism #10 (Penguin Classics, 1968), p. 33 (italics in original).
2. As Roger Schank recently wrote: "Ultimately, AI will be assimilated into every other discipline. . . . The ability to create better and better knowledge systems will allow people in every field to develop new ideas and to find new approaches to their oldest problems. AI will encourage a renaissance in practically every area that it touches." Roger Schank, *The Cognitive Computer* (Addison–Wesley, 1984), pp. 221–22.

INDEX